Hotel Front Office

N & LEIG
CC

Stanley Thornes Catering and Hotel Management Books
Series Editor: John Fuller

Hotel Front Office

Second Edition
Bruce Braham, FHCIMA, Cert.Ed., R. Dip.

Stanley Thornes (Publishers) Ltd

To Chubby and Dan

Originally published 1985 by Hutchinson Education

Reprinted 1990 by
Stanley Thornes (Publishers) Ltd
Delta Place
27 Bath Road
CHELTENHAM
GL53 7TH
United Kingdom

Second Edition 1993

01 02 03 04 05 / 10 9 8 7 6 5

A catalogue record for this book is available from the British Library.
ISBN 0 7487 1632 7

Typeset by Tech-Set, Tyne & Wear
Printed and bound in Great Britain at The Bath Press, Bath

Contents

Preface to first edition

The work of a hotel receptionist is frequently underestimated both during the education of potential staff in technical colleges and by hotel managers who are often preoccupied with other parts of their business. However the receptionist in a hotel front office is the one member of staff who will affect, one way or another, the satisfaction of guests. Indeed it is often not realized that in many cases reception is the only department in a hotel that a guest has to make use of during the course of his or her stay.

Historically many technical colleges were established on the foundation of expertise gained from practical skills such as those demonstrated in a kitchen or restaurant. The senior staff were consequently craft-orientated and lacked an appreciation of the skills required in office work, especially where a hotel front office is concerned. To many craft lecturers the work of a hotel receptionist was therefore totally alien, and education of students, besides those destined for the kitchen or restaurant, was frequently tolerated, but often regarded as unnecessary by those who had never been exposed to its operation.

Luckily in more recent years courses have become much more business-orientated and now it is widely appreciated that in a hotel the majority of revenue comes from the letting of bedrooms and comparatively little from the spin-off trade in the restaurants, so the importance of teaching front office skills has largely been established. The onset of computerization has meant that computer applications in a front office have become a necessary part of any student's education. To enter the industry without such knowledge would leave the student at a distinct disadvantage.

In the industry itself those managers from a craft background have similarly tended until recent years to overlook the importance of the front office, sometimes delegating responsibility into the hands of a supervisor with the necessary technical knowledge. But in the same way that a manager needs to know whether a chef is honest, he or she also needs to know the intricacies of front office work, so that revenue is maximized and there is no opportunity for fraud.

Interestingly, many managers are now faced with the situation where their hotel operation is becoming totally accommodation-orientated as has been the case in the United States for some time where 'apartment hotels' are well established. With the onset of time-share and self-catering in this country, the traditional manager is now confronted by the situation where in many sectors of the hotel industry there are businesses being created that possess no formal food or liquor facilities whatsoever.

The importance of reserving, servicing and obtaining payment for accommodation is therefore of the utmost importance and the need for expertise has never been greater. While the industry is rapidly changing, especially where new technology is concerned, there is an identifiable need to bring up to date in one volume the techniques for ensuring that a front office is run as effectively as possible.

Hotel Front Office therefore attempts in as down to earth a way as possible to outline the importance of a front office and its staff to the operation of a hotel.

The definition of what is (and what is not) a hotel has first to be established, as this is often a cause of confusion. If one examines the definition of a hotel used by the organizations involved in giving star-ratings, it will be seen that it is any establishment with six or more letting bedrooms. The average person, though, when asked about hotels will immediately picture an establishment with several hundred bedrooms in a city centre such as the London Hilton in Park Lane. This book gives the student or the hotelier the information he or she requires to work in or establish a front office system whether this be in a Hilton or what might be called a large guest house.

Hotel Front Office has been written not only with the student in mind, but also to give assistance to persons actively involved in the industry who may seek a different solution to a particular front office problem. Therefore many potential systems are discussed, but where items such as computers are concerned, the book deals in generalities. Progress with technology is so fast, that to deal with a specific system would be misleading and out of date by the time the book is only a few months old. Therefore *Hotel Front Office* will tell you how a computer may assist you in a front office and how the information it produces may be best handled, but it will not deal with any one particular system.

New technology, though, will never replace the need for the right kind of person to be employed in the front office and it should be appreciated that many people receive much more satisfaction from exercising social skills and handling finance, than from creating a particularly intricate dish in the restaurant. It is to this breed of person that this book will appeal as well as to those who find themselves in charge of or working in a front office.

The last philosophical point that *Hotel Front Office* has deliberately taken under its wing is to illustrate that the hotel industry and its detailed systems are truly international. No opportunity has been overlooked in an effort to show that a technique or system operated in a hotel in this country may just as effectively be utilized overseas and references and illustrations also make this point.

Personally I have found the hotel industry challenging as well as very enjoyable and regard myself very much as an industrialist in the educational sector. Therefore I hope that *Hotel Front Office* will give you an answer to the particular problem you wish to solve and that it may assist you in avoiding the more obvious pitfalls into which many have fallen before.

Bruce Braham
Canford Cliffs, Poole, Dorset

Preface to second edition

'A hotelier is a person made up of the usual chemical compounds ordained by nature, but must have a personality and many virtues the average mortal does not possess.

The hotelier must have the diplomacy of a Kissinger, the social grace of the Queen Mother, the speed of a Concorde, the smile of a Greek God, the patience of a saint, the memory of an elephant, the thick skin of a rhinoceros, the strength of an Atlas, the staying-power of a mother-in-law, the fitness of a centre forward, the grooming of a duke, the voice of an Olivier, the eye for profit of a Vestey, and last but not least, the hotelier must have a love of humanity, for humans show their worst side when they are tired and hungry. Being gracious to guests as well as to associates shows a mastery of the art of hospitality.'

Albert Elovic

Historically the development of what is now widely recognized as the hospitality industry began when people started using facilities away from their homes as long ago as biblical times. However, as a commercial operation, hospitality in Europe began when the infrastructure developed and when people travelled they found the need to stop at firstly monasteries and subsequently inns and taverns where there was the rudimentary provision of a bed as well as food and drink. Indeed the evolution of the hospitality industry, particularly hotels, has always closely followed improvements in methods of travel. The Romans provided *diversoria* at strategic points along their highly efficient road system and later the pilgrims travelling on foot and on horseback stayed at the monasteries in the Dark and Middle Ages. Merchants chose to reside at manor houses and eventually the stagecoach brought about the use of inns as places of rest as well as locations at which the horses could be changed. The railways subsequently spawned hotels – each of which were seen to give the private railway company's a competitive advantage – at the major stations. The institution of the Grand Tour exposed the wealthy youth to overseas cultures that they imported into their own countries, such as the undoubted gastronomic expertise of France. At the turn of the century Escoffier and Cesar Ritz began their great influence on hospitality. In more recent times the advent of mass mobility has brought about the concept of the motel and since the Second World War hotels have grown up at many new destinations easily accessible to aircraft and, particularly, the jet. The hospitality industry, where the hotel has been concerned, has therefore been evolving almost since time began.

There are a wide variety of definitions of 'hospitality'. The word itself is derived from *hospice*, a medieval house of rest for travellers and pilgrims. A hospice was also an early form of what is now called a nursing home and the word is clearly related to *hospital*. Therefore hospitality does include hotels and restaurants but also includes other kinds of institution that offer shelter, food, or both, to people away from their homes.

These institutions have common management problems in providing food and shelter – problems that include erecting the building; providing heat, light and power; cleaning and maintaining the premises; and the preparation and service of accommodation and food to the customers. Of course, this is all expected to be undertaken with liberality and goodwill.

In preparing the second edition of *Hotel Front Office*, I have deliberately tried to widen the concept of where the skills of an accommodation manager may be put to good use to show that what is contained within these pages may be applied to organizations other than hotels. These was also a need to update the technology of running a front office and to make more reference to areas such as legislation and VAT. All these have been incorporated to make the book even more useful to those studying the subject area in theory as well as those actively involved in day-to-day operation.

Bruce Braham
Canford Cliffs, Poole, Dorset

Acknowledgements

The author and publisher are grateful to the following for their permission to reproduce illustrative material:

Bath Travel, Bournemouth
Bournemouth and Poole College of Further Education
Carlton Hotel, Bournemouth
Centraal Hotel, Amsterdam
Holiday Inns, Slough
Holiday Inn, Walldorf-Heidelberg

Hotel du Cheval Rouge, Versailles
Hotel garni Gunther, Boppard am Rhein
Hotel Ibis, Bagnolet, Paris
Hotel Ibis, Amsterdam
Trusthouse Forte, London

The author is also very grateful to Vivian and Vera Braham, who helped with proof reading.

1 The role of the front office and reception

Reception work is vital to any hotel

The work of the front office and reception departments in the hotel industry can be most satisfying and enjoyable for the right type of person who is aware of the intricacies of the job. On the surface the receptionists' skills and the variety of work with which they are faced may not be apparent to someone unfamiliar with the hospitality industry. It would appear, after all, and in many cases quite rightly, that receptionists are working in most congenial surroundings which are far preferable to those found in the average office, and that they are meeting a wide variety of different people from many differing backgrounds. They may well be lucky enough to be provided with live-in accommodation by their employers and will almost always be entitled to meals while on duty, which could mean that they are able to eat in restaurants sampling dishes from the same menu that the guests receive. It is also obvious that their skills will enable them to travel in an industry which is truly international, having potential sources of employment worldwide. Indeed, the average customer to a hotel sees a smiling receptionist behind a desk for a few seconds on arrival and probably never dreams of the amount of detailed work that has to be under- taken when not actively involved in welcoming customers.

The variety and technicality of the job of the receptionist, which are also skimmed over in popular television representations of the hotel receptionist's work, depend very much on the professionalism of the establishment and its management systems but are rarely evident to the casual observer. Equally, the size and type of hotel will determine the work undertaken in reception; for example in a small hotel there may be just a few receptionists employed, while in a large establishment reception is one department of a larger front office organization. Whatever the size of hotel there are, though, several common areas of work for which reception is responsible and the tasks undertaken by reception staff may be sub-divided into the following important areas:

1   *Welcoming arriving guests* By carrying this task out correctly guests may be put at ease at the time of arrival and welcomed to the hotel which is to be their temporary home for a period of time. Guests that are treated in an insensitive way on arrival may prove to be problematical during the rest of their stay.

2   *Completing the hotel register* The legal formality of registration must be fulfilled by the receptionist who sees that all customers supply the details required for a record that may be inspected by the police from time to time. Useful marketing information may also be collated at this time.

3   *Recording reservations* The selling of rooms is the profit-maker in all hotels and consequently vital to an effective hotel business. Reservations are also very detailed and taken for many different lengths of time so they must be recorded accurately as mistakes may be extremely embarrassing and could alienate guests.

4   *Compiling guests' bills* The bill that is presented to a guest on departure involves many items of expenditure that have been incurred by customers in different departments of the hotel throughout their stay. These many small items have to be co- ordinated and collated on to one bill accurately so that the guest is not inadvertently overcharged or undercharged. Billing must also be carried out swiftly so that a guest's bill is always instantly ready should the guest wish to check-out.

5   *Providing information* The reception desk is the

focus of the hotel to many guests and therefore the receptionist has to be able to answer all types of enquiries not only about the hotel but also about the surrounding area and its activities.

6   *Dealing with complaints* The reception desk is looked upon as the 'gateway to management' and therefore many guests will come to reception to find the manager in the event of a complaint. The receptionist must therefore be prepared to handle all types of complaint, sometimes from customers who will be in an emotional state of mind.

7   *Selling the hotel* Not only must receptionists be able to sell rooms but they must also be aware of the facilities of the other departments within the hotel so that they are able to sell them effectively. This is known as 'in house sales' and is a means of encouraging guests to make use of the hotel's facilities such as the restaurant.

8   *Providing security services* Hotels, because of their nature, have several different types of security problem which receptionists must be aware of and prepared to play their part towards preventing. They will be keen to see that customers pay for their stay at the establishment and will operate a deposit system so that the effects of a customer becoming a 'walk out', or leaving without paying, are minimized. They will operate a safe custody system so that guests may leave their valuables and they may well operate the room key system, sometimes with the benefit of computerized keys, ensuring that only the correct guest receives the key to his or her bedroom.

9   *Undertaking communication* A hotel provides a complex series of services to its guests and in order that all are co-ordinated communication is essential. As reception is the department that is recording the guests' requirements when they make their reservations it is up to the staff there to inform the other departments in the hotel of the details and state of the business. Reception also contains all the means of communication so logically it becomes the co-ordination centre of the business, thereby able to influence its effectiveness greatly.

10   *Maximizing occupancy* Occupancy is a statistical term used to describe how full or occupied are the rooms in the hotel. One of the major aims of reception is to maximize the number of rooms sold therefore bringing in as much revenue to the business as possible.

These are the basic tasks that the reception function in an hotel has to fulfil but the staffing and scope of the office will almost certainly depend upon the size of the establishment concerned. Indeed the systems utilized to cope with these tasks have to be moulded around the type of business being undertaken by a particular hotel and therefore will vary considerably from one establishment to another.

In order to keep clear in our minds the difficult concept of which type of system may be employed in a particular type of hotel, throughout the book we shall be referring to three imaginary establishments which will, through their description, illustrate the various parameters and considerations that have to be borne in mind in operating an effective reception.

The Ship Inn

The Ship Inn is a small hotel of twenty-five bedrooms situated in a popular tourist destination on the south coast of England. Originally it was a house built at the end of a terrace for a skilled worker in the nearby shipyard which utilized the trees in the local woods as the medium from which ships were built. As steel replaced wood in the building of ships the village fell into disrepair and the house became an inn with five bedrooms for sale, but as tourism grew in importance to the area an extension was built on the back of the hotel providing a popular restaurant with a commanding view of the estuary. The public bar was also supplemented by the addition of a lounge bar and a new wing of twenty purpose-built rooms was added as the market for these became apparent. At the peak of the season the hotel – having failed to obtain planning permission for a permanent facility from the local authority – operates a field at the back as a short-term camp site welcoming both tents and touring caravans.

The Ship is owned and has been run by the same family for twelve years and has resisted overtures that have been made by several large companies to take it over. It is a free house, thereby not having any particular ties to one brewery, and has established itself as the centre of village life, particularly out of season.

Like many small hotels it runs on an informal 'family' atmosphere with many of the staff undertaking several responsibilities apart from their own specializations. The owners, for example, spend much of their time either watching over the restaurant and bars or actively involved in the housekeeping role maintaining the standard and cleanliness of the

Figure 1   *The Ship Inn*
(a)   The Ship Inn from the village street
(b)   The Ship Inn showing the terrace and restaurant

(a)

bedrooms. A full-time chef is employed to look after the kitchen operations, and several local staff operate the restaurant under the supervision of the owners.

As far as reception is concerned, due to the small number of arrivals and departures on each day one full-time receptionist is employed; she also acts as a secretary to the owner and assists with correspondence and accounts. Because of the large number of individual tasks for which she is responsible it was thought necessary to recruit her from the local College of Further Education where she had obtained a formal bookkeeper/receptionist qualification. On her days off and when she is not on duty her tasks are taken over by whichever member of the owner's family is available. It is a feature of the Ship that most of the staff as well as the owners themselves are able to step into anyone else's job to help out should the need arise.

The Ship therefore requires a relatively simple reception system and the managerial structure even though extremely informal may be illustrated as shown in Figure 2.

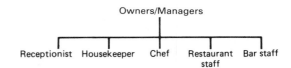

Figure 2

(b)

The Majestic Hotel

The Majestic is a luxury five-star hotel of 150 bedrooms that was built in Victorian times by a private railway company near the terminus of their line in a city centre in the Midlands. The concept behind the hotel was originally that its fine standard of service and quality would help tempt railway passengers away from rival lines. Due to the topography of the site of the railway terminus, though, the hotel had to be built half a mile away from the station, which turned out to be a blessing in disguise as it gave the hotel an air of tranquility that would not otherwise have been possible. The city in which it finds itself is famous for its manufacturing industry; consequently the hotel is a natural centre for conventions and exhibitions for which it has ornate function accommodation. The hotel has also undergone considerable renovation since the Second World War, when it was lightly damaged in the bombing, so that now all the bedrooms have private bathrooms which have been created within what were extremely large bedrooms. The hotel is operated by a hotel company that has interests throughout the Midlands and which maintains the hotel as the flagship of its business.

Being a luxury establishment and therefore required to provide the highest possible standards of both accommodation and cuisine, the hotel supports a highly specialized staff. Indeed, many of the tasks that were undertaken in the Ship Inn by an individual are undertaken by a small department at the Majestic. For example, the Majestic provides a full room service for all meals and this alone requires separate staffing from the service of food required in the restaurant and banqueting.

As far as the management is concerned the size of the hotel and the quality of service necessitates specialization in order that effective supervision and control may take place. The general manager fulfills the executive functions of management while a deputy

Figure 3   *The Majestic Hotel*

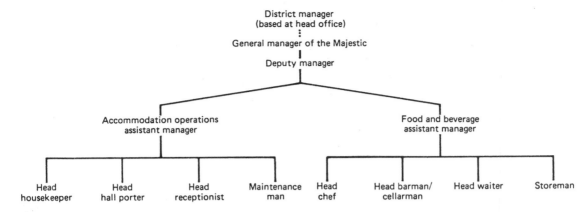

Figure 4

manager takes on the day-to-day operational tasks within the hotel. In order to improve communication and liaison the hotel operation is split between two assistant managers who are responsible for either of the departments involved with the letting of accommodation or the service of food and liquor. These two assistant managers are therefore termed the accommodation operations and the food and beverage assistant managers and each is responsible for the effective and profitable operation of their specific areas. Each of the members of the management team may also become a duty manager at some time, possibly each day, therefore being available to supervise the entire hotel operation for a certain period of time and to deal with customer relations.

Where reception is concerned the accommodation operations assistant manager supervises a head receptionist and a small number of receptionists on each of the two shifts operated each day. During the night the night porters on duty take over any reception responsibilities that may occur out of hours.

The managerial structure of the Majestic, being a typical medium-sized hotel in a group, is as shown in Figure 4.

The International Hotel

The International Hotel is a modern purpose-built hotel with 600 bedrooms constructed near a major airport which has direct flights to numerous destinations throughout the world. It is one of this country's most modern hotels, offering a high standard of comfort and an extensive range of facilities to its numerous guests. The hotel has a three-star rating as it was built deliberately with the intention of undercutting the pricing of existing hotels near the airport. Consequently standardization of the rooms and services is an essential part of the operational philosophy as dictated by the multi-national hotel company which owns it.

The hotel has been built a short distance outside the immediate perimeter of the airport so as to appeal to the motorist driving on the nearby motorway link; its situation on a large intersection helps this aim considerably. The hotel has a car park capable of accommodating over 1000 cars to cope with this market and many customers also find it convenient to leave their cars here while undertaking air trips overseas.

The International is little used by guests for holidays and it is almost exclusively a hotel for the traveller who stays for one night on average at the start or finish of a journey overseas. The short average stay of customers puts extra pressure on the reception and housekeeping staff as they have to deal with an unusually high turnover of customers, leading to bedrooms being used more than once each day at peak periods. All of the International's 600 attractively decorated bedrooms have private bathrooms and the hotel is well equipped with function rooms, a choice of restaurants and bars and provides excellent facilities for conferences, meetings and banquets.

The accommodation departments in the International are grouped together under a rooms division manager who, like the assistant manager at the Majestic, has overall responsibility for the

Figure 5   *The International Hotel*

profitable operation of the bedrooms. Many of the departments, because of the nature of the business, have to be operational twenty-four hours each day and reception is no exception. Reception, though, is looked upon as one small part of the total front office operation at the International and consequently a front office manager is needed to supervise and organize nearly seventy staff in the total front office. It will be seen that much of the work undertaken by individuals in reception at the Majestic is carried out by a separate department of the front office at the International.

Being a typical large hotel the managerial structure of the International Hotel is as shown in Figure 6.

The accommodation unit

Whatever the type or size of hotel when referring to the work of the front office and reception the department has one basic function within the purpose of the business. This function is to sell rooms profitably. Indeed, whether we are referring to the smallest of

hotels like the Ship, or the largest like the International, the purpose of their operation is to sell rooms profitably so that their business remains solvent.

It is sometimes easy to forget in an industry that relies on giving a good personal service to customers that the purpose of an hotel is to make profit at the end of the day. Consequently, as we shall see in a later chapter, the reception staff have to be geared up to sales and have to have an intimate knowledge of the rooms that they are selling.

At this moment it is worth broadening our outlook on the work of reception, as rooms are not only being sold within hotels – it should be realized that the techniques applied to hotels may also be used in other types of business where accommodation is being bought by customers. If one steps back and analyses what a hotel guest is buying in staying in a hotel room, basically it amounts to the use of an area of the hotel for a certain period of time. The room itself may vary from a tudor panelled period room with a four-poster

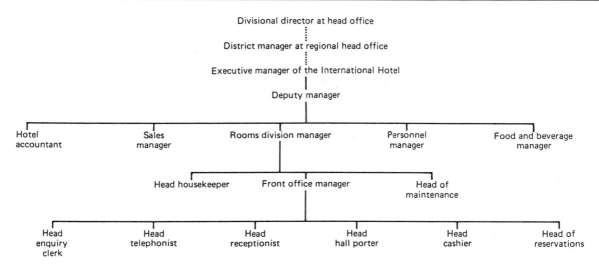

Figure 6

bed, as one might expect to find at the Ship, to a functional modern facility with a bathroom en suite which one would take for granted at the International. Where time is concerned guests may stay for one night as a minimum; even though shorter periods may sometimes be negotiated, or, in the case of some hotels, there may be residents who stay indefinitely. Financially an accountant analysing our business would probably not refer to rooms but would be happier using the term 'units of accommodation'. The term 'accommodation unit' may be more readily understood when one looks at the types of accommodation unit that may be on offer in other businesses which are concerned with their sale to customers.

To illustrate that hotel rooms are by no means the only type of accommodation unit in existence we shall briefly investigate a number of other alternatives that show that the skills of the hospitality/accommodation manager may be deployed in alternative ways. Throughout the rest of the book it should then become apparent that the hotel skills being described may be readily transferred to other similar accommodation operations.

The Super Ferry

Alan Whicker, in his TV series about the luxury liner *QE2*, referred to the ship as 'a resort hotel that chases the sun' and what an astute analogy that was. If you agree with that definition there are in fact many 'floating hotels' in operation today ranging from the large luxury cruise liners to the smaller cross-channel ferries. In both cases the purser is really equivalent to the hotel manager and the accommodation units that are being sold profitably are the cabins on offer to travellers during the period of their voyage. Obviously the standards of cabins will vary, even on one large ship, and one could be dealing with luxury apartments equivalent to a suite of rooms in a hotel, or, at the other end of the scale, the couchette or small cabin commonly found on the small cross-channel ships. Indeed, on many of these ferries the accommodation unit reserved for travellers may even be as small as a reclining seat situated in a large lounge with many similar seats close by.

Many passengers have traditionally perceived car ferries as being merely a means to an end in allowing them to make a sea crossing as comfortably and quickly as possible with the opportunity to purchase a cheap bottle of spirits from a duty free shop. In reality, of course, where ship-borne hospitality management is concerned there is a lot more to it than that and ferries are in many ways *floating hotels*. Modern ferries offer not only extensive cabin accommodation and lounges to cater for various perceived markets but also carvery, self-service and waiter service restaurants, children's play areas, cinemas, discos, bars and shops. Additionally some ferries even possess swimming pools and casinos.

The recent history of shipping has seen the whole

Figure 7   *A twin and a double accommodation unit at the Majestic Hotel*

car ferry concept being critically examined as a result of the Channel Tunnel. The operators of the Channel Tunnel forecast that it would quickly handle 78 per cent of cross-channel passengers and this means that action had to be taken to modernise the existing ferry concept if the firms involved were to stay in business. They therefore had to accept that change was on the way and that they would have to invest heavily in newer ships and better port facilities whilst offering higher standards of service.

The concept they adopted had already been successfully operated in Scandinavia where the jumbo, cruise or super ferry had already been proven. Super ferries are generally much larger than the older ships possessing an unparalleled variety of facilities and services – shops, for example, have become 'department store' in style. The very size of super ferries leads to economies of scale (bigger ships reduce the number sailings thereby lowering overheads – fuel oil and crew – and, by carrying more passengers and cars, the unit cost is reduced) by which they are able to respond to any threat from the competition in the form

of a price war. Ferry operators too have now accepted that they are in the hospitality business and have identified an intention to make the ferry crossing an intrinsic part of an enjoyable holiday experience. The perceived rest that the car's driver and passengers are able to take advantage of is regarded as a unique selling point of a ferry.

The publicity surrounding the Channel Tunnel raised awareness of ferry crossing enormously and stimulated growth in the early 1990s whilst passengers themselves had become more sophisticated than their predecessors, being more inclined to go it alone and explore overseas. The effects of the Channel Tunnel have been repeated around Europe and the almost universal growth in bigger and better ships has meant that the economics of travelling by ship have remained competitive.

Against this success there was not only the problem of the 'Chunnel' itself in the Eastern English Channel but there were also two other serious considerations that ferry operators had to bear in mind on a much wider basis. Firstly, the single European market spelt

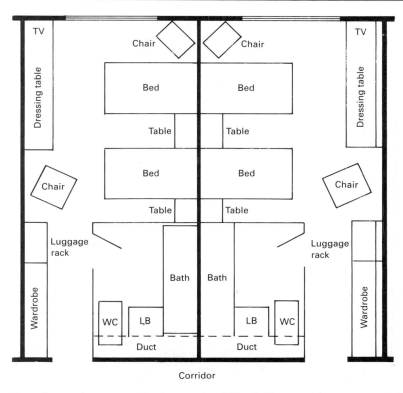

Figure 8 *Typical floor plan of two twin rooms at the International Hotel. They are like many hotels built back-to-back to save on building costs as they share common main services.*

the end of duty free shops which had previously produced somewhere in the region of one third of their revenues. Secondly, VAT on fares and ship's stores became payable at about the same time. The ferry business therefore had to invest not only to compete but also to replace existing income and contain rises in expenditure.

The example we are going to examine is the imaginary Super Ferry *Corfe Castle* owned by the equally fictitious Continental Steam Navigation Line.

The origins of the Continental Steam Navigation Line stem from the middle of the nineteenth century and over the next hundred years it matured into a worldwide shipping company serving all parts of what was then the British Empire. As the company grew it bought other similar shipping related organizations until the present day when its ferry operation is but one division of a multinational business encompassing many diverse occupations such as the shipping of

containers as well as the operation of supertankers and land-based transport.

The Continental Line fleet has been extensively modernized in recent years in order to compete with the Channel Tunnel and the concept of the super ferry has fully materialized. The *Corfe Castle* is a ship twice the size of existing ferries and capable of handling 1250 passengers and 850 cars. The recent investment by Continental Line has been to fund innovations such as club class lounges with an executive differentiation for business travellers, department store style shops as well as variations on the previous tariffs. These new price structures include special fares for skiers, students and motorhome owners. Additional incentives offered by the Line to passengers include holiday motor breakdown insurance in co-operation with one of the major motoring organizations, a Bonus Club for frequent travellers on the Line's ferries giving discounts on gifts, travel and weekend breaks and an

Figure 9 *The Super Ferry,* Corfe Castle

arrangement with a national hotel chain whereby ferry passengers qualify for heavily discounted hotel room rates. The Continental Line also offers inclusive hotel and self-catering holidays in France and Germany, making use of the ferries.

The Continental Line recently advertised the position of 'Senior Hotel Manager' when they were seeking to recruit a person who would have the responsibility for managing the onboard passenger related business on the *Corfe Castle.* The advertisement that appeared in the press for the job is shown in Figure 11.

The advertisement clearly illustrates the fact that the hotel manager will be responsible for what is in effect a floating hotel boasting a wide variation in cabins as its accommodation units. Many of those facilities and cabins may be seen in the deck plan of the *Corfe Castle* (Figure 10) and in Figure 12.

Whilst these accommodation units are only occupied for a relatively short period of time they are still reserved and serviced in an identical way to the bedrooms in a hotel.

Retaining the theme of floating accommodation units, a popular way of spending a vacation is to hire a barge on a canal or a small cabin cruiser or yacht on a waterway. Whether one is talking about the Norfolk Broads as a location or the Greek islands, where flotilla holidays are popular, the boats themselves are really floating accommodation units and may be treated as such when it comes to dealing with them from the business point of view. We have already mentioned that at our imaginary *Ship Inn*, there is a camp site at the rear of the establishment. Here the customer may well bring their own accommodation unit in the form of a tent and they just purchase the right to erect it on a particular site for a defined period of time. In some cases the site operators themselves provide tents which in reality are very cheap accommodation units for the operator to invest in. On a more professional basis caravans, whether static or

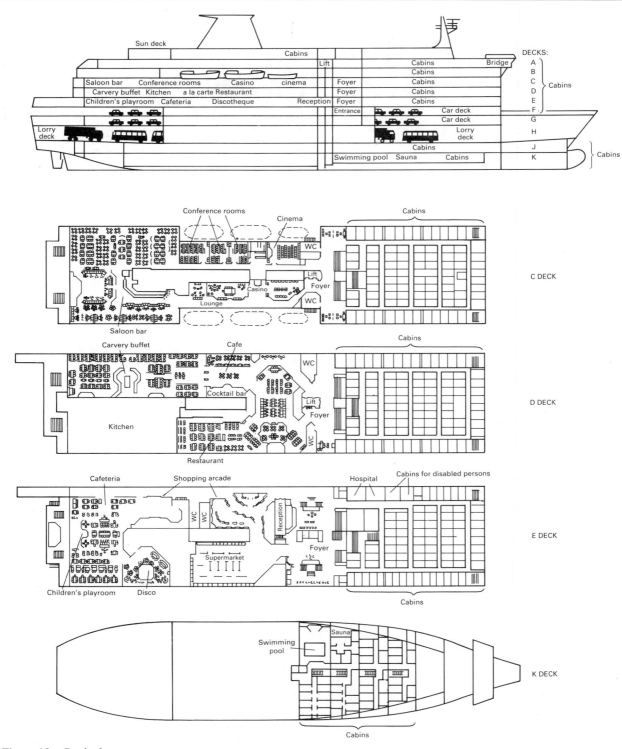

Figure 10 *Deck plans*

continental *LINE*

SENIOR HOTEL MANAGER

Highly attractive salary and employment package associated with a large company. Relocation where appropriate.

Continental Line is Europe's leading car ferry company operating six routes and carrying over 9 million passengers annually.

Recently, we have strengthened our position in the market place being a successful company with worldwide interests in the ferry and leisure business. This has resulted in an innovative restructing programme, to position our ferries firmly in the leisure rather than transport market. This creates unique opportunities for contributing to our new business concepts, and for providing expertise in a demanding and exciting environment.

The Senior Hotel Manager will be responsible for the effective and efficient management and development of the *total* on-board passenger related business. This includes the financial profitability and quality of all aspects of the on-board offer.

This is a ship based appointment, responsible for the Hotel, Food and Beverage, Retail and Passenger

Information teams, inclusive of Free Flow, Restaurants, Duty Free and Tax Free shops and in some instances a significant hotel offer on-board. The work is demanding and varied and we aim to respond to our guests with imagination and flair. Responsibility rests with you to motivate individuals and groups in line with company policy, and to provide a sound personnel role on board.

You will probably be a General/Area manager with several years experience within the Hotel, Catering or Retailing business, with a turnover of at least £2 million and 30+ staff.

A good sound basic level of education is required with MHCIMA or Retailing/Marketing (NEBSS) equivalent. A second European language would be and advantage.

If you feel excited at the prospect of managing at this level and can meet the challenge and demands of such a role please write in confidence enclosing a curriculum vitae and current photo to:

Mrs I. Cotton, Personnel Department, Continental Line Wharf House Southampton, Hampshire.

Tel: 1134 - 567891

Continental Line is an equal opportunities employer

Figure 11   *Recruitment advertisement*

touring, may be referred to as types of accommodation unit and they too vary in quality from the luxurious to the functional but the business principles are just the same as for any other type of accommodation unit.

Sunset Quay

Sunset Quay is predominantly a caravan and chalet park situated on a West Country peninsula near to its own beach and possessing spectacular views across the bay. It markets itself as a 'mini seaside resort in its own right' offering a wide range of facilities to its customers which have qualified it as an English Rose Award winner.

The facilities available at Sunset Quay include a variety of shops such as a foodstore and gift centre selling fresh and frozen food, groceries, sweets, toiletries, newspapers, stationery, beachwear and gifts.

There is an in-store bakery too, providing fresh bread daily. In addition there is also a hire centre, launderette and a photographic processors. Sporting facilities include the outdoor heated Hawaiian pool and sundeck as well as the climate-controlled indoor water park which possesses a waterslide, jacuzzi and a poolside cafe. Sailing may be undertaken as well as subaqua diving. Additionally there is the Kylie Night Club which is not only a family clubroom but also a centre of entertainment for all ages, including children. The Tasmin Amusement Centre with electronic, pool and video games is popular too. The licensed bar and beer garden overlook the water park and are often pressed into service as the venue for both cabaret and entertainment.

Whilst most of the customers like to self-cater the site does possess a restaurant, an ice-cream parlour and barbecue facilities.

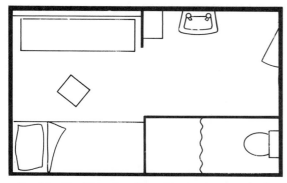

Special cabin, 2/4-berth, with washbasin, shower and toilet

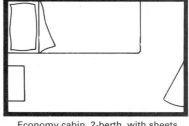

Economy cabin, 2-berth, with sheets,
blankets and pillows provided

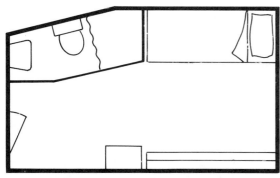

Special cabin available with 4 and 2 berths,
with washbasin, shower and toilet

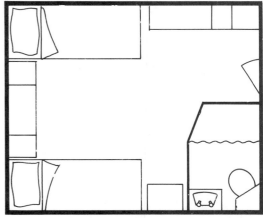

De-luxe cabin with 2 berths, toilet, shower, washbasin,
settee, colour TV and refrigerator

Figure 12   *Cabin accommodation units on the* Corfe Castle

Whatever your definition of hospitality there is little doubt that Sunset Quay is an integral part of the overall hospitality industry, though some observers might regard it as an unconventional member. Through its various facilities Sunset Quay does provide its guests with food, beverages, accommodation and environment in return for remuneration.

Interestingly all of the caravans are privately owned and therefore the accommodation on offer to holidaymakers is provided by the private owners through Sunset Quay. It should be realized therefore that the private owners fund a large proportion of the capital cost of the accommodation units directly themselves. The park has a licence for 1300 caravans all of which are privately owned. The owners buy both a site and a caravan and pay Sunset Quay an annual site fee. The owners may either let out their caravans to holidaymakers if they so wish whilst some actually live in their caravans for most of the year. Others choose to use their caravans as a second holiday or weekend home. Some sites are more expensive than others depending on their position and whether they are connected to full facilities or not. The more expensive sites have concrete bases and are linked to a gas main. Additionally they have a proper car parking space and dustbin enclosures. All the vans have access to satellite television.

Sunset Quay has recently invested in a number of chalets which are situated in the grounds and which provide another alternative type of accommodation for those wishing to stay. The 100 chalets, or A-frame lodges, on the site are owned and operated by Sunset Quay itself. Like the caravans they all possess a private bathroom, including basin, toilet, bath or shower. A well-equipped kitchen with a modern cooker, fridge, cupboards, crockery, cutlery and pans is standard and

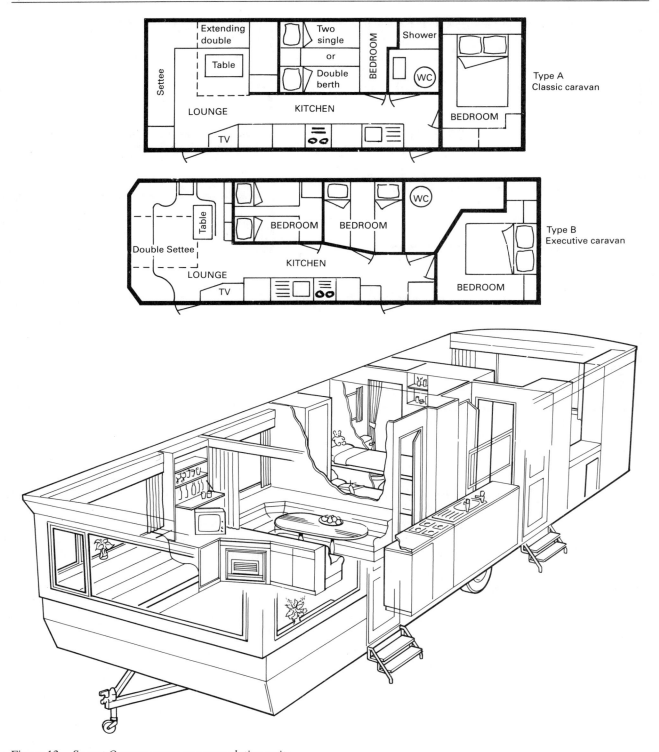

Figure 13 *Sunset Quay caravan accommodation units*

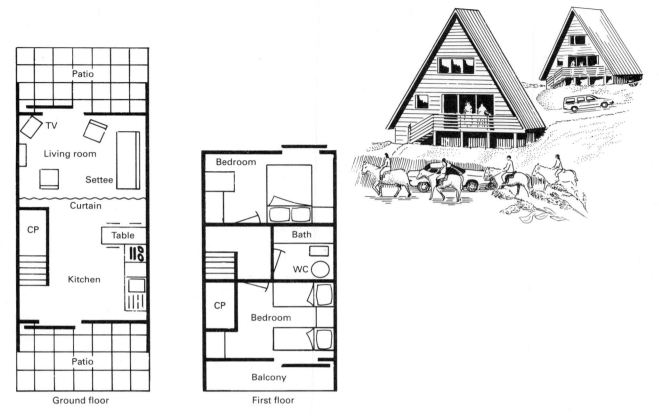

Figure 14   *Sunset Quay chalet accommodation units*

in most cases a microwave, dishwasher and washing machine is included. A colour television is provided in all the chalets and caravans, whilst there is also access to relayed video films and satellite television. The chalets have proved particularly popular with families and are, of course, another low capital investment type of accommodation unit.

Due to the way in which Sunset Quay is structured, the management team are mainly in existence to perform a co-ordinating function. Much like a hotel there is a general manager, assistant manager and a range of departmental managers in charge of sales, reservations, bars and entertainment. Other departments such as the restaurant, cleaning and maintenance are contracted out. Sunset Quay managers, whilst only in direct control of the chalets where accommodation is concerned, are therefore responsible for monitoring and making sure that the contractors maintain closely defined standards in their particular specialist areas.

Sunset Quay boasts 260 staff including the cleaners supplied by the contractors. The park is open for ten months of the year from March to December and is closed in January and February for essential annual maintenance.

If one steps back and analyses what Sunset Quay provides physically it becomes apparent that it is an 'exploded hotel'! The accommodation units are in fact scattered around the site but perform exactly the same function as the bedrooms within a traditional hotel.

Costed in the same way as a hotel, but with their source of revenue being somewhat different, are the accommodation units that one may find in the educational sector of the hospitality industry. There are, after all, halls of residence in universities and schools where accommodation units ranging from study bedrooms to dormitories are being provided for, in this case, students rather than guests. In a hall of residence the domestic bursar is the equivalent of the hotel manager looking after the allocation and servicing of the accommodation as well as the provision, in many cases, of meals. Some halls of residence may, though, be self-catering while many halls closely resemble hotels during the educational vacations when they are transformed into conference venues or even accommodation for holidaymakers.

Having mentioned self-catering there are many establishments in operation that may be termed as apartment hotels where no formal provision for the service of meals is made. This has been popular in the United States and parts of mainland Europe for some time and self-contained flats of varying sizes are normally the accommodation units. Some operators rent villas or chalets as their particular type of accommodation unit and are frequently using the time-share method of generating revenue from their operations. Time-sharing means that the accommodation unit is bought for a particular period of time for so many years by the customer. For example, a time-share flat might be bought by a customer for the first week in August for the next ten years and he/she then has the right to occupy it for that period during that time. Other customers would have similar rights throughout the rest of the year. Going full-circle in our discussion of accommodation units, quite a number of traditional full-service hotels are now offering time-share facilities on some of their accommodation units to guests, so it is a philosophy of the costing of accommodation with which we must be familiar.

Having therefore seen that hotel rooms are by no means the only type of accommodation unit in existence it may be concluded that there are many types of business in which reception and front office techniques may be applied. As we progress through this book many of the systems discussed could just as easily be adopted to the operation of accommodation units in these other spheres.

The key to maximum profits is maximum room occupancy

A basic part of the receptionist's work is to sell the accommodation in the hotel, whether this be directly to a customer at the front desk or by means of the efficiency with which advance reservations are handled. Many hotels are let down by the inefficient business practices of their reception staff, such as bad telephone operation, which loses potential accommodation sales. It is only the hotel with excellent systems and attitudes which will maintain its business against the stiff opposition found everywhere in the hospitality industry today.

The reception staff will only show the correct attitude towards sales if they are encouraged and given a good example by an enthusiastic management who themselves demonstrate a positive approach towards sales.

There is far more profit to be made out of the sale of a bedroom than out of an equivalently priced meal. Consequently managers spend a substantial amount of their time in encouraging accommodation sales and treat bar and restaurant revenue, for example, as useful spin-off income once customers have been attracted to the rooms. Rooms, though, can only be let once for a specific time; if the sale has been lost and not re-booked it is impossible to sell it again. This is in stark contrast to food, which may be stored until the market is there for it to be consumed. Neither is it possible to increase dramatically the number of rooms available to meet a sudden surge in demand, so accommodation sales have to be approached carefully in a planned and ordered way.

Therefore many hotels are now adopting aggressive selling techniques, sometimes spearheaded by a sales manager, to approach customers rather than just sitting back and waiting for them to find out about the hotel themselves. Conference, tour and travel agency business is chased to increase the occupancy of rooms, sometimes at notoriously low business times. Discount rates of many varieties are employed and all the skills of marketing, with the eventual knowledge that the key to maximum profits is the maximum occupancy of rooms.

A good first impression is vital to the guest and the business

The receptionist should remember that customers at the hotel are making that establishment their temporary home for the duration of their stay and are therefore entitled to the courtesy and treatment that they would normally expect in the comfort of their home surroundings. In other words, customers are, in their own minds, spending a considerable amount of money on the understanding that they will receive this very service while staying at the hotel; they should not be allowed to be disappointed.

Many potential customers have never actually seen the hotel in which they are going to spend their holiday or business trip at the time that they make their booking. They may well have referred to a guide book of some sort, have been recommended by a travel agent or have just phoned around until they found an establishment that fulfilled most of their wishes. The impression given to a customer is therefore most important and, as we shall see expanded in later chapters of the book, extends to the method of dealing with customers not only in face-to-face situations at the front desk but also with potential guests via the telephone or correspondence.

At this stage, though, we shall concentrate on the vital first impression that a customer receives on arrival at the hotel, possibly never having seen the establishment before.

Guests will probably find themselves in a large and unfamiliar foyer and may well be nervous having a misgiving at the back of their mind, perhaps brought about by past experiences, that they may not be expected or that their reservation has not been recorded accurately. It is up to the reception staff to put customers at ease as soon as possible and to welcome them to the hotel, thereby reflecting the hotel's personality. Indeed many customers may only come across the front office staff during their stay; therefore this department, above all others, reflects the attitude of the hotel to them so that the impression they receive will be most important as it could well be their only impression. The reception area is, of course, the first and last business contact that every customer has with the hotel, so it is up to the receptionists to make sure that they turn what might otherwise be a cold and impersonal building into a friendly and hospitable place.

It is therefore important that the people recruited for reception staff have the right personality: those who are aloof, reserved or even uninterested in customers will be devastating to the impression of the hotel. Many customers who complain to the manager subsequently during their stay may well have been aggrieved initially by the lack of understanding from an uncaring receptionist when they first arrived. Had they received the idea that the hotel was a warm, cheerful and friendly place on arrival they might otherwise have overlooked small lapses in the service elsewhere but so often, unfortunately, this is not the case.

The reception staff should aim to give the hotel a 'guest-pleasing' personality so that the customer approaching the reception desk should gain an impression of friendly competence. The guest who is mishandled in one way or another is unlikely to return to the hotel, while the satisfied customer is a mobile advertisement for the establishment and may become a regular as well as recommending the hotel to all his or her friends. It can therefore be seen that not only should the reception staff possess the skills to give a customer a good impression for purely business reasons but that a warm welcome, as part of this impression, is essential as it is a part of good manners.

Reception is the communication centre of the hotel

Like any business a hotel is dependent upon effective communication between its various departments to be able to work efficiently. In the commercial world the salesperson in a shop must keep the ordering department aware of the number of sales made so that in turn the warehouse is up to date and can forward replacement goods. An accounts department will also be involved in the shop to ensure that the money taken from customers is both recorded accurately and actually collected from those people who may have purchased goods through both cash and credit facilities. The only way in a shop operation that all this may be co-ordinated is through close liaison, whether it be in the form of paperwork or through electronic office systems, but the aim is the same: to be able to provide customers with their requirements as efficiently as possible.

In a hotel the same organizational problems arise and the aim may be described as being to create happy guests. Many of the problems that occur with customers may be traced back to a lack of communication somewhere along the line, so a hotel must aim for a systematic approach leading to smooth, errorless operations. It should be remembered that the product that a hotel is selling is generally a room for a set period of time or a meal in a particular atmosphere and if something goes wrong – for example a customer's booking is lost – one can naturally expect a guest to become extremely aggrieved. In the case of a lost booking the error might have been made at the time the reservation was taken by the particular clerk which may actually have been many months ago. The paperwork relevant to the particular customer may inadvertently have been lost or accidentally erased from the system. The receptionist may have over-looked the guest's details when preparing a breakdown in advance of room allocation; whatever the reason

and whoever was responsible a dissatisfied guest is standing at the reception desk and must, probably legally, be accommodated or compensated. The art of communication is therefore to create teamwork within the operation of the hotel so that this type of problem does not exist.

Perhaps the most important part of communication, as far as the guest is concerned, is that not only is the hotel able to record his or her reservation but also the

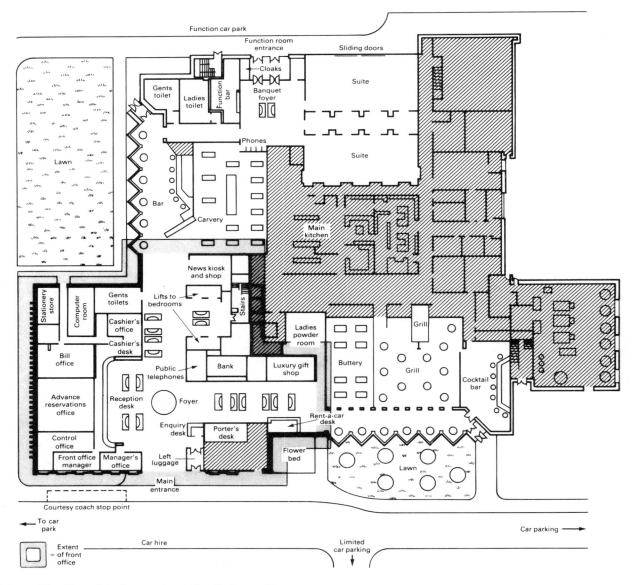

Figure 15   *Plan of the International Hotel's front office*

individual requests that are peculiar to each customer and vital to that person's stay. For the reservation clerk to forget to record that a customer has particular dietary problems at the time the reservation is made may well lead to embarrassment for the restaurant manager and chef should this not have been made aware to them in advance. Another common example might be that customers have asked and been advised that they may check-out of the hotel at an unusual time, say, in the middle of the night. If they subsequently arrive at the cashier's desk to find everything locked up for the night there may be a difficult problem, involving both use of diplomacy and social skills for the night staff to have to overcome. All these types of very individual problems may be avoided by a systematic approach to communication and by utilizing well-proven methods of communication. These will be outlined in Chapter 4. At this time though the importance of creating teamwork within a large and diverse hotel structure should be emphasized and consequently management will be concentrating on creating an atmosphere of harmony which in itself will lead to effective liaison and therefore communication.

What is the difference between the term 'front office' and the term 'reception'?

Before moving on to the detailed chapters of this book it will be wise to establish what is meant by the terms front office and reception, as confusion may occur if these two are not explained at an early stage especially as they appear regularly throughout the book.

The term front office is best explained by reference to the physical layout of hotels of varying sizes. For our purposes the International is the best one of our three imaginary hotels to refer to (see Figure 15).

In this size of hotel it may be seen that there are a large number of departments in their own right grouped around the foyer area of the hotel to deal with guests not only on arrival and departure but also throughout their stay. Because they are situated in the foyer area, which is easily accessible to guests, for convenience they are grouped together under the all embracing title of the front office. All those departments may therefore be legitimately referred to as being part of the operation of a front office in a large hotel and indeed they may warrant a front office manager to oversee their everyday work.

It may be seen that the reception desk is one small part of the total front office and therefore in this size and type of hotel forms a single department within the complete front office. In smaller hotels, though, the reception comes into its own with the merging of jobs under the responsibility of a smaller number of staff. Consequently in these smaller establishments it would be wrong to group the individual jobs into the term front office especially as in the very small establishments, such as at the Ship Inn, there may be only one receptionist. Therefore in smaller hotels the work of dealing with customers on arrival and departure as well as during their stay is termed reception.

We could therefore sum up by saying that reception is one part of the work of a front office in a large hotel while it embraces all the work undertaken by a front office in a smaller establishment.

2 The receptionist

The most important aspect of reception is the person behind the desk

The infectious sincerity of the young lady in the building society advertisement beams a now famous 'Good morning', warmly inviting us to penetrate the Woolwich's portals. Wouldn't it be nice if the same sincere feeling of welcome and homeliness were conveyed to all guests hoping to stay in hotels?

All too often guests who have travelled a long distance and are both tired and hungry arrive at their hotel only to be greeted by supreme indifference from an uncaring receptionist. It is not uncommon to feel that as a customer one is trespassing on the receptionist's precious time and getting in the way by actually daring to bring business to the hotel. Instead of being treated as someone whose business is valued the customer is reluctantly herded into an accommodation unit with the interest that an anonymous occupancy statistic deserves. Is it therefore surprising that so many customers never bother to return and apparently take their valuable business elsewhere?

Where marketing is concerned it is pointless spending small fortunes on attracting customers if the product is not up to standard: the best way to scare a potential sale away is to convince the guests that they are unwelcome. Now, when markets are so competitive and the customer has a choice of so many different hotel destinations, it is undoubtedly the establishment that treats its customers as friends and individuals that will thrive.

So bad has the situation been that the *Automobile Association Guide to Hotels and Restaurants* has in the past been very critical of hotel receptionists after examining the reports of its inspectors. 'You don't get a warm welcome in most of Britain's hotels,' said the guide. 'Our inspectors feel welcomes overall could be greatly improved. Hotels don't seem to realize that first impressions are what stick in the mind and a poor welcome and reception can be very indicative of what the service is like for the rest of the stay. How many times have you gone to a reception desk and there is no one there or the receptionists are chatting and finish their conversation before turning reluctantly to the guest?' Despite this warning it is evident that the situation has changed little in many establishments.

Many customers arrive at a hotel never having seen the premises before, other than in a brochure, and the first staff they come into contact with are invariably the receptionists. They are to be found behind their desk which is deliberately situated near the main entrance to enable them to carry out their main responsibility, which is to welcome customers. This word 'welcome' should not be forgotten as the basic task of reception staff is to greet the guests much as anyone would welcome friends who are visiting their homes. It should not be forgotten that guests are making the hotel their temporary home and they should be able to expect the same amount of courtesy and civility that they would normally receive in the domestic situation.

Guests should ideally, therefore, be welcomed without delay and the formalities of room allocation and registration dispensed with as soon as possible. Customers are often nervous in new surroundings and in a tense frame of mind in an unfamiliar foyer, and the caring receptionist should aim to put them at ease swiftly, thereby removing this psychological worry. Many guests may be nervous after past experiences of hotels when their bookings have gone astray or their details and requirements have been incorrectly recorded so they may therefore be more tense than normal.

Where it is the receptionist's duty to 'break the ice' she should be ready to greet customers in 'Woolwich-style' with a smiling passing of the time of day and a cheerful natural 'May I help you?' The manner in which this is done will influence guests and help put them at ease and the formalities may then be carried out. A popular maxim to remember is that 'There is nothing as nice as a cheerful word of greeting' and in a similar vein, 'The sweetest music to anyone's ears is the sound of their own name.' The conscientious receptionist will endeavour to remember regular or past customer's names thereby making them feel like an individual and therefore a welcome friend; but care must also be exercised as an error of identification may be most embarrassing. Reference to arrival lists and guest record cards will help lessen the risk and give the guests the impression that they are individuals and that the staff have marvellous memories for detail.

The receptionist, apart from social skills, must possess the ability to present a hygienic appearance. 'Hygienic' may not at first sight appear to be the correct adjective to use in these circumstances but a scruffy individual in reception will sow seeds of doubt in the mind of the guest about the staff in the other areas of the hotel who, for example, may be entrusted with preparing meals. Receptionists need not be fashion models, in fact this might be discouraged, but they should be well-groomed people presenting a neat appearance to customers. Hair should be well cared for and make-up unobtrusive while uniforms should be clean and well pressed. An important facet where the receptionist is concerned, when helping guests to complete registration forms and handing out key cards, is that he or she is well manicured.

Should our receptionist possess a good appearance as well as social skills the guest should on arrival form an all-important favourable impression. As the receptionist is in the front line greeting customers he or she is the person who, more than anyone else, can affect the guest's entire stay. If the first impression is bad guests will continue to doubt the hotel or even look for trouble as they will have a nagging worry in their mind that the organization is not all that it should be. The consequence of this is that what might have been a minor problem to the guest may sometimes proliferate into a major complaint. One cannot stress too heavily the importance of this first impression which is almost always attributable to the ability and competence of the receptionist and his or her social skills.

The best solution if guests are receiving the wrong impression is not necessarily intensive training, although it may be advisable from time to time to remind existing staff of their responsibilities, but an occasional on-the-job training session. The accommodation manager who is aware of the importance of reception will tackle the problem by recruiting the ideal staff initially as it will be very difficult to alter the ways of existing staff if bad habits have become established.

It should be obvious at an interview if a potential member of the reception staff is capable of dealing amicably with the public. Someone whose personality is dour and uninteresting will not be friendly and sociable towards customers and it is these facets of personality that are essential in a receptionist. A warm and outgoing attitude will indicate the type of receptionist that will benefit the business and this is what the skilled interviewer should look for. It should not be necessary to prise these areas of personality out of an interviewee and if, indeed, this actually proves to be necessary the applicant is not suitable for the job. The interviewer should be looking for the type of person that he or she warms to initially as this first impression at the interview may well be a true indication of the impression that guests will receive at a future date.

With the high number of applicants for vacancies the initial 'sift' of applications is usually carried out by means of referring purely to the academic qualifications presented. Even though school or professional qualifications are a good indication of competence – after all one is unlikely to employ a completely inexperienced receptionist – there are more important criteria to be satisfied that can only be assimilated at a face-to-face interview. The receptionist's personality and consequent attitude are more important than paper qualifications when they are continuously expected to deal with customers. Training in the mechanics of reception work is far easier to impart than trying to change an individual's character.

Hoteliers should realize the importance of correctly applied social skills among the reception staff and that customers are likely to be dissatisfied in some cases and are therefore unlikely to return to an establishment. Some customers may only come into contact with the

A guide to species of reception bird

The ostrich
Buries head in nearest cover. Avoids customer contact at all times. Emerges when the coast is clear.

The screech owl
Attacks customers and keeps them at bay; snaps violently if provoked. Treats telephones as intruders.

The peacock
Struts round reception to display its plumage - not to be hurried as this may ruffle its feathers.

The cockatoo
Bags of confidence; expects others to be as well informed. Puts guests firmly in place.

Company cormorant
Calls 'Company policy, company policy' at the slightest sign of complaint.

Docile duck
Lethargic, disinterested, habitually yawns, usually looks in opposite direction.

Guzzle goose
Consumes large quantities of coffee and sticky buns - sprays intruders with both.

Jackdaw
Collects sundry rubbish and hoards it on reception counter.

Lesser crested mumbler
Never opens mouth, especially when making telephone calls.

Knitting nestler
Scatters miles of shapeless knitting round it wherever it goes.

Nicotine bird
Fumigates all and sundry. Litters surrounds with copious droppings.

Greater crested christmas bird
Well adorned with all available tinsel. Highly psychedelic make-up. Do not approach - usually crackers!

The dumb lounger
Usually drapes itself on nearest object - rarely seen upright. When approached calls 'Eh, eh, y'wot'.

Flurried flapper
When approached turns bright red, flaps arms and throws all papers in the air. Can never find anything; finally flies off in a flurry of confusion.

The vulture
Pounces on all and sundry - its word is law - avoid at all costs.

Nightingale
Sleeps all day - plays all night. Not offensive.

Migrant bird
Migrates whenever needed, only returns when guest has gone.

Perfect bird
Suspected to be nearly extinct, but now being re-introduced at certain sanctuaries - your help urgently needed.

Figure 16   *Tongue-in-cheek memorandum issued to managers to encourage the selection and training of reception staff*

reception staff during their stay and need not necessarily speak or even see any other member of staff. On the basis therefore that 'the best advertisement for an hotel is a satisfied customer' the reception is arguably the most important marketing tool in a hotel and the most important constituent of reception is its staff.

What is meant by social skills?

Undoubtedly the constant exposure that receptionists have to both the public and the other staff in hotels is an integral part of their work and consequently the way that they react to people in face-to-face situations is going to affect the image that the reception portrays in the minds of these other people.

Speak to people: there is nothing as nice as a cheerful word of greeting.

Smile at people: it takes seventy-two muscles to frown, only fourteen to smile.

Call people by name: the sweetest music to anyone's ears is the sound of their own name.

Be friendly and helpful: if you would have friends be friendly.

Be cordial: act as if everything is a genuine pleasure.

Be interested in people: you can like everyone if you try.

Be generous with praise: cautious with criticism.

Be considerate of the feelings of others: it will be appreciated.

Be thoughtful of the opinions of others: there are three sides to an argument: (a) yours, (b) the other person's, (c) the right one.

Figure 17   *Some social skills reminders issued by Holiday Inns to their staff*

We have already discussed the implications of first impressions to a customer arriving at a hotel but it is worth reminding ourselves that it is unlikely that a guest who is received badly will return again to the establishment. Equally, a long time after the details of a guest's stay, such as the total of the bill or the standard of the bedroom, have been forgotten, the attitudes with which the staff have dealt with the customer will remain clear in the mind. People like to exist in a friendly atmosphere and if this has been created by the staff in a hotel it will not only be memorable to the guests but it will also encourage them to return. As reception is the department in all hotels that the guest is bound to come into contact with, which is not necessarily the case for all the other departments, it is essential that the correct attitudes are fostered not only by hiring the correct staff initially but also by reminding them through training of the importance of social skills.

Not only will receptionists who are 'skilled socially' find that their relationships with customers become easier but also that their dealings with the other departments and their staff in the hotel will improve. We have all, for example, heard of people who have suffered 'personality conflicts' with others and the consequences of these occurring within one's hotel between staff can be dire in the extreme. In the accommodation departments or rooms division inter-departmental liaison is vital especially between the reception and housekeeping. Without effective communication reception will never accurately know

the rooms that have been cleaned and serviced by housekeeping and are consequently ready to let. Communication may be affected in the reverse direction as well so that housekeeping might not be aware in sufficient time of those rooms that are about to be filled by customers. A personality conflict leading to a breakdown in communication between these two departments could damage the hotel's reputation by, for example, leading to guests having to needlessly wait in the foyer for their rooms to be completed or accidentally being shown to rooms that are still being serviced. Many of these types of error, instigated by personality conflicts in some cases or a pure lack of social skills in others, could have been overcome had the reception staff been selected for their competence in social skills or been made aware of their importance through training.

The term 'social skills' is rather off-putting and perhaps it would be good to define in a clearer way exactly what is meant, particularly it should be realized that social skills are something that we all possess but it may be that they need improving to deal with certain situations. Perhaps above all receptionists will use their personalities to help their social skills and indeed much of these are really a part of an individual's personality. For example, in dealing with people at the front desk, tact and common sense are vital to overcome some of the difficult situations that may arise and receptionists are going to have to be alert to spot the different types of person with which they are confronted. It may be left to their discretion as to whom they will be asking for a deposit on arrival; therefore they must be astute and able to sum up people very quickly not only for the hotel's benefit but also for their own protection. Receptionists must, even when under provocation, be polite to customers at all times and be the type of people who understand that a hotel is part of a service industry so they must be capable of, and indeed willing to give, service to customers. The correct voice, also important on the phone, should be one of their assets and where this is concerned they should not be too loud when having personal conversations with customers as, after all, they do not want their discussions broadcast through the foyer to all and sundry. Receptionists should speak slowly, especially to foreign and elderly customers, and avoid the use of slang or hotel jargon. A customer is not going to understand that 'as a chance customer you are being charged a deposit on the NCR in case you might be a walkout!' It is too easy for hotel receptionists to lapse into this type of hotel jargon which is used in everyday conversations in the office but which is totally alien to the guest who becomes even more aggravated or confused than before an explanation was offered. Where receptionists' manner in conversations is concerned it is all too easy for them to become dominant over guests who are not going to take kindly to being ordered about by someone who they are paying to offer them a service. This must be monitored carefully so that it does not get out of hand.

It has been said that 'The guest is always right' and basically this is the attitude that should be instilled into receptionists. One must accept that one will never be able to please all of the customers, human nature being what it is, but if one accepts that guests are right it will help to avoid the possibility of getting into arguments at the front desk. Indeed these should be avoided at all costs and the cheerful or friendly receptionist who is always polite to customers will be a difficult person for a guest to have an argument with. If one does not ignore customers and tries to be helpful while being pleasant and eager to serve there will be few problems in dealing with the public.

Guests will subconsciously grade hotels that they have stayed at by the way in which they were treated. Social skills will not only make the receptionist's work easier but they will assist the business by encouraging customers to return 'to that friendly hotel where I felt like an individual and part of the family'. Discourteous staff at reception may sometimes be blamed for guest dissatisfaction but if adequate training is given reception will be a happier place in which to work. It is evident that in approaching a reception desk most customers are seeking guidance of one type or another and by the correct application of social skills a receptionist should quickly be able to find out the customer's requirements and fulfil them. It should be remembered, though, that just as no two receptionists are alike no two customers are the same, and just as we are able to suffer moods, then customers are subject to similar feelings. As a result a receptionist must be the type of person who is not only sympathetic to the feelings of others but also interested in people so that the customer is always dealt with with the utmost courtesy. Don't be surprised, though, if customers are sometimes suspicious of courtesy, unfortunately, in many cases, they are not used to receiving it in everyday life.

Later in this chapter we shall look at the importance of the appearance of the receptionist which is another facet of personality which helps greatly with the social skills and consequent guest relations. One's appearance helps one's confidence upon which the guest relies. Very quickly they need to know that their reservation, for example, has been recorded carefully and that there have been no mistakes that might stop them checking in swiftly. They therefore need to be able to gain an impression of confidence from the staff behind the desk. A receptionist should be cordial, but not to the extent of appearing insincere, and with confidence will be able to take control of conversations with guests thereby showing interest and a desire to be helpful. Sincerity should be reinforced with a smile for customers, helping to put them at ease, and where possible the customer's name should be used. There is no doubt that the use of the guest's name is one of the quickest ways of making a guest feel at home but one should always be careful as mistakes may lead to embarrassment. If in doubt the use of 'Sir' or 'Madam' should be taken as the safe option but the cultivation of a memory for guest names should be encouraged. It is essential, to avoid possible confrontations or embarrassment, to always remain neutral in conversations with customers. One should keep off the more risky subjects, remembering that even though the guest you are conversing with may not be sensitive, the customer standing nearby may well be. Criticism of other guests must never occur whether to the individual concerned or to another guest as one never knows what might be passed on. Conversely, the people to whom you are speaking may wonder what you are going to say about them behind their back. The motto therefore is to avoid gossip where possible.

Several personal attributes as well as good grooming are necessary for all front office staff

Having seen how front office staff should interact with others using basic social skill guidelines it should be becoming apparent that the reception staff are important public relations people for the hotel. The way in which they speak to customers and deal with awkward or complicated situations will greatly affect the image guests build up in their minds of the hotel.

Not only is it important to use social skills to the best possible advantage but the receptionists themselves must present an impeccable outward appearance to customers as there is no doubt that this will also reflect the image of the hotel to the customer.

Remembering that guests are making the hotel their temporary residence for a short period of time and that very personal services are going to be provided, such as the provision of meals and a bed for the night, should guests on arrival be greeted by a slovenly, unkempt member of staff then doubts are going to be raised in their minds over the efficiency and perhaps hygiene requirements of the establishment. They could not be blamed for wondering what standards the management are imposing behind the scenes in areas the guests do not visit, such as the kitchen, if the staff who are in contact with guests are allowed to present such a poor appearance. It is therefore extremely important that all staff who are going to come into contact with guests should present a clean and tidy appearance thereby complementing the overall image of the hotel.

Remembering our three hotels it should be appreciated that the type and standard of the hotel will largely determine the uniform that the front office staff are required to wear if, indeed, a uniform is appropriate. At the Ship Inn, for example, the atmosphere is largely informal and the single receptionist will be allowed to select his or her own clothes for work. The Majestic, on the other hand, boasts a large front office staff providing a very traditional service to customers, there being both male and female staff working in the front office. An interesting requirement of the work of the receptionists here is that one of their duties is to escort customers to their bedrooms on arrival so that they have to emerge from behind their reception desk and therefore extra care has to be taken to select appropriate footwear. As the hotel is projecting a traditional image the uniform is selected so that all staff will endorse this luxury atmosphere and therefore black skirts and white blouses are appropriate for the female staff, and morning suits for the male staff. The International Hotel, on the other hand, is a busy travellers' hotel where the staff in the front office are under great pressures dealing with large quantities of customers in a hotel which is presenting a businesslike as well as a modern image. In this case a common uniform of brighter colours is appropriate to the staff and at various times different themes have been tried including trouser suits for the receptionists which were thought appropriate to the hotel. The status of various members of staff is, in fact, indicated by different types or colour of uniform at the International.

It may therefore be seen that there are varying requirements as regards dress in different types of hotel but basic guidelines may be followed whatever the establishment. Above all the dress selected for reception staff should not be startling as this may sometimes cause offence to customers. This should be carefully watched where staff are allowed to select their own dress as it is much more important to be able to work adequately in one's garments rather than to be an impractical leader of up-to the-minute fashion. In general the lessons have been learnt and a combination of blouse and skirt or a tailored dress will be appropriate in most situations for the female receptionists. The colouring will depend on management policy but in general sober pastel colours are encouraged where the hotel image requires this, with suits commonly black or charcoal grey in luxury establishments. As an accessory, incidentally, do not forget that an identification name tag is most useful to allow guests to identify staff.

No uniform will achieve its image-building aims if it is not kept properly and the receptionists should be encouraged to maintain their uniforms to the required standards. Obviously they should be repaired if damaged but a hotel should provide both laundering and dry cleaning facilities for uniforms or a dress allowance if necessary to give an incentive to staff to keep their uniforms in the best possible condition. The management may lead by example here and should not be unwilling to comment on the standard of dress in reception. They will also realize that pride in receptionists' appearances may well reflect their attitude towards their work and all the reception staff should be encouraged to maintain the best possible standard of appearance.

With regard to accessories, in many cases jewellery may be encouraged in moderation to complement a businesslike appearance but this should not be taken to extremes. For example, a large number of bracelets will be most impractical if using a touch-sensitive keyboard on a computer terminal. Needless to say, female staff will be required to wear tights in reception and usually stipulated colours will be laid down in managerial policy. They should, of course, not be laddered. Regarding footwear, in general it should be remembered that receptionists spend most of their working days on their feet. Comfort and practicality should therefore take precedence over high fashion, with high heels being discouraged, particularly if staff have to walk around the hotel; they may prove dangerous on stairs or in slippery conditions such as those frequently found in the back areas of kitchens. The shoes themselves should be kept clean and in a good state of repair.

The presentation of the receptionist's hair is important. If hair is unkempt the effect of the uniform may be negated completely. There are so many differing styles that to stipulate any one would be impractical but generally hair should be well cared for and preferably kept off the face in order to avoid the receptionists constantly having to brush hair out of their line of sight which is not only tiring for them but irritating to customers. Receptionists' manicure is important as their hands are in constant public view, as forms are being examined at the front desk, keys are being handed over and paperwork is being exchanged. They should keep their hands clean and nail varnish should be well maintained and not allowed to become chipped or in a poor state of repair. Makeup in general is a matter of personal taste but should be simple and obviously be considered to complement the uniform.

It is common for male front office staff to be asked to wear a morning suit consisting of a black jacket, and sometimes waistcoat, with pinstripe trousers, a white shirt and grey tie during the day. In the evenings they may well be required to change to a dinner suit with a white dress shirt and black bow tie; this always was, and still is, the traditional dress in a luxury hotel. In other styles of establishment, for example the International, a business or lounge suit might be appropriate with a light coloured shirt and an appropriate tie. In American-orientated hotels a blazer and slacks are commonplace. Whatever the requirements of the management the same standards of cleanliness and smartness should apply to both sexes and where male staff are concerned they must be well-shaven and have neatly groomed hair, again to complement their uniform.

The importance of the dress of reception and front office staff must never be underestimated; indeed, it should be a natural asset of the staff that they present themselves in a manner which indicates both efficiency and a pride in their work.

We are now building up a picture of the type of person who is best suited to work in a reception office and the various facets should be formalized by the management so that they know what to look for at the time of recruiting staff. The formal way in which either the rooms division manager or the personnel manager in a large hotel will record what is required of reception staff is by drawing up a specification of the ideal attributes and qualifications that one looked for when recruiting. This formal layout is called a *job specification* and the same layout may be used for all staff in the hotel. A typical job specification for a receptionist is shown in Figure 18.

The job specification will be used at the time of recruiting staff and will be particularly useful for reference in compiling an advertisement and, when application forms are returned and interviews take place, it will act as an excellent check-list.

The receptionist's work is both varied and interesting

Having laid down the qualities and attributes that one is looking for in the 'perfect' receptionist the next important thing to do is to work out exactly the duties and responsibilities that each member of the front office staff will have. This is called compiling a *job description*, and is very different from the job specification.

The job description will give a sense of security, to a new member of staff, especially if issued soon after employment commences, as it should make clear his or her exact responsibilities so that there is no confusion or overlapping of work with other staff. The job description is in fact a reference for the individual member of staff and supervisors so that both know exactly what is expected of the receptionist.

A typical job description for a receptionist is show in Figure 19.

From the job description it will be seen that the work expected of the receptionist may be varied and perhaps it is now time to examine some of the operational aspects of the work of reception.

In all but the smallest hotels the function of reception as regards welcoming guests and dealing with their enquiries has to be fulfilled twenty-four hours each day and therefore a complex shift or rota system has to be utilized to cover all the available hours. It should go without saying that the same staff may be expected to work for only an eight-hour day and therefore the staffing totals in the front office frequently have to be quite high to cover eventualities throughout the whole day and night.

In large hotels, such as the International, a 'straight shift' system will be worked by the receptionists which basically divides the working day into three eight-hour shifts. In some older organizations staff went off duty and came back later in the day to complete their work but the 'straight shift' system is far preferable in that it allows staff to work straight through; once they have finished work they are free to go home rather than having to wait around to start work again which can be most frustrating.

The shifts are timed around the peak periods of work in reception which, of course, depend on the movements of customers. In the food and beverage departments such as the kitchen the obvious peak periods are at meal times while in reception they coincide with the arrival and departure of guests. There are consequently two peak periods in reception unlike the three that may be encountered each day in the food and beverage departments. The arrival of guests will tend to take place in the late afternoon and early evening and so there will be a shift on duty at this time to deal with the bulk of arrivals. Guests tend to depart in the early morning and so there must be a shift on duty to deal almost solely with guests who are checking out. Therefore, this shift has to be on duty fairly early in the morning. In a hotel like the International there may be sufficient guest movements to require there to be a third shift on duty during the night especially as there is an airport nearby. The majority of customers, though, may well arrive and depart during normal hours so the night shift might only consist of a skeleton number of staff. In some hotels the night auditor, whose specialist work is described fully in Chapter 7, may well undertake the night reception responsibilities. In the Majestic Hotel there may well be very little movement of guests during the night and consequently the night porters are entrusted with the night reception duties, but the normal two shifts would be operated during the day in the same way as the International.

The reception hours of work could therefore be described as follows:

Reception straight shifts:
Early or morning shift – 7 a.m. to 3.30 pm.
Late or evening shift – 3 p.m. to 11.30 p.m. approximately
Night shift -11 p.m. to 7.30 a.m.

Two points should be noted from the hours above which are approximate and may vary between one hotel and another due to differences in business. The shifts, especially the evening shift, will finish work when everything in reception is complete. The evening is particularly reliant on, for example, the restaurant and bars closing so that the monies taken may be recorded before the reception staff go off duty.

More important, from the managerial point of view, it will be seen that there is a half-hour overlap between each shift. This is formally called 'handover time' and should be allowed for in completing all reception rotas. The reason is so that there is a stipulated time when the two different sets of staff on each shift may discuss important communications that may need to be passed on between them. For example, the monies in the safe and till must be agreed so that the evening shift, say, does not inherit any error made by the morning shift, and details of bookings and room changes by guests need to be exchanged. A useful tool to have to hand is a reception incident book which will

Majestic Hotel — Personnel department

Job specification.   Position: Junior receptionist

	Essential	Preferred
1 Personal data Age Home circumstances Marital status	18-25 Living locally	Live-in Single
2 Physique Health Speech Manner Appearance	In good health Fit Good stamina Clear without impediment Pleasing personality Natural Well groomed	Extrovert
3 Educational and technical qualifications (a) Secondary: GCSE A-level (b) Further education (c) Higher education	English language Mathematics	French German Computer knowledge English language Mathematics City & Guilds Reception BTEC Diploma NVQs RSA typing First aid certificate

4 Work or other experience		Full-time or work experience
		  in hotel of similar standard
		Good reference from previous
		  employer if applicable
		Knowledge of computer
		  application in hotels

5 Mental abilities	Common sense Verbal ability Mathematical ability	
6 Social skills	Gregarious Tactfully persuasive	
7 Initiative	Self-starter Able to work without supervision	
8 Emotional stability	Ability to withstand stress Maturity	

Figure 18   *Job specification*

Majestic Hotel — Personnel Department

Job description.   Position: Junior receptionist

1   <u>General information</u>

    Immediate superior: Head receptionist and/or shift leader
    Work area: Reception office
    Hours of work: 5-day 40-hour week
                              An 8-hour straight shift will normally be worked
                                each day.
    Salary/wages: £   per week
    Overtime: Overtime will be paid for complete hours worked
                                in excess of 40 hours at a rate of £   per hour.
    Accommodation: Staff living in the hotel will have accommodation
                                and board deducted from their salary at the
                                following daily rate: £   per day
    Meals: Meals on duty will be provided free of charge in the hotel
                                restaurant or canteen.

2   <u>Job summary</u>

By job knowledge and personal attitude the junior receptionist is responsible
for the smooth operation of the reception office while undertaking the many tasks
both during the arrival and departure of guests and throughout their stay. Along
with colleagues, he or she will help to maintain the reputation of the hotel.

3   <u>Job content</u>

The junior receptionist will be expected to carry out the following tasks as a
matter of course:

(a) welcoming guests and allocating accommodation
(b) completing the register in accordance with the law
(c) recording reservations
(d) compiling, presenting and receiving payment for guests' bills
(e) providing information and dealing with enquiries
(f) dealing with complaints when necessary
(g) selling the hotel and maximizing occupancy
(h) maintaining the security arrangements of the hotel
(i) ensuring effective communication throughout the hotel and
     maintaining liaison with other hotel departments
(j) undertaking miscellaneous secretarial duties
(k) carrying out any other duties that the management or the head
     receptionist may deem reasonable.

Figure 19   *Job description*

contain all the necessary information of complaints, lost property, changes in reservations and late check-outs, that each shift leader has completed and will have signed by her successor. There may then be no dispute that information was not handed over. If shifts started and finished at identical times the reception staff would be inclined to rush through handover, but with a formal half hour there is plenty of time to liaise.

With basic two shifts, only one of which would be worked by an individual receptionist each day, it is possible to arrange duties so that both days off and afternoons or mornings off may be accommodated to the greatest satisfaction of staff. In some hotels individuals work all evening shifts one week and then all morning shifts the following week so that they are left at least part of each day for family life.

Another way to organize the shifts has great benefits to the management while it may give each member of staff a long break each week. Let's imagine that our member of staff is going to have Sunday and Monday off and the shifts could be arranged according to the rota shown in Figure 20.

With this arrangement it will be seen that the member of staff has from 3.30 p.m. on Saturday until 3.00 p.m. on Tuesday off, therefore giving a long break. The problem is that on two days during the week she will have to work an evening followed by a morning shift which, though, has its compensations in that she may be able to carry on the work she began the night before. Managerially this is an advantage. Thursday, being the middle day, is flexible so that either an evening or a morning shift may be worked on that day. On the evenings that the member of staff is being asked to finish late and start early again the following morning, it may be policy in some hotels to offer reception staff accommodation for the night to avoid the necessity for a return journey home. This system of working the shifts is used in quite a few hotels and generally staff like the idea of a long break but other methods of working may be utilized rather than letting shifts become monotonous.

What does a hotel receptionist do?

Having seen that the receptionist may work varied hours we should examine briefly the work undertaken in a hotel by the receptionist. In many cases the detail will occur in later chapters of the book but it will be as well at this time to be clear in our minds of the scope of a receptionist's job in various types of operation.

In small hotels, such as the Ship Inn, the receptionist probably has the most demanding job of all, being either the only receptionist, or one of a very small number of receptionists, employed by the hotel. In our example of the Ship Inn, there is only one receptionist and the reasoning for this is quite simple, in that the volume of customers, with only twenty-five bedrooms, is such that a single member of staff can cope with the work. It should be made clear, though, that the number of rooms is not the only criterion upon which staffing levels are determined. Another most important point to bear in mind is the type of business being catered for and the consequent tariffs that are being charged. The Ship Inn is not the sort of hotel where guests stay for one night only and being a resort hotel catering for holidaymakers the tariff in operation will run for probably a week in duration or longer. Guests may therefore book for time periods of a minimum of seven days which has the effect of concentrating the work of reception into one day. In many resort towns the peak day of reception work is Saturday or 'changeover day' when the weekly tariffs start and finish and virtually all the arrivals and departures take place. Changeover day is therefore busy from early morning with check-outs right through to the late evening until all the new arrivals have appeared. On this day the reception may

Monday	Tuesday		Wednesday	Thursday		Friday	Saturday	Sunday
▨▨	E	M	▨▨	E		E	M	▨▨

E = evening shift   (3 p.m. – 11.30 p.m.)   ▨ = time off
M = morning shift   (7 a.m. – 3.30 p.m.)

Figure 20

well need supplementing with extra staff while during the rest of the week the work of the receptionist may be relatively relaxed without the pressure of large numbers of arrivals and departures.

In small hotels receptionists have to be extremely competent at their work because it is in this size of establishment that they literally have to be 'Jacks of all trades' as they will be responsible for undertaking all the jobs that may be specialisms in larger front office operations. They will have to know everything, from the legal requirements of accommodating customers to the intricacies of accounting, in order to prepare the guests' bills; therefore they must be real experts at their work, having to take sole responsibility.

The Majestic Hotel is an example of a medium sized hotel operation and with 150 rooms and a varied clientele the receptionist's work becomes more specialized. We have seen that shifts are operated in this type of hotel to cover the long hours of reception operation and the work in the front office is undertaken by considerably more staff. Being a city centre hotel there will undoubtedly be a greater variety of customers which in itself will lead to a more complicated system of tariffs. Business customers, visiting firms in the city, may well wish to stay only one night, while conference delegates may be at the hotel for at least a week. There may well be tourists staying for a few days at the hotel, and some may come in the form of coach tours, therefore reception may be swamped by large numbers of customers in one go. To cope with the variety of the work a larger number of staff is required but the receptionist's work is more specialized, but no less difficult, in this type of hotel largely consisting of dealing face-to-face with customers at the front desk on arrival and departure. This is still the type of hotel where it will be unlikely that there will be totally separate departments for each specialism so receptionists must be capable, for example, of dealing with both reservations and cashier's duties as these will be expected of them as part of their everyday work.

The very large hotels tend to offer very specialized work to their staff with the sheer volume of customers to be dealt with. Using the International Hotel as our example, this establishment has 600 bedrooms that due to the nature and situation of the hotel are very heavily used throughout the year. An airport, after all, tends to be busy continuously and therefore the hotel

requirements of people travelling through the area will not diminish either during the day or over a week. The pressure is virtually continuous. The International will deal with travellers who stay for very short periods of one night and therefore it may be seen that if the hotel is full this could mean that 1000 individual customers could leave and then be replaced each day at the hotel. The work of dealing with this number of arrivals and departures necessitates specialized staff in separate departments and thus the work of the receptionist is very restricted. Indeed a receptionist at the International may well deal solely with the welcoming, checking-in and room allocation of guests on arrival and may help the cashiers with departures at check-out time. The other specialist work such as the compiling of the guests' bills and reservations will be undertaken by other departments in their own right. The work of the receptionist at the International will no doubt be specialized and pressurized due to its volume; in order that staff receive satisfaction from their work, management should be fully aware of this problem and rotate staff through jobs in various offices.

What work is undertaken during a typical day in reception?

Every hotel develops its own method of work that is peculiar to that particular establishment, but there are many general items of work that are common to all hotels and which vary very little. Unlike the food and beverage departments in a hotel where there are three main pressure times during the day which obviously coincide with breakfast, lunch and dinner, the reception and front office in virtually all hotels has to deal with departing guests during the morning and arriving guests during the early evening. If the hotel is running the suggested straight shift system this means that the morning shift is primarily handling departures and the evening shift the arrivals.

A typical day in the reception of a hotel operating on the two shift system will start at seven in the morning with the reception staff opening up the office and discussing with the night staff any developments with regard to arrivals and departures that have occurred during the night. Any money that the staff such as the night porters have taken will be collected, checked and receipted ready for its combination with the takings in general. Dealing with money, the floats that will be required later in the day by the coffee shop and restaurant as well as the bars will be made up ready for collection. Once the cash has been checked any bills for later arrivals or early departures will be entered into the accounting system and a balance of the previous day's business calculated and checked before the accounts are closed.

As they occur the vouchers that have been issued for early morning teas (EMTs), newspapers and phone calls will be entered into the accounting system for the new day and the bills for any expected departures will be prepared up-to-date in anticipation of their checking-out. By this time departures will be taking place and it may be necessary to help the cashier's staff if there is a queue forming or if they are under great pressure. Meanwhile the incoming post will have arrived and that referring to reservations will be recorded by the reservations clerks and correspondence will be checked.

When the bulk of the departures has taken place there will be secretarial duties to undertake such as preparing the menus for typing for lunch and dinner. The money that has been taken from departing customers in settlement of bills will be totalled during the morning and checked against the paid bills before being entered into a paying-in book and taken to the bank. At the time that the banking is done a request for change will be given so that the hotel has sufficient small change to cover all the transactions during the next twenty-four hours.

At maximum check-out time, which is usually midday, those guests who were expected to leave and who have not yet done so will be checked to see if they wish to stay on or whether they are in fact going to leave late. Liaison will take place with the housekeeping department at this time to check the rooms that have been used by guests who have not yet left but who should be doing so.

During lunch entries will be made into the accounting system to record the food and beverage transactions and then, by 3 p.m. the accounts will have been balanced and checked in preparation for handover to the evening shift.

Between 3 p.m. and 3.30 p.m. the two shifts should liaise over guest's details regarding arrivals and departures that may have a bearing on the work of the evening shift and all financial figures should be agreed and signed for. During the afternoon arrivals will occur and they should be welcomed, registered and allocated rooms and it may be policy for reception staff to show the guests to their accommodation. During the afternoon the following day's *arrivals, departures* and *stays* lists will be compiled and distributed to the various departments.

All charges incurred by customers during afternoon tea, dinner and in the bars will be posted onto the bills as they occur including those new bills opened for new arrivals. During the evening a close watch will be kept on the occupancy level of the hotel to see if an over-booking situation is going to occur or whether there are still rooms available. Towards the end of the shift the night porter's information will be compiled giving details of rooms free to let and the names of any late arrivals and the rooms they have been allocated. The accounts will be balanced and a daily report completed for the management before the floats and takings are accepted and checked once the restaurant and bars are closed. At the completion of the shift the reception safe will be locked and the keys handed over to the manager on duty so that everything is left secure.

3 Advance reservations and sales

As a hotel relies on the effective letting of its bedrooms for the majority of its eventual profit, the manner in which advance reservations and sales is undertaken is important to the entire operation. If the rooms in the hotel are not sold properly all the effort placed into ensuring that guests, once installed, enjoy their stay is wasted as the business relies on the maximum occupancy of the accommodation.

Advance reservations are orders that are received by the hotel and are of necessity a very good indicator to an accommodation manager of the levels of business likely to be encountered during the ensuing days and months. Indeed, unlike many other types of commercial business the 'orders' are received sometimes many months in advance so a very accurate picture of the pressures of business in the future may be assembled. The reservations themselves may contain a large amount of vital detail, peculiar to each guest, that must be accurately recorded and communicated: it should be remembered that a mishandled reservation can be one of the major sources of complaint and loss of business that a hotel can encounter. As a consequence the staff undertaking the vital work of dealing with reservations must not be underestimated, as the right people given the correct systems to operate may improve the levels of business undertaken by the establishment in a significant way. Despite all the money ploughed into marketing and advertising it is often the staff handling reservations that will, in many cases, be the persuasive force in encouraging a guest to stay at the hotel.

Effective salespeople must know their customers

There is no doubt that guests who stay at the hotel and who are treated with civility and feel that they are people rather than statistics will return and possibly recommend their friends to do the same. Guests like to be recognized and remembered and therefore a large part of the receptionist's time should be taken in trying not only to understand who the clientele of the establishment are but also to build up a rapport in order to make guests feel like individuals.

First, it should be obvious that to categorize the personalities of guests is impossible as a reception desk will be exposed to every possible aspect of human nature at one time or another. Guests will range from those who are charming to those who are abusive; they will lavish tips or demand their money back; they will be extrovert or shy, confident or nervous and will all, as individuals, require a most tactful method of reception and application of social skills.

It is far easier, though, to categorize the market segments from which the customers emanate shown in the type of hotel chosen. Broadly, our Ship Inn is catering for holidaymakers and tourists, the Majestic Hotel for businesspeople and convention delegates and the International Hotel for travellers be they on business or holiday. These basic judgements may be reached very quickly, but how accurate are they? The sales staff of the front office need to know accurately the guests and their requirements before being able to sell effectively. The front office contains a wealth of information which already allows some basic market research to be undertaken and with a small amount of modification a detailed profile of the market and its customers may be created to help with the sales. One of the best sources of information about guests is the register which is filled in on arrival and, apart from the legally required details such as name and nationality, questions concerning the reason for the guest's stay, the type of transport used, the length of stay and the next destination may help build up a detailed picture of the typical guest. Not only will this help the front office staff but it will also be of great assistance to the marketing and sales department in a large hotel or the management who have this responsibility in smaller hotels. Although compiling the analysis of all the questions asked at the time of registration may seem forbidding the use of a computer to do this for you is ideal and as long as the program is well thought out a satisfactory series of conclusions in either printed or graphic terms may be achieved.

The analysis of guests does not stop at the completion of the register on arrival; to complete the picture the hotel's staff need to know the more detailed views of the customer during his or her stay. One way of doing this is to leave a questionnaire in the guest's room; this may be used in market research as well as enabling the hotel to find out the views of the customer on subjects that would be unlikely to be discussed in detail in ordinary conversation. Again, the results of this continuing process should be analysed by all the departments involved, eventually resulting in a detailed picture of the hotel's clientele.

A typical questionnaire is shown in Figure 21.

The questionnaire may turn out to be a most effective method of obtaining information and comment from customers, but, like most research, only a percentage of those left in rooms will be returned; it should also be remembered that, human nature being what it is, guests are prone to air their dislikes rather than their likes. A complete picture will therefore not always be presented.

Another method of collating information about customers is the use of a *guest history card* which may be most useful in those hotels where the time and trouble is taken to attempt to treat customers as individuals. Of our three hotels this could be possible at the Ship Inn and the Majestic Hotel but at the International, due to the volume of guests, the guest history card system may be so laborious and time-consuming to operate that an alternative may have to be found. The philosophy of the guest history card is that it contains relevant information about customers that may be used not only for marketing but also for allowing a personal service to be given to guests on subsequent visits. They are a tremendously useful memory-aid for staff and management who, by their use, may appear to have superb memories for guests and their requirements.

On the guest history card will be recorded the likes and dislikes of customers so that on a future visit they may be accommodated so that their stay automatically becomes relatively trouble-free. For example, the guest may have made it known that she is a vegetarian or that she likes a quiet room so when her card is examined before her next visit both these requirements may be catered for and preparations made. Special dates may be recorded, such as a birthday or an anniversary, so that if these occur again during the guest's future visits they may be noted if the guest is the type of person who will not be embarrassed. Handled correctly by management the apparent memory of the hotel for its guests may appear most impressive to the guest where this particular use of the cards is concerned. It may be that when a guest makes a reservation she asks for the same room that she stayed in last time, therefore the reservations clerk should examine the card so that this request may be accommodated. The dates or previous stays at the hotel will also be recorded on the card, so that it is easy, for example, for receptionists to remind themselves when a particular customer last stayed at the hotel. This may be a pleasant way of welcoming that customer on arrival during the course of conversation. It may also be useful to record the credit rating of customers so that for a future visit it may be seen whether the customer was able to settle his bill and what kind of credit facilities management may offer on a return visit.

The cards themselves will be kept in detail, particularly for VIP guests and regular customers and should be filed alphabetically in reception where they may be referred to by both the front desk and reservations staff. It is often possible to utilize the reverse side of a registration card for the guest history so that all the relevant information is kept in one place. Many hotels keep the cards virtually indefinitely but it will become apparent that some guests are not going to return so emphasis is placed on the retention of those cards for VIPs and regulars. It may well be that in hotels the size of the International that the storage of this information is best carried out on a computer where it may be analysed and recalled swiftly. But whether held on cards or within the memory of a computer, the information is most useful for allowing staff to know their customers as well as enabling them to give a personal service.

By the use of this guest history system a number of

Guest questionnaire

| The International Hotel |
| Guest's comments help us to further improve our service |

Client's name (optional) ....
Home address ....
Business address ....
Profession ....
Date ....
Room number ....

Did you make your room reservation through:
Central reservations ....
The hotel's reservation desk ....
A travel agency ....
Your company ....
The company you are visiting ....
Other ....
You did not reserve ....

How did you hear of the hotel?
Staying in another group hotel ....
From our brochure ....
From friends or colleagues ....
From your travel agent ....
Through your company ....
From advertising on posters ....
In the press ....
On the radio ....
In the cinema ....
Other ....

Object of your journey:
Business ....
Holiday ....
Conference ....
Other ....

How did you arrive?
Car ....
Plane ....
Train ....

Please give us your opinion of:	Very good	Good	Average	Poor
The reception desk				
Welcome on arrival				
Courtesy				
Efficiency				
Telephone service				
Your room				
Size				
Comfort				
Quietness				
Temperature				
Cleanliness				
Bathroom				
Breakfast				
In the restaurant				
In your room				
Quality				
Quantity				
Service				
Punctuality				
The restaurant				
Quality				
Choice				
Service				
Courtesy				
Atmosphere				
Overall you think the hotel is				

Other remarks ....

Please seal and return the questionnaire to the reception desk. Thank you.

Figure 21 *Guest questionnaire*

customers will, of necessity, appear whose presence in the hotel may be thought to be undesirable in the future. Consequently a separate listing of customers is kept which is sometimes referred to as the black list. This should be part of the guest history files and the names contained should be known intimately to all staff handling reservations so that, if necessary within the law, undesirable customers are not permitted to return to the hotel; or if they are permitted the relevant management are informed. Unfortunately every hotel will have customers who have in the past defaulted on the payment of their bill, left the hotel deliberately without paying, become drunk or been annoying to fellow guests so that they are not welcome on subsequent visits. Therefore all reservations staff should be aware of these people so that they are not inadvertently allowed into the hotel. The guest history black list should be referred to if there is any doubt over the acceptance of a particular guest, although it will be seen later in the chapter that the excuse given to stop a customer returning should be kept within the law. Just saying that the hotel is fully booked is not necessarily the correct way out of this situation. The reservations staff or receptionist must use extreme tact in refusing a customer and remember that all the information on the guest history cards and black list is confidential. While referring to the black list the reception will also receive regular details from the local police of persons, including their alias names, involved in payment and hotel fraud locally. Photographs may well be included and the staff should refer to these and take the relevant action advised by the police should any of these people actually try to book into the hotel. The best way of remembering the contents of the black list is to have an alphabetical list at the front desk and beside each reservations clerk so that names are not forgotten.

The point should also be made that the guest history and black list do not just contain the names of individuals but also of companies whose business may not be encouraged in the future. Just as individual guests default on payment the same may well happen

Majestic Hotel

Name:..

Address–home :.. Nationality:..

business:.. Profession :..

change :.. Credit :..

Arrival date	Departure date	Room number	Rate	Remarks

Figure 22 *Guest history card*

This layout could also be a guideline for the display on a computer VDU upon which the reservations clerk or receptionist might be able to recall the name of any guest. This would be the best system at the International where the contents could easily be compiled automatically from registration and reservation details on programs run in parallel with larger organizations, consequently their names should be listed should their presence not be required in the establishment. It should also be realized that, even though names appear on a black list, not every customer will be refused a return visit, as a warning on arrival from the manager may be sufficient to stop a previous situation from occurring again.

A typical guest history card might be laid out as shown in Figure 22.

Front office staff must know the product they are selling

Just as the understanding of the requirements of the guest are necessary to the front office staff an intimate knowledge of the product they are selling is equally essential. On the surface the product would appear to be bedrooms or an accommodation unit for a period of time but in fact the total product of a hotel is far more complex than this, and involves the entire range of services offered by the establishment as well as their exact pricing.

It is therefore vital that new members of staff joining a hotel, even if they have considerable experience in the hotel industry elsewhere, are made to complete a check-list of the business for themselves so that they are quickly able to deal with all the possible questions with which they may become involved, both at the time of selling rooms as well as during their everyday work in dealing with customers in residence.

The check-list itself will be very detailed and might start with an analysis of the location of the business itself so that questions asked by the potential customer on how to reach the hotel are easily satisfied. Receptionists must know all about the public areas of the hotel purely so that they may be able to show guests the way or at least direct them to the facility they want to find and they must know all about the restaurant and bar facilities available. The reception desk may well have to hand a selection of the day's menus as well as details of the opening times of the various bars so that queries may be answered. The floor and lounge service details should be known so that guests can be informed of the correct procedures for obtaining these services while all the shops, kiosks, swimming pools, car hire desks, banks and similar operations found in a hotel must be understood by the receptionist.

Apart from a physical tour of the hotel a detailed check-list may be completed and kept to hand by the receptionist. A suggested common format is shown in Figure 23 and its completion should be a part of induction.

A major part of the check-list refers to the rooms in the hotel and we should examine this more carefully as this is where the new member of the front office staff needs the most knowledge. It is apparent that in many hotels the reception and front office staff are selling rooms that they have never seen and therefore an essential part of their induction and regular training is to tour the hotel accommodation to familiarize themselves with the layout of the rooms and their quality. Indeed, in some hotels the staff who are on late shifts and who are required early the next morning are encouraged to spend the night in vacant hotel rooms; this quickly gives them a knowledge of the facilities of the rooms that are being sold. In a busy hotel this may not be practicable so other ways have to be found of reminding the reception staff of what the rooms are like. One idea is to keep colour photographs of each room at the front desk which not only act as a reference for receptionists but also enable them to show potential guests the room(s) they are about to occupy. This is a useful aid particularly in hotels like the Majestic where rooms of the same type may vary dramatically in their size, furnishings and situation. At the International, on the other hand, which is a purpose-build modern hotel, rooms are standardized and so photographs of the typical single, double, twin and family bedrooms may be kept, while the suites on offer may vary considerably and are therefore recorded individually. The Ship Inn is small enough for the receptionist to know the individual rooms; even so, photographs may well be useful, saving the laborious task of showing the guest a room prior to it being sold. In all the hotels, though, should the guest require, a good method of selling a room is to actually take the customer to see it.

Many hotels find the use of room cards (also known as room record cards, room history cards or room index cards) a great help as they provide a record of not only the usage of each room but the fixtures and fittings. If kept in the back of the reception desk these cards allow receptionists to recognize rooms as well as telling them of the names of the guests that occupied the room in recent weeks and any complaints that may have been received. The cards will inform them about

HOTEL PRODUCT CHECK-LIST — Reception staff should know the following:

Hotel bedrooms and suites

(a)   Room numbers and location of each room: *floor, aspect, access*.

(b)   The type of accommodation available: *single, twin, double, suite*.

(c)   The number of visitors each room takes: *extra beds, cots*.

(d)   Additional facilities: *private bath/shower/bidet, balcony*.

(e)   Relationship with other rooms: *inter-connecting doors, sitting room, public bathroom/shower/toilet, maids service room*.

(f)   Room facilities: *wash basins, bedside lights, telephones, intercom, radio, colour or black and white TV, maids service bell, iced water cabinet, mini bar*.

(g)   State of furnishings: *newly redecorated, good, poor, old-fashioned*.

(h)   Emergency drill for each room in case of fire.

Tariffs

(a)   Hotel rates: *per person/per room, per day/per week*.

(b)   Details of following tariffs: *room only, room and breakfast, demi-pension, en pension, inclusive terms, children*.

(c)   Special tariffs: *high/mid/low season, Christmas/Easter, bargain breaks, discount rates*.

Standing arrangements

(a)   Service charge.

(b)   Value added tax.

(c)   Advance reservations deposits.

(d)   Price and service times of all meals in restaurants.

(e)   Room and floor service facilities and charges.

(f)   Acceptance of dogs and pets.

(g)   Car parking, garage, petrol, car wash and repair facilities.

(h)   Telephone call charges.

(i)   Corkage charge.

(j)   Prices of all drinks, liquor, cigarettes and snacks.

(k)   Acceptance of cheques, travellers cheques, credit cards.

(l)   Sales ledger credit arrangements.

(m)   Acceptance of travel agency and company business.

Hotel facilities

(a)   Number and position of public cloakrooms, lifts and staircases.

(b)   Position and amenities of lounges, TV and writing rooms and restaurants.

(c)   Opening hours and facilities of bars, games rooms, ballroom, sauna, swimming pool, solarium, hairdresser, shops and display cases.

(d)   Outdoor facilities such as beach tents, tennis courts, swimming pool, and refreshments.

(e)   Provision of packed lunches, early dinners and late suppers.

(f)   Hall and night porter services including theatre tickets, taxi hire, car hire, laundry, dry cleaning and valeting.

(g)   Range of banqueting and conference facilities.

Figure 23   *Hotel product check-list*

the standard of decoration and may be most useful in enabling lost property to be forwarded to a customer quickly. These cards are at their effective use in the Ship Inn with its guests who are staying a long time, but in the Majestic and International the information would be best recorded on the program of whatever computer system is in operation so that the receptionist could obtain the details from a visual display unit (VDU). The layout of an appropriate room card could also be copied to provide the display on a computer's VDU and might be as shown in Figure 24.

Once the rooms themselves have been recognized in the mind of the potential sales person their pricing must be thoroughly understood. In the hotel industry the tariff is the price list; this may be highly complex, depending upon the business undertaken by the particular establishment. While the obvious aim of a tariff is to present the hotel's pricing clearly to the guest it should be emphasized that a complex tariff structure in a hotel may become extremely difficult for the reception to operate and therefore one thing that

should be kept in mind in creating a tariff structure is its ease of operation.

One of the problems in trying to keep a tariff simple is that it may have to be capable, particularly in a hotel like the Majestic, of catering for businesspeople, holidaymakers, conference delegates, tours, children and long-stay residents throughout the year. The pricing will undoubtedly be reviewed at regular intervals, to keep pace with inflation, thereby creating a problem with those customers who reserved accommodation in advance under the previous pricing, and may well entail different prices for the same room both during and out of the main season. There could be special tariffs to encourage business at low periods, such as at weekends; at Christmas a special inclusive tariff for several days may be operated. These are just some of the possible variations of a tariff within a single establishment.

Bearing in mind that one of the aims of a tariff is to attract customers to the hotel, a keen eye should be kept on the pricing of locally competing hotels by the

Ship Inn			
Room number: 21		Type: Twin + bath. Can take extra bed or cot.	
Floor: First floor new wing.		Aspect: Balcony over estuary.	
Decor: Standard + colour TV		Last decorated: 29/3	
Arrival date	Departure Date	Name	Remarks
2/8	9/8	MR/S DENNIS	
9/8	23/8	MR/S JACKSON	
23/8	30/8	MR WELLS	RADIATOR LEAKED
30/8	6/9	MR/S GREGORY	

Figure 24 *Room card*

manager to ensure that the tariff is suitable for the particular market catered.

It is also common throughout hotel tariffs to find that the 'unit of costing' varies between the room and the guest. As a consequence some tariffs will be described as 'per room' and others 'per person', the latter probably being more accurate in bookkeeping terms and the former being easier for the reception staff to operate. It is important though, to make it clear to the guest as to which of the units of costing is being applied so that they are fully aware of any price implications that either may have on their eventual bill.

The types of basic tariff on offer to guests are similar worldwide although they are often given different names: the word 'tariff' is common in hotels with a British method of operation, and 'plan' is used in hotels with an American background. This should not confuse the receptionist as it means just the same as tariff.

Room only or European plan

This is the most basic type of tariff and is commonly found in city-centre luxury hotels like the Majestic. The basis of the guest's bill is therefore a room charge; every other service on offer in the hotel is charged separately. The paperwork and bookkeeping involved in completing a guest's bill is therefore increased dramatically. It also has the effect, with the price-conscious guest, of losing potential revenue because the customer has the opportunity of opting out of services such as meals.

Room and breakfast or Continental plan

This is a favourite type of tariff in transient hotels such as the International where breakfast is automatically costed into the basic price. It may well be worthwhile costing in the price of full English breakfast as the bookkeeping is certainly simpler, although some hotels will quote a separate supplement if full English rather than continental breakfast is taken. Breakfast is traditionally one of the accounting bottlenecks in the hotel and using a room and breakfast tariff eradicates the problem where, with separate charges, guests may checkout before their breakfast details have reached reception. The tariff does have the advantage of allowing a forecast of the number of breakfasts needed

to be given to the breakfast chef, thereby simplifying his work and reducing the possibility of food waste.

Demi-pension, half board or Modified American plan

This entails guests paying one price for their room, breakfast and one main meal. Depending on the type of hotel – for this tariff may be found in both city-centre and resort hotels – the main meal taken may be lunch or dinner. As far as guests are concerned demi-pension tariffs have the advantage of allowing them to miss one of the main meals so that, for example, in a resort hotel they may stay on the beach all day, returning for dinner. In a city-centre hotel, such as the Majestic, they may wish to go out in the evening to the theatre and it may then be more convenient to miss dinner. To the hotel the demi-pension tariff entices customers into the restaurant for at least one main meal, thereby increasing the amount they spend in the hotel; there are, of course, possibilities of extra drink purchases.

En pension, full board or American plan

This is commonly used where guests are staying a long time and allows them to pay for their room, breakfast, lunch, dinner and sometimes afternoon tea in one price. The guest therefore obtains maximum exposure to the food and beverage departments but, in common with demi-pension, there have to be some accounting adjustments made within the hotel accounts to record the financial position accurately. While the guest is aware of paying only one price an allocation will be made to each cost head within the hotel records so that it may be seen how much money was taken for their accommodation and how much for their individual meals. This enables the accommodation and food and beverage departments to assess their income on a fair and more accurate basis.

Inclusive terms

These may be quoted to customers and may be tailored to any particular requirement. All that an inclusive tariff means is that a certain number of hotel services are covered by a single price. For example, it is common to quote inclusive terms to conference delegates where a single price might include an en pension tariff plus morning coffee and afternoon tea, the hire of the conference room and the use of its associated facilities, early morning tea and a morning newspaper. The final price may be quoted for the entire period of the conference rather than on the more normal daily basis, thereby simplifying the accounting as far as the conference organizer is concerned.

Bargain breaks

These are a type of tariff introduced to encourage the use of hotels during otherwise slack periods, and are really a type of inclusive terms operated over a short period. The original intention was to bring customers into business hotels over weekends when their normal clientele were not in residence. Indeed, weekends are the quiet time in many commercial hotels and bargain breaks may be most effective in encouraging extra custom. So successful was this type of tariff when it was introduced that it is now common to find it in operation throughout the year in all types of hotel. The detail differs from one hotel to another but it is usual for the room and all main meals allowed in the price from dinner on Friday evening until luncheon on Sunday afternoon and the room to be available for Friday and Saturday nights. In some hotels a bargain break may be quoted to a guest for any period exceeding two days residence in the establishment and need not be restricted purely to weekends. The bargain break is therefore a form of discount tariff available to all guests showing, as it does, a saving over the full cost of the services involved if bought individually.

Children's tariffs

These are a common means of encouraging family business to hotels but they may be most difficult to operate if clear and precise instructions are not compiled at the outset. Usually a discount or a free stay will be given to children sharing their parents' room and it is important within the tariff to stipulate the age range involved. Some hotels give varying amounts of discount the older a child gets but this is a most cumbersome method and very difficult for reception to operate; it is far easier to give a free room rate to babies and a percentage food reduction to adolescents. The room reduction will depend on whether they are sharing their parents' room or not.

'Seasonal' tariffs (e.g Christmas or Easter)

These allow a seasonal package to be put together to cover both the room, meals and entertainment for the period of the celebration. It is usual for Christmas tariffs to run from Christmas Eve through to after Boxing Day but the exact length depends on how Christmas falls within the week as the tariff would be unlikely to finish at the weekend. The tariff and its detailed programme might also run on to include the New Year's celebrations.

While using the term seasonal to refer to Christmas it should be made clear that, especially in resort hotels, the pricing of rooms will vary due to the seasonality of the business. The high season will undoubtedly be more expensive; this may be during the peak weeks of summer, in a resort hotel like the Ship Inn, but in Switzerland for example, the peak season in the mountain hotels is in the New Year when the snow is at its deepest for skiing.

So far we have examined the tariffs that would readily be found in the printed tariff sent to potential guests and which are found near the information rack detailing the rooms in reception. Consequently these prices are commonly referred to as the *rack rates* but they are by no means the only tariffs that customers will be paying in the hotel.

Discount tariffs

These will be found in any establishment and at the Ship Inn could be given to travel agents in the form of a 10 per cent commission or at the International to airline personnel. The principle, though, is the same: a discount may be given to organizations which send the most business to the hotel. The consequence is that the company, for example, who uses the Majestic hotel most will receive the largest discount off its room bills. Discounts are, though, strictly negotiated in advance by the management and reception staff should ensure that they do not involve themselves in giving discount rates to customers unless it has been specifically cleared by their superiors. The accommodation manager has the sole task of increasing the occupancy of the hotel, and the usage of discounts to attract custom is one of the prime sales tools. Other incentives may be used, such as the 'two-for-one' tariff common in conference hotels where delegates are encouraged to bring their spouses free of charge as far as the room is concerned and which proves most popular.

It may therefore be seen that the arrangement of tariffs can be most complex in some hotels where a combination of many of these discussed may be in operation alongside each other. The front office staff as a whole have to be familiar with their operation and detail so that the customer is not inadvertently overcharged, undercharged or embarrassed by errors.

Selling is an essential part of the work of the staff

Having assembled a detailed knowledge of the requirements of the customer as well as the standard and facilities of the product the next step is to make sure that this information is used to the best possible advantage in selling to the customers.

There would appear to be a natural reticence in some staff to actually undertake selling to customers as sales is an intimidating technique to the uninitiated. Indeed, a salesperson is someone, in the minds of many staff, who pressurizes customers unbearably until achieving a goal and who is identified more with commodities such as secondhand cars rather than quality hotel accommodation. Nothing, in fact, could be further from the truth and that sort of pressurization of customers need never be undertaken in a hotel; the selling function is purely the use of common sense to try to assist potential or existing guests with their requirements. Really, the aim of sales in a hotel is to keep as much business within the particular establishment as possible and if this is borne in mind by the reservations staff, sales in the formal way will become quite natural and guests will never be placed into awkward situations.

Selling really starts at the time that the initial contact is made with the hotel by the guest which may be some time before an actual reservation is placed. Often a guest will write to a hotel for a copy of its brochure and tariff and even the manner in which this communication is treated can effect an eventual sale. All enquiry letters should be examined in detail as they often contain individual requests or questions. 'Can the hotel cope with disabled guests?' or 'Is your chef capable of producing vegetarian diets?' may be the type of question slipped into a letter. It is essential that these types of question are answered individually with a reply letter so that the guest is convinced that your hotel is interested, not merely leaving it to chance that the questions are answered in the brochure. The personalization of correspondence, which may be assisted greatly in hotels by the use of a word

processor, is an essential part of sales as the potential guest needs to feel like a person and not an occupancy statistic. One may also be certain that if the potential guest has contacted several hotels the one that takes the personal attitude towards him or her will receive the business. Selling has therefore started at this early stage of a reservation in a subliminal way purely by following the courteous use of good manners by replying personally to a guest's enquiry. Imagine how much nicer it is to the potential guest to receive a personalized reply answering all the questions rather than a brochure stuffed into an envelope with a 'With compliments' slip. Which hotel would you go to if you were the customer?

So selling is taking place in some cases before a customer is encountered, but the part of selling that worries staff most is in the face-to-face situation at the desk, or over the phone as happens with many reservations. Here, the selling becomes a natural part of the conversation and entails trying to satisfy the guests' requirements as much as possible. In handling reservations for rooms the guest is keen to know both the standard of comfort of a room as well as the price and the selling obviously hinges around these two parameters. By a careful assimilation of the way a conversation is going with a customer his or her requirements will become obvious as to the quality of accommodation required. Many guests will require detailed guidance as to the best type of accommodation to fulfil their needs whereas others will have fairly strong predetermined ideas of what they want. In either case they should not be pressurized but assisted. There is nothing worse than over-doing sales but the last thing one wants staff to be is passive recorders of reservations without placing any effort into guiding customers. It may, after all become obvious that a guest requires a better standard of room than that offered and in this situation by careful reference to the facilities and cost of the room the customer may well accept an alternative. Approach to the customer should be friendly and courteous, as always, and the alternative accommodation should be presented in a favourable way. The room should be described and reference made, from personal knowledge, of the fact that there is a television, that the room has been newly redecorated and possesses air conditioning during the current hot weather; the guest will thus become aware of a picture of what he or she is buying. In extreme cases, as is often the norm on the continent, it may be necessary to show the guest the room, as the higher the price the more the guest needs to know about his purchase. Should the guest have any worries, for example, about the quietness of the room or the nearness of the lifts, members of staff must show interest and do their best to fulfil the guests' needs.

Where alternative accommodation is concerned one of the worst 'sales killers' is the use of a bad phone technique. The use of phones is examined in detail later in the book but often if a guest phones for 'a double room for the twelfth' the answer so often comes back 'Sorry, we are fully booked on that date' and the conversation ends. The customer is therefore lost and the business has gone elsewhere. If only the reservations clerk had gone on to say 'But I could fit you in on the thirteenth,' or 'Would you be prepared to take a twin room rather than a double?' then there are two possibilities that could have been explored that were missed. It may well be that the guest wants to stay at the hotel so much that he will change the date of his stay or be prepared to accept a different standard of accommodation. He might even have accepted two single rooms instead of the double but we shall never know because the reservations clerk killed the conversation dead and lost any chance of keeping the business.

It will therefore be seen that sales as such are really dealing with the requirements of customers and trying to accommodate them where ever possible using a courteous manner. The intuitive reservations clerk or receptionist, though, will spot potential customers whose business may be improved by offering them or encouraging them to reserve a more expensive room than the one that they have initially expressed an interest in. The guest who is undecided is the one who may be encouraged to better a reservation while the short-stay businessperson is probably unlikely to be open to alternatives and to resist further suggestions. In fact, any sales resistance means failure and the creation of a dissatisfied customer must be avoided at all costs. Resistance therefore is an indication of failure and may well come from inexperience on behalf of the staff involved.

Sales techniques must be encouraged by the astute accommodation manager as there is no doubt that properly applied they will increase business, but the obvious pitfalls of inexperienced or over-zealous staff should be watched as they may have the opposite effect to that desired.

How does the law affect reservations?

The handling of bookings and reservations is the most important part of the business of the hotel and consequently both the hotel itself and the guest are protected by law against problems which might occur in dealing with the letting of accommodation. It is vital that all staff who are involved in bookings are fully aware of the legal requirements and implications of the various laws so that the hotel does not become involved in legal actions, thereby destroying the goodwill of the business. Guests should also be made aware of their obligations in reserving accommodation.

The first confusing part of the law that must be understood is that most hotels are, in fact, 'inns' in the eyes of the legal profession. Under the Hotel Proprietor's Act 1956 an inn is an establishment where accommodation is being let without restriction to all travellers; indeed, an inn has a duty to accommodate any travellers provided there are rooms available, and if they would appear to be properly dressed, able to pay their bills and unlikely to upset other guests. Legally, therefore, whoever is dealing with reservations either in advance or at the front desk could refuse to accommodate a customer only if the hotel cannot provide the accommodation requested, if the customer is not able to pay for a room or if he or she were scruffy in dress or under the influence of alcohol. From the previous discussion on the exclusion of guests who might be on a black list it will be seen that there are only certain reasons that may be used legally to refuse a guest accommodation at what will legally be an inn. The point should be made at this time that the vast majority of hotels are in fact inns ranging from our Ship Inn-type of hotel right through to the International Hotel. The Ship Inn is legally an inn while in law the International Hotel and all similar establishments such as the Majestic are also inns.

In the same context it should also be noted, as indeed it is a part of many tariffs, that a traveller may also expect food and drink at any time of the day and night. Consequently all inns provide refreshments throughout twenty-four hours and while it is quite 'legal' to provide a snack at night the only excuse for not providing food or drink is that there is none in the hotel. Drink, incidentally, does not mean an alcoholic beverage in the eyes of the law.

Another part of the Hotel Proprietor's Act that all staff should be aware of is that as employees of the proprietor they are dealing with guests and making decisions on his or her behalf so they must realize that their actions and conversations are in fact representing the proprietor and consequently must be treated as such.

Under the Hotel Proprietor's Act the only type of establishment where the requirements of an inn do not apply is the private hotel which is deliberately restricting its custom to particular groups or types of person. In this case the proprietor has absolute discretion over who he or she is willing to accommodate but it will be realized that the vast majority of establishments are in fact inns and therefore obliged to cater for all travellers.

The next part of the law that the front office staff should be familiar with at the time that bookings and reservations are being made is the law of contract. This may sound intimidating but purely provides that the arrangement that is made in a booking is honoured by both the hotel and the guest and should either party default compensation may be claimed. The law of contract therefore ensures that the hotel provides the accommodation that it promised and the guest pays for that accommodation and provided that this is carried out both parties are happy.

It is important to realize that in order for a contract to be formed where a booking is concerned an 'offer' of accommodation has to be made to the customer who must then 'accept' this offer. In other words, our customer must be told by the hotel that a certain room at a certain price will be available for a period of time for him and once he has accepted this offer a contract exists between the hotel and the guest. These are the meanings of the terms 'offer' and 'acceptance' that are used throughout the process of forming a legal contract.

When the various types of reservation are discussed it will be seen that bookings are in some cases handled many months in advance and in other cases almost instantly when a customer arrives at the front desk and enquires if there is a room available. Consequently it will be evident that a contract need not be a written document; indeed, it may quite often be a verbal agreement. Many reservations are made over the phone and the conversation, provided it contained an 'offer' and an 'acceptance', is a binding legal contract that is enforceable by law. Needless to say wherever possible it is preferable to confirm conversations in writing as it is far easier to prove a written rather than a verbal contract.

The problem with contracts occurs when either party wishes to cancel his or her agreement. Normally this is the guest who no longer requires to take up the offer of accommodation which he or she has accepted. Legally the hotel may claim compensation if unable to re-let the accommodation but in practice many hotels will not do this in order to maintain goodwill with customers. There may, after all, be many legitimate reasons why a customer may no longer be able to take up accommodation previously booked. The hotelier may, though, decide to pursue the matter if an individual or organization persistently cancels rooms. Legally it should be realized that it is quite permissible to claim compensation if one of the parties to a contract defaults on the arrangement.

Where reservations are being made at the front desk the management and staff should be aware of the Tourism (Sleeping Accommodation Price Display) Order 1977 which insists that the tariff in operation at the hotel is visible at the reception desk. This was a legal requirement introduced in the wake of the introduction of value added tax to ensure that every opportunity is given to guests to make them aware of the full price that they are going to be paying for their stay. The tariff display must include the full cost of both the room to include any taxes and service charges as well as any meals included in the price.

Should the front office staff who are dealing with bookings and reservations be aware of the obligations of the law that is relevant to this part of the operation of the hotel, it will make them much more aware of potential problems should they not operate the relevant systems correctly. All new reception and front office staff should be reminded of the legal obligations at the time of their induction since this aspect of their work is so important.

Reservations are received by many different methods

The staff dealing with advance reservations in the hotel are going to be faced with a logistical task in sorting out all the requests for accommodation so that they may ascertain the volume of business expected on any particular night. One of the major problems is that reservations may be received by a variety of methods all of which possess their own intricacies and problems which must be overcome so that a true picture of business is achieved. Having seen the legal side of receiving reservations care has to be taken with all the reservations to ensure that the law of contract among other legal constraints is conformed with, and this is not always easy where some kinds of reservation are concerned.

Probably the most common way that a reservation is received is by *phone* and certainly the larger the hotel the more reservations that will be coming in by phone. By phoning the hotel there would appear to be an urgency on behalf of the guest to place a reservation and therefore it is usually the method used by people wishing to book almost immediately if not on the very evening of the call itself. In many cases the guest has chosen to phone because there is not time to exchange a letter with the hotel so care has to be taken that the law of contract is conformed with verbally. In some cases there may well be time for a letter of confirmation to be sent or even a telex message and where this is the case the reservations clerk should ask for this to be done, thereby confirming the verbal conversation in writing. It should be remembered that the phone is an expensive method of communication over long distances and therefore the reservation must be handled as quickly as possible so that the guest is not having to wait and therefore pay a lot of money for the call. Thus the reservations clerk must have all the information needed to answer a reservation close by the phone and instantly available. It is also easy for phone conversations to be abbreviated and for information to be inadvertently forgotten so clerks should have a checklist acting as a memory aid in front of them so that details are not omitted from the conversation.

In hotels dealing with business customers it is not uncommon to find that the *fax* or *telex* accounts for a large number of the reservations. A fax or telex machine is a common method for most companies to communicate and when reserving a hotel room they have the advantage of giving an instant written message. Messages may also be sent and received when an operator is not at the machine so that reservations and confirmations may be sent throughout the world without having to wait for offices to open in different time zones. Legally both the fax and the telex are a great assistance as a written message is received.

In resort hotels reservations are usually received by *letter*, which is fine legally but has the disadvantage that the reservations information has to be extracted from many different layouts of letter and the reservations staff have to decipher many variations in handwriting. Once this has been done, though, a letter forms a firm part of the contract with the customer and if replied to quickly and efficiently overcomes any misunderstandings that might have occurred without there having been the benefit of a discussion at the time the reservation was made. Letters usually imply that there is plenty of time to exchange information before the date that the customer is due.

It is common for reservations to be received by *computer* in many hotels whether the information be coming from another hotel within the group, a travel agent, a central reservations office or a reservations bureau run by a marketing consortium. Soon it will be common for customers to reserve hotel accommodation from their own TVs, particularly cable TV, in the comfort of their own lounges. Whatever the source of a booking by computer it is handled in the same way as fax or telex reservations but has the advantage that a print-out may be produced to a common format thereby easing the compilation of information in the reservations office.

Many reservations may be placed in person by the potential guest or someone acting on his or her behalf at the front desk and this has the advantage that all the problems may be discussed there and then. Of course many guests reserving in person may well be 'chance' customers who have just arrived, hoping to find a free room and may therefore be accommodated within minutes. Legally the offer and acceptance will, of course, be made verbally. Some guests may be so impressed with their stay at the hotel that they reserve a future visit at the time of departure, in this case care must be taken to ensure that their booking is recorded and not omitted.

It may therefore be seen that there are several widely differing methods by which reservations may be received. Many hotels are daily having to deal with all of these methods of making reservations, and while it is true to say that the resort hotel will receive mainly letters and the business hotel will specialize in phone and fax reservations, each has to be able to deal with any of the potential sources of booking. Consequently the system that is used in a hotel for recording advance reservations has to be most adaptable but also capable of collating the information into a common format no matter what its source.

The reservation system – booking the right person into the right room on the right night

It is a fact that virtually every hotel has its own peculiar system for recording reservations and many of these systems are not only inefficient but frustrating in their complexity for the staff who are expected to operate them. Often a basic system has been introduced when a hotel first opened and in the ensuing years changing managements have brought along their ideas and preferences so that the

reservations system has become highly modified. At worst a reservations system may be so complex to operate that the occupancy levels of the hotel are adversely affected.

There is no one common system that may be used in every.type of hotel, no matter what the hardware salespeople tell you, and almost every system, be it computerized or manual, will have to be adapted to the situation peculiar to the individual establishment. Every hotel, for example, will differ from its neighbour in the number of rooms and their types that are on offer to guests. In our examples the Ship Inn has twenty-five rooms and the International 600, so the same system could not possibly be used in these two hotels. While this may seem an extreme illustration even among hotels of the same size there will be a considerable number of differences between types of room, tariff and level of service to make a common system impossible, so throughout this section of the explanation of the handling of reservations we are

	Ship Inn (small resort hotel of 25 rooms)			Majestic Hotel (medium-sized city centre hotel of 150 rooms)			International Hotel (large airport hotel of 600 rooms)	
Uniform method of recording incoming reservations	Reservation form		Personal computer screen display	Reservation form	Whitney card	Computer screen display	Reservation form	Computer VDU
Quick visual reference of reservations	Bedroom book	Conventional chart	Personal computer screen display	Density chart	Whitney advance booking rack	Computer screen display	Computer VDU	
Record of reservationd details		Bookings diary	Personal computer memory	Bookings diary	Whitney advance booking rack	Computer memory	Computer main memory	
Communication method of reservation details to hotel departments	Arrival, departure and stays lists							
	Typed	Print-out		Typed	Print-out	Screen	Print-out	Screen

Figure 25　*Reservations system*

going to examine what could be used in our three imaginary hotels.

Before looking in detail at the types of system that are commonly in operation let us look at the basic requirements of any advance reservations system.

We have already seen that reservations are placed at hotels by a variety of different methods and the first objective of our system should be to collate all this information, no matter what its source, into a *uniform record* that may easily be understood by any of the staff who are dealing with reservations. This uniform record should also contain the basic information that we need to obtain from guests concerning their stay at the hotel. The way that a uniform record is achieved of bookings is normally by the use of a reservations form.

The second important requirement of a reservations system is that we can see at a glance how many rooms are available for letting on particular days in the future. We therefore need a *visual reference* which may give us this information quickly and this may best be achieved by utilizing some form of reservation chart.

Third, there is a mass of information that we need to record ranging from the dates of the booking to the individual requests that a guest may have; consequently our reservations system must have a *detailed record* of each particular booking. In many hotels this may be kept on a computer or a bookings diary may suffice.

Fourth, and probably most important, the reservations system chosen must be *adaptable*, because not only will it have to deal with the run-of-the-mill bookings but there will be cancellations, overbookings, early departures, unforeseen extensions of stay and a myriad of alterations that may have to be catered for during the normal course of business.

One item that is common to manual reservations in most hotels is the use of abbreviations to cut down on the large amount of writing that may take place during the course of bookings. To write out, for example, double room and bathroom each time a reservation is taken for this type of room is time consuming and therefore the following abbreviations should be used where possible:

− Single room
+ Double room
= Twin room
B Bathroom
S Shower

Manual reservation system suitable for the Ship Inn

The Ship Inn is a typical small resort hotel and we should remind ourselves that the bulk of the business is holidaymakers staying for periods of a week or a fortnight. Unlike many resort hotels, the Ship Inn does remain open throughout the whole year and therefore the reservation system has to be operational for fifty-two weeks. Many resort hotels close over the winter to reduce their overheads when there is insufficient business for them to remain open and in these cases the reservation system is extremely basic. Quite often the hotel is open for a season of only thirty weeks, thus each bedroom is let for a maximum number of only thirty times each year, but with some customers staying a fortnight even this figure may be reduced. The level of information having to be held, therefore, in a reservations system in a seasonal resort hotel is minute compared with a busy business hotel where guests stay on average one night.

The Ship Inn receives the majority of its reservations by letter several months before the guest is due to stay but there has been a trend in recent years for the customers increasingly to book at a late date when, for example, it looks as if a good period of weather is going to be prolonged and then a certain number of reservations come in by phone. The reservation system therefore has to cope mainly with bookings by letter but has to be capable of being used for other types of reservation as well.

The receptionist has long since found it impossible to use the guest's letters themselves as the prime part of the reservation system because they appear in many different layouts and types of handwriting. Originally they were used, but it was discovered that the owner's family, who take over the reception work when the receptionist is off duty, found it difficult to understand the many details involved, so like many hotels a reservation form was introduced to provide a uniform record of the reservations (Figure 26).

The reservation form at the Ship is used mainly as a place where each reservation's information is collated and as such is completed by the receptionist each time a letter is received so that every booking is recorded in the same uniform way. The reservation form really comes into its own when a phone reservation is received as it keeps a check-list in front of the receptionist so that she does not forget to obtain any

```
        Ship Inn Reservation Form

    Date of arrival _____        | Single         |        |
                                               | Single/bath    |        |
    Date of departure _____         | Double         |        |
    Name _____         | Double/bath    |        |
    Address _____         | Twin/bath      |        |
            _____         | Twin/shower    |        |
    Telephone number _____         | Extra bed      |        |
    Booking placed by: _____         | Cot            |        |
    Name _____         | Other          |        |
    Address _____

            _____

    Telephone number _____

    Terms _____ Time of arrival _____ Signature _____ Date _____

    Remarks _____

             _____

             _____  _____

    _____
         Please confirm in writing     |    Unclaimed rooms will be
                                        |    released after 6 p.m.
```

Figure 26   *Reservation form*

vital information. It may be seen that the reservation form may also be used as a method of informing guests of certain conditions of their booking, hence the request to 'confirm in writing' and the reminder that 'unclaimed rooms will be released after 6 p.m.' so that embarrassment is removed should the guest otherwise have been unaware of these stipulations.

The reservation form therefore standardizes the recording of reservations so that all staff involved may quickly see the relevant details which are completed for any type of booking. We have noted that the form may be easily used for letter and phone reservations but it may just as easily be used for reservations made in person at the front desk or for reservations received by fax or telex or from external bureaux. The form is the basic part of the booking around which the entire reservation system revolves.

Looking in detail at the layout it will be seen that the first item of information requested is the date of arrival and departure. Especially on the phone this allows the receptionist to instantly tell the customer whether rooms are available or not as there may be certain dates that are fully booked. Having established that the dates

are clear it is then necessary to find out the exact room requirements and consequently the boxes on the righthand side of the form are utilized. Here the types of room, peculiar to the particular hotel, are laid out so that a tick or a number of rooms required may be quickly inserted into the relevant box. It should not be forgotten that the form may be used for tour or travel agency bookings or reservations that require more than one room, so sufficient space should be left for numbers of rooms required to be entered. Having recorded the room requirements, including problems like costs or extra beds which may be needed, the name and address of the customer should be taken along with a phone number in case a query arises at a later date over the booking. If the reservation is placed by a third party, such as a travel agent or someone's secretary, their details are also taken as it should be understood that the person making the booking is not necessarily the person who is going to stay. The tariff or terms should be recorded and guests asked their time of arrival, so that it will be clear whether they are going to arrive after 6 p.m; or not; the 'remarks' section of the form should then be completed. It is most important that any particular requests, requirements or remarks are recorded at this stage as this is the first part of the system of communication that will cater for these requirements when the customer eventually stays at the hotel. The last part of the form to be completed is the space for the receptionist's signature and the date the booking was made to act as a means of checking should there be a query at a later date.

Having recorded all the reservations in this uniform way the next step is to provide a 'visual reference' so that the state of bookings may be ascertained at a glance. In a small resort hotel there are basically two alternative ways in which this may be done. The first is by the use of a *bedroom book* and the second is by the use of a *conventional reservations chart*.

The bedroom book is the simplest of all solutions and ideally suited to the small resort hotel where bookings last for a period of a week or a fortnight but the Ship Inn is really the maximum size of hotel at twenty-five rooms in which it might be handled successfully. As may be seen from the layout the bedroom book consists of one page for every day that bookings are taken which, in some resort hotels, may mean just for the period of the restricted season of perhaps thirty weeks. The bedroom book has the room numbers on the left-hand side and a reminder of their type with columns for the guest's name, the number of persons in the party, remarks and the date of departure alongside. The receptionist will fill in the details of the guests staying on each night in the hotel on each appropriate page of the bedroom book. In our example we have a bedroom book filled in with the current details for 8 August and we can see that there are plenty of vacancies at this time for that night. It should be noted that the provisional booking for Mr Smart has been recorded so that room 25 is not let inadvertently to another customer until we have heard from Mr Smart. All the entries are made in pencil to allow for adjustments and cancellations.

In a small hotel the bedroom book may also provide enough information, along with the reservation form, to give the hotel its 'detailed record' and therefore the reservation form and the bedroom book cold comprise the complete reservation system (Figure 27).

An interesting variation on the bedroom book is used by the Hôtel du Cheval Rouge in Versailles, France. Rather than a formal layout of a page the floor-plan of the hotel is reproduced on each page of that hotel's version of the bedroom book. In this hotel, which has forty-three bedrooms, many customers stay for only one night and therefore the system has to cope instantly with a large number of chance arrivals at the front desk which is in fact at one end of the bar. One of the drawbacks of the formal bedroom book is that it is sometimes difficult to find the correct type of room for a customer quickly but at the Cheval Rouge the 'visual reference' is very powerful and thanks to the detailed drawings the right type of room may be located swiftly. Conveniently the layout of the hotel includes a courtyard and it is in the space left by this that details of the persons occupying rooms is recorded in an informal way against the appropriate room number. A separate reservation form is kept with the bulk of information concerning each reservation and that acts as the 'uniform record' and the 'detail record'.

The floor plan of the Cheval Rouge (Figure 28) shows the use of the room numbering to indicate the floor upon which each room is situated; this is a system common to many hotels. The majority of the rooms on the first floor, in this practical example, are therefore indicated by the use of numbers in the one hundreds and all the second floor rooms start their numbering with 'two'. In a very large hotel with many floors this system can be most useful in indicating to staff the floors upon which particular rooms are located. You will notice also on the plan that the locations of stairs as well as the facilities of each room are indicated clearly to simplify the reserving of a particular type of room, as well as to enable guests to be shown on the diagram the best way of walking to their accommodation.

We have already mentioned the drawbacks of the bedroom book which primarily involve the difficulty of locating a particular type of room for a guest and this problem multiplies if that room has to be reserved over a long period of time for one guest's stay.

As a consequence there is an alternative system of 'visual reference' which is suitable for the small resort hotel of up to fifty rooms like the Ship Inn. The use of a *conventional reservation chart* may be most satisfactory in this size and type of establishment giving as it does a view of at least a whole month's reservations on a single sheet. In some hotels that are very small the conventional chart may even run to three months on a single sheet.

Ship Inn Bedroom Book					
8 AUGUST 19_____					
Room number	Room type	Name	Number of persons	Remarks	Date of departure
10	= B				
11	+				
12	+				
14	= S				
15	–	JAMES MR J	1		9TH AUGUST
16	= B				
17	– B				
18	+ B				
19	– B				
20	= B				
21	= B	DENNIS MR/S G	2	A/C TO NEWBOLD TRAVEL AGENCY	9TH AUGUST
22	– B				
23	+ B				
24	– B				
25	= B	SMART MR/S B	2	PROVISIONAL BOOKING	16TH AUGUST
26	+ B				
27	– B				
28	= B				
29	– B				
30	+ B				
31	= B				
32	– B				
33	+ B				
34	= B				
35	– B				

Figure 27   *Bedroom book*

The layout of the conventional chart is quite simple, having as it does the room numbers down the left-hand side along with their types; a useful item of information to show also are those rooms that may interconnect such as 29/30 and 32/33 in our example. Across the top of the chart are the dates for which rooms may be reserved so that in fact each square on the chart represents a 'room night'.

The way in which reservations are recorded is that once an appropriate room has been found for the relevant dates a pencil line is ruled in against the room number and under the dates to show on which nights

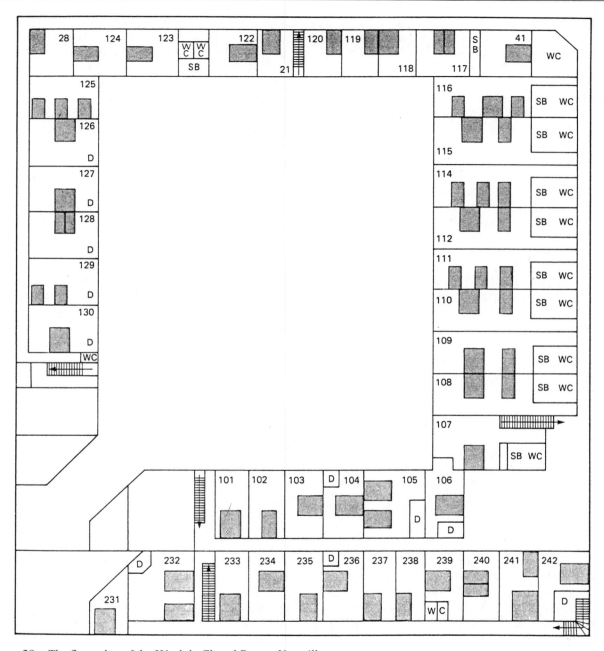

Figure 28 *The floor plan of the Hôtel du Cheval Rouge, Versailles*

that room will be occupied. The guest's name is then written in to identify the individual reservation and we may therefore see from our example that a customer by the name of Brown will be sleeping in room 10 for the nights of 9,10,11,12, 13 and 14 August. The small 'arrow heads' are placed at the end of each reservation to indicate when a particular reservation starts and finishes otherwise, as for room 21, it might be difficult to establish which of the guests is occupying the rooms on specific dates. All the entries are made in pencil so that alterations to accommodate cancellations, unforeseen departures, extensions of stay and room changes may be made with ease. The chart detail may be inked-in in some hotels only after the particular day has passed in order to provide a permanent record of the business but while the chart is in operational use only pencil should be used.

All reservations including chance customers should be recorded immediately on to the chart in order to avoid the possibility of 'double booking' customers or putting two reservations into the same room. It will be noted that on the conventional reservations chart specific room numbers are being allocated at the time a reservation is placed and therefore it is most important, with a limited number of rooms of the same type, to ensure that double booking does not take place. A problem area with this is when provisional offers of accommodation are sent out to guests for their confirmation and so even these provisional reservations must be shown on the chart, by the use of a dotted line, so that another guest is not inadvertently booked into a room which has already been offered. The example on our chart of the recording of a provisional reservation is that of Mr/s Smart in room 25 and once his booking has been confirmed it would be ruled in on the chart.

It is also important that any rooms that are taken out of service for any reason are recorded on the chart for the duration of the time that they are 'off'. It may well be that decoration has to take place or repairs and if the fact that the room is not usable is not recorded on the chart the consequence might be that guests are allocated these rooms by mistake, so in our case room 17 has been shown as a room taken 'off'.

The conventional reservation chart (Figure 29) works well in the small hotel where reservations tend to be for long periods and also where the reservation is placed a long time in advance, giving plenty of opportunity to allocate specific rooms. The chart gives a good 'visual reference' of how business is shaping up for the future and therefore it would be quite ideal for the hotel of the size and type of the Ship Inn.

It would, though, be wrong to use a conventional reservation chart in larger hotels or those types of establishment where short stays are the norm, because the chart would become very confusing to operate. Not only would a large number of alterations have to take place to fit in specific requests for rooms over specific dates, but there would be very little space on the chart to write in even the guest's name for a one-night stay. The effect of using a conventional chart in a large short-stay hotel is that the continuous occupation of individual rooms, a necessity for profitability, does not take place; consequently the overall occupancy figures for the hotel are reduced. The chart would be both cumbersome and frustrating for the staff to operate and therefore it should be avoided in hotels of more than fifty rooms and where the business is primarily for short stays.

The conventional chart, though, is ideal for a hotel of the size and type of the Ship Inn and could even be modified to cope with the camping business attached to the hotel. If camping spaces were put on a separate chart down the left-hand side, leaving the same range of dates across the top, the conventional chart format could quite easily be used when dealing with hotel reservations in unforeseen situations. This perhaps shows how hotel systems may be adapted to cope with different accommodation businesses.

It can be seen, though, that the conventional chart in itself carries very little information about the detail of a guest's booking other than the person's name and the duration of stay in a particular room. A method of recording all the detail is therefore required and a *bookings diary* is the best solution (Figure 30).

The bookings diary is a useful 'detail record' as it sorts the reservations that have been received into their date of arrival. This is most important so that preparations can start to be made for the influx of guests on certain dates in the future and the bookings diary gives this very neat display of detail by arrival date. The diary itself has a page for every date for which bookings are accepted and upon which customers may arrive at the hotel. It is most important that the actual date being referred to is clearly printed at the top of each page so that reservations are not mistakenly placed on the wrong page and consequently the incorrect date. In most hotels the range of dates covered by the diary will be at least one year ahead especially in a resort hotel where reservations may well be being made for the following summer season. In hotels that are situated in conference towns or accommodate conferences themselves the dates covered in the diary may well run

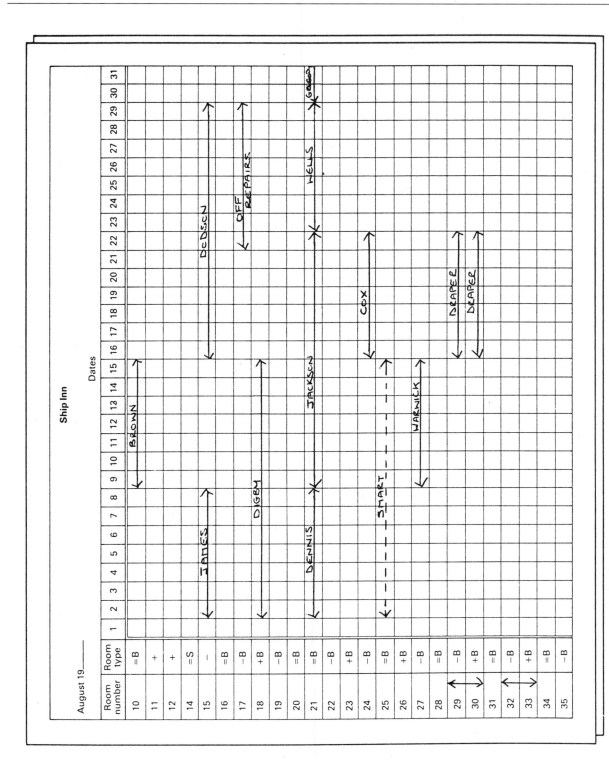

Figure 29 *Conventional reservation chart*

The Ship Inn — Bookings diary							
Bookings for: Saturday 9th August							
Date of booking	Name	Number of persons	Type of room	Rate	Date of departure	Remarks	Room number
23/3	BROWN MR/S J	2	= B	FULL BOARD	16/8	ONE BEDBOARD ROOM NEAR STAIRS	10
2/4	JACKSON MR/S D	2 + BABY	= B	FULL BOARD	23/8	ONE COT	21
6/4	WARWICK MR D	1	- B	1/2 BOARD	16/8	ROOM OVERLOOKING ESTUARY / REGULAR	27
12/5	STONE	1	= B	FULL BOARD	23/8	CANCELLED BY LETTER 12/5	31
12/5	VINE	1	= B	FULL BOARD	23/8	"	31

Figure 30   *Part of a page from the booking diary*

into several years ahead as it is common to arrange large conventions this far in advance.

All reservations are entered into the diary as soon as they are made so that each page will display information in the order that the bookings were placed for that particular date. In a small hotel a book might well be quite sufficient to handle the quantity of information for arrivals on a particular day but in a larger hotel a loose-leaf system may have to be employed to cope with the larger number of arrivals and their details. The details may be taken from the reservation form and is particularly useful in recording the individual requirements that guests may have, enabling these to be communicated to the relevant departments prior to their arrival. For example, in our diary Mr and Mrs Brown have asked for a bedboard to be placed onto one of the beds in their twin room. This is because Mrs Brown suffers from back trouble and needs to sleep on a rigid surface; as she is not very mobile she has also asked for a room near the stairs. From this information, which will be transferred to an arrivals list at a later date, the reception can place the Browns into room 10, which is near the stairs, and the housekeeper will be warned in advance to place a bedboard onto one of the beds. Thanks to the initial preparation of the bookings diary with a large amount of detail this sort of customer request may be catered for. Where the 'rate' column of the diary is concerned it is sometimes the policy not only to show the type of tariff the customer is paying, as in the case of the Ship Inn example, but also the cost, which can mean more to the staff undertaking the billing in a hotel where there is a wide-ranging variation in tariffs. At the Ship Inn the tariff is weekly by room, so that a description of 'full board' or 'half board' is quite sufficient. If a diary is to be used in a hotel where room allocation is not carried out until the guest actually arrives then a 'room number' column is not required, but at the Ship Inn this is done in advance and therefore a record is made in the bookings diary.

All reservations are recorded in the diary, including chance reservations, tours and groups, so that a complete 'detail record' is built up. Cancellations are simply ruled out in the diary and not completely obliterated just in case customers arrive at the hotel, as does happen, to claim their room, having forgotten that they cancelled and still expect their accommodation to be available. Another complication is where people of different names are accommodated in the same room; both their names should be recorded, if this is in fact known, so that messages or mail may be forwarded to them during their stay in the hotel. In our example of a diary Miss Stone and Miss Vine were to have occupied room 31 but they have in fact cancelled so the diary has been adjusted accordingly. If you look at the conventional chart you will see that there is no record of their potential occupation of room 31 so the room is free to let once again to the next customer who might want a twin room with bath for those particular dates.

As far as a small hotel is concerned the Ship Inn system of utilizing a reservation form and then a bedroom book or a conventional chart and a bookings diary would be quite sufficient to cope with the volume of information where reservations are concerned, but, in any larger establishment, with a predominately short-stay business, alternative systems that are more suitable are necessary.

Manual reservation system suitable for the Majestic hotel

The Majestic Hotel is not only considerably larger than the Ship Inn, boasting as it does 150 rooms, but the business being handled varies dramatically in that the average length of stay in the city centre is two nights rather than the week experienced in the resort hotel. You will remember that in the resort hotel each bedroom could be let for as few as thirty times each season, while at the Majestic the rooms may each be let in the region of 200 times each year. At the seasonal resort hotel of twenty-five rooms this means that approximately 750 reservations have to be handled, assuming that the hotel is full each season, but at the Majestic a similar calculation might reveal as many as 27,000 bookings with which the reservations system will have to cope. Although the information required to be stored on each individual reservation is virtually identical, whatever the hotel, the sheer number of bookings indicates that a vastly different system has to be employed to cope with the volume.

It is still of great value if the hotel uses a reservation form similar to the Ship Inn example in its reservation system because there is no substitute for 'recording uniformly' the information coming in from all the different booking sources. It is likely at the Majestic that all types of reservation will be handled including considerably more tours and convention reservations as well as bookings from central reservations offices and marketing bureaux. The reservations form is also useful as a check-list so that information is not forgotten but is recorded in the same manner no matter what its source. The only alteration that would have to be made to the Ship Inn's reservation form for use at the Majestic would be to tailor the types of room to those now available at the Majestic.

The Majestic is the type of hotel that may well have a problem achieving maximum occupancy due to the number of cancellations that occur. Consequently the management will use a policy of *overbooking* to try to alleviate the effects on the business. Overbooking means that the hotel accepts more reservations for rooms than there are actually available in the hope that this will compensate the hotel against cancellations. Customers who do not show up are called 'no shows'. Guests leaving earlier than originally anticipated may also cause problems where occupancy is concerned so our reservations system must be able to handle overbooking accurately. The point should be made that overbooking is a managerial decision and the amount and frequency will vary from day to day in the hotel once it is seen how business is going. Obviously indiscriminate overbooking can lead to big problems in the hotel if all the guests arrive, including those who are overbooked, because under the law of contract they all have to be provided with accommodation.

It is therefore essential that the reservation system incorporates a 'visual reference' or reservations chart upon which overbooking may be shown accurately so that the accommodation manager may see at a glance the state of bookings and be able to make policy decisions on overbooking. Bearing this in mind as well as the fact that at the Majestic, unless there are specific requests for actual rooms, room numbers are not allocated to particular guests until they arrive then a *density reservation chart* is the most suitable.

Perhaps in statistics most of us are used to the idea of a histogram or a bar graph being used to illustrate quantities or volumes whatever the subject of the investigation; the density chart is purely a histogram showing how many rooms of particular types have been booked on each night of a particular period. The only issue that often confuses people is that, unlike the normal histogram, the density chart is upside down so that the columns run from a base at the top of the chart rather than the bottom (Figure 31).

In our density chart example the part of the chart we are looking at is for the month of August and like other charts the nights are clearly indicated across the top of the chart. The total rooms in the hotel have also been divided up into their particular types; at the Majestic there are twenty-two twin rooms with bath, so this portion of the density chart is dealing solely with those twenty-two rooms. The scale down the left-hand side of the density chart is purely a descending numerical

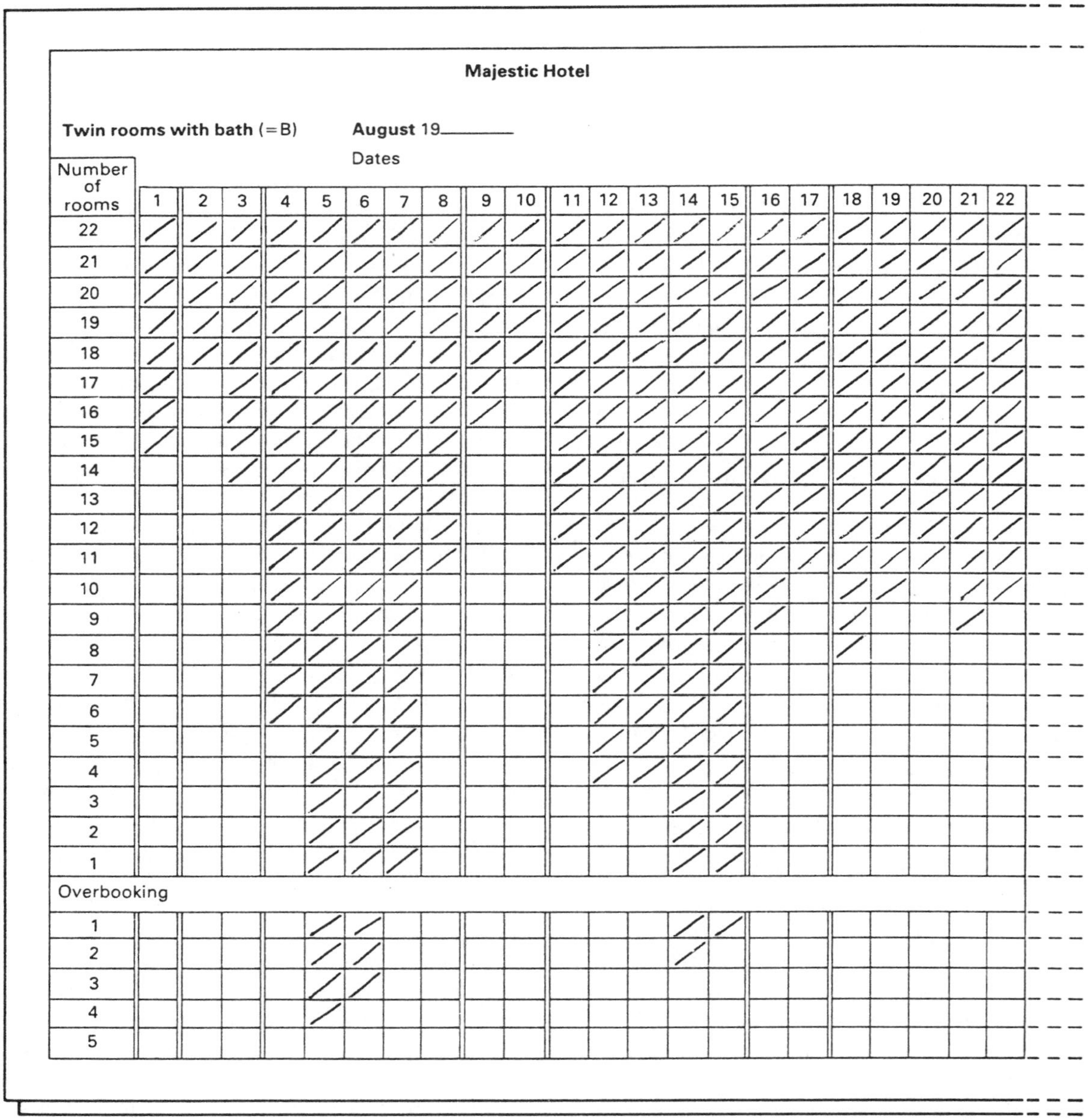

Figure 31   *Density reservations chart*

scale showing at a glance how many twin rooms with bath are left free to let on each night giving the member of staff a very quick 'visual reference'. Each time a reservation is taken for another twin room with bath a pencil dash is placed in the next available space at the bottom of the particular columns for the nights concerned until those columns are full; overbooking then may be considered for which there is space at the bottom. The aim, of course, is to fill up the chart with dashes which would mean that the hotel is completely full, but on our example there are only five nights where this is the case and on only four of those has it been felt necessary to overbook.

To illustrate the speed with which a reservations clerk may see whether there are rooms available it can be seen as quickly as you read this that there are fourteen rooms left on the 1st, seventeen on the 2nd and thirteen on the 3rd, etc. It is therefore much quicker and easier to use than trying to spot the same information on a conventional chart where all types of rooms are intermingled. The point should be made that there will be separate density charts for the other types of room in the hotel and we are just looking at the portion for those twin rooms with bath.

The density chart works well in those hotels where all rooms of a particular type are similar both in their physical facilities but also as far as price is concerned. Provided the chart has been kept properly the guests leaving will provide sufficient rooms for those arriving; the actual room numbers are not allocated until the guest's arrival. This overcomes problems of rigidity in the previous system where the occupant of the room has not vacated, leaving the new guest to wait around for a particular room already allocated. The guest may, in fact, be shown to the next room of the type he or she requires, as it becomes available rather than having to wait for a particular room, provided similar rooms are standardized.

The type of density chart that we are referring to is a printed version upon which pencilled dashes are placed to show each reservation of a type of room, but there are other forms available. Another common version uses coloured pegs to indicate different types of room but this has the problem that the pegs become worn and may fall out of the chart if it is not erected at an angle. This may not sound too much of a problem until one tries to find out where the displaced peg came from, which is almost impossible, so that one's

reservations are inefficient. The density chart, though, is very easy to record cancellations on, as all one does is erase dashes or remove pegs at the base of the particular columns for the nights that the cancellation covers. When the next reservation for those nights comes in the squares may be used again to continue the progress towards maximum occupancy. It should also be made obvious that, compared with the conventional chart, the density chart is ideal for recording overbooking accurately so that a complete picture is kept in front of the management. It also doesn't matter on the density chart whether a reservation is for a month or one night so that it is far better suited to coping with the short-stay business because there is relatively little detail shown, not even the guests' names, as this would be very difficult.

As the density chart is purely a record of the quantities of rooms reserved for particular nights, in order for it to be used even more reliance has to be placed at the Majestic on the use of a *bookings diary* to show all the details about customers. The diary will show where it is possible to find the length of stay of each customer as this is not evident from the density chart. Basically the information held will be the same as that in the diary at the Ship Inn but of necessity, due to the size of the Majestic, the diary will take the form of a loose-leaf system able to hold information on potential customers booking into 150 rooms. Therefore there will be more than one page for each day holding the information about arrivals on that day.

The first manual system that might be used in the Majestic-type of hotel is therefore the reservation form followed by the density reservation chart and then a loose-leaf bookings diary. This is quite a common reservations system to find in the medium-sized city-centre hotel where the guest length of stay is short.

An alternative reservation system that could also be used in a medium-sized hotel is the *Whitney* system which became very popular in the days before computers were commonplace. The system is produced by the American Whitney company, from which it takes its name, and is very popular in hotels with an American link as, until recently, it was virtually the universal system used to handle reservations in America. The Whitney system has the advantages that it economizes greatly on paperwork which is often a disadvantage of the manual reservations systems, and allows the various components of an effective reservations system to be combined together comprehensively.

The whole system revolves around the use of Whitney cards which are of a deliberate design and size and filled in by the reservations clerk at the time the reservation is placed (Figure 32).

One can either obtain standard cards printed by Whitney themselves or design one's own cards as long as the size is kept and the information that one would expect on a reservation form is included; this is what the Whitney card is initially replacing, being the 'uniform record' in the Whitney system. The cards themselves may be printed in a large number of different colours so that various types of guest and tariff may be recognized. For example, standard reservations may be indicated on white cards while red cards may be used for VIPs and yellow cards to distinguish that a particular guest is staying as part of a convention booking. The colour coding is something peculiar to each individual hotel and differs widely but suffice it to understand that various colours are very useful in showing different types of guest or tariff.

Once the information has been recorded onto the appropriate Whitney card this is placed in a metal holder or slide and taken to the advance reservation rack which is a major feature of the Whitney system. The rack is usually situated on the walls of the reservations office and consists of a large number of vertical columns arranged into the dates for which reservations are being taken into the future. Needless to say that in a large hotel the advance reservation rack takes up a considerable amount of space but it is very logical in that at least one column will relate to the date for which our Whitney card has been completed (Figure 33).

The Whitney card, still contained within its holder, will then be dropped into the appropriate column for the date of arrival and then into the correct place so that an alphabetical record of guests due to arrive on that day is completed. All the holders may be moved around and new reservations may easily be inserted so that a useful alphabetical listing of arrivals for particular dates is gradually created. The Whitney advance reservation rack has therefore neatly become our 'record of detail' thereby replacing the need for a bookings diary and has the added advantage that the guests are listed alphabetically, unlike previous methods. It is also argued that the rack provides a useful 'visual reference' as to how business is building up but in practice a reservation chart on the density principle would help make the exact number of reservations taken easier to control. Just like our other reservation systems the Whitney must be adaptable and therefore cancellations are recorded by ruling out the details on the appropriate card, which is not thrown away, but kept on the rack in case the customer arrives. Also, separate Whitney cards are provided to indicate reasons for rooms being taken 'off' and these too will be placed onto the advance reservations rack as a reminder to booking clerks (Figure 34).

The Whitney system of recording reservations is therefore most useful and, if required, may be extended, by the use of the same cards, to handle the arrival of guests and the room status problems during a guest's stay as will be seen in a later chapter. The only drawback is the amount of space required in the reservation office for the racks which may be extremely large in any size of hotel. This, though, is outweighed generally by the fact that one Whitney card may follow a particular guest through his or her stay and may act in

Room	Name	Date
	Address	
Remarks:		

Figure 32   *Whitney card*

Figure 33 *A Whitney advance reservation rack*

turn as a reservation form, a bookings diary and a guest history card thereby economizing greatly on the work of the reservations staff.

Having seen in the Whitney system the second of the manual reservation systems suitable for a medium-sized hotel such as the Majestic we must move on to examine the computerized reservations systems that may be employed as an alternative.

Computerized reservation systems suitable for the Ship Inn, Majestic and International hotels

Computers may be regarded as 'electronic filing cabinets' and as such are ideally suited to dealing with large amounts of information which need to be extracted in a number of ways. Consequently a computer is an ideal tool for a hotel to employ for storing the information concerning reservations which in total may be equivalent to a vast amount of paperwork had a manual system been used. We have already discussed the fact that at the Majestic Hotel in the region of 27,000 reservations may have to be recorded annually but at the International even this

large figure is superseded. Boasting 600 rooms and with an average guest length of stay of one night the reservation system at the International has to be capable of dealing with 219,000 reservations during the course of a year. This is assuming that each room is let once a day but there may even be times at an airport hotel where rooms are let more than once during a 24-hour period so there has to be a spare capacity within the system to allow for this added increase in business peculiar to the particular establishment. Overbooking will add to this total too.

The computer that is selected should easily be capable of handling this quantity of information and has the added benefit of eliminating a large amount of the boring, time-consuming work that might otherwise be done by hand in reservations and allows the front office staff more opportunity to devote themselves to guest relations.

It should be appreciated that an increasing number of hotels are employing computers within their establishment for a number of applications, the majority of which require the numbers of guests and their details as a foundation for their successful operation. It is therefore essential in installing an

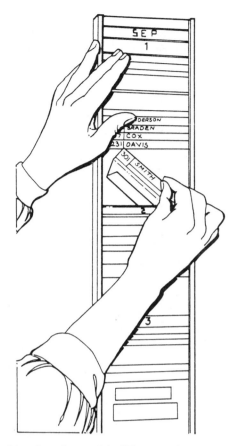

Figure 34   *On column of the Whitney advance reservation
rack*
*All cards are placed under date of arrival and then in
alphabetical order*

integrated computerized hotel system to start with
reservations and then to build in applications that
depend on this information.

It may be seen from Figure 35 of the applications in
a complete integrated computer system that reservations
is the basic application upon which the rest of the
system depends. It is therefore most important that the
reservations part of the computer system is constructed
carefully so that the demands placed on this
information from other applications are met in the best
possible way.

The basic components of the reservations systems
that we have examined already still have to be met by
the computer in that there is still a necessity for a

'uniform record', a 'visual reference', a 'detailed
record' and for the system to be 'adaptable'.

At the Ship Inn reservations might be handled easily
by a small stand-alone personal computer. In both the
Majestic and the International it is likely that there will
be specialized staff dealing with reservations and in
the International's case it is almost certain that there
will be a separate reservations office dealing with
the large number of bookings being handled.
Consequently the reservation system may have to be
operated physically in at least two different places with
reservations being made both behind the scenes
with reservations clerks and at the front desk itself
when receptionists are handling chance customers.
Consequently, the best approach is to utilize dumb
terminals linked to a central reservations memory and
store which enable both reservations locations to
gain immediate access to the reservations program
(Figure 36).

The term dumb terminal with a visual display unit
(VDU) simply refers to a television screen upon which
the necessary information concerning a reservation is
displayed in easy-to follow 'menu' configuration.
Rather than using a reservation form, as was the case
in the manual system, a reservations clerk can now
type in the same information, using the terminal's
keyboard, which will be displayed on the screen and
instantly transferred into the computer's store from
which it may be accessed in any number of ways at a
later date. The display used on a VDU is important in
that it must be easy to follow as well as acting as a
check-list so that when a phone reservation is being
handled nothing is accidentally forgotten.

In order to speed up the operation while a
reservation is being placed and to avoid having to
write the details and then transfer them from a
reservation form into the computer at a later time,
various codes are used to simplify the process. These
codes will obviously vary from one hotel to another
but if properly thought out at the time the computer
software is being designed they will enable the
reservation process to be much speedier which, of
course, will please the customer and cost them less for
their phone calls.

The 'menu' display that will be followed by the
reservation clerk in the diagram holds much of the
information that would be required on a reservation
form in a manual system. In order that the various

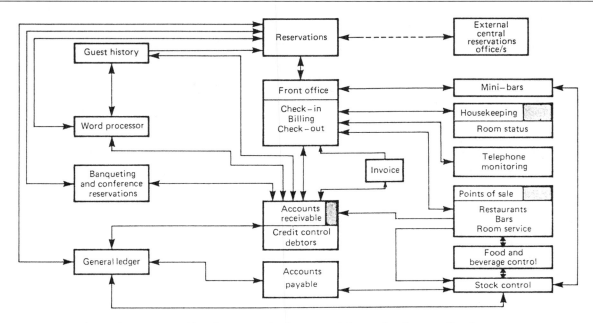

Figure 35   *A typical complete integrated hotel computerized system might require these applications*

codes are not forgotten these may be kept on a card alongside the screen where they may be referred to quickly.

To explain some of the items on the display the top line is concerned with the date of arrival, which would include the naming of the actual day as well as the date, the number of nights that the guest is staying, the date of departure, the type of room and the tariff arrangement. Underneath there are two further opportunities to confirm the amount the guest is paying with the 'Rate' and 'Plan' headings all designed to make the details of payment exact. There is also opportunity to name up to two guests and to specify how many adults and children there are in the party and whether any extra beds or costs are required and, if so, how many. Next follows a space in which the customer's address may be inserted along with, should it be a company booking, the name of a company and the person to whom an account should be sent or a copy of the confirmation. The name and details of whom to contact by phone in the event of problems with the reservation is also taken underneath before a large space for any requirements or remarks made by the customer concerning his stay.

At the bottom in the left-hand column any room

number allocated is recorded followed by the method of payment, the number of any voucher used for payment or credit card, the expected time of arrival and the date that entries might be being recorded taken. In the centre column the area and source of booking are recorded for marketing reasons, as well as the hotel source if placed by another hotel in a group, together with the status of the reservation in the sense of whether it has been confirmed or not or if confirmation has been requested. In the case of a travel agency booking their ABTA number is required followed by the details of the percentage commission that they have negotiated for their booking. The amount of any deposit received is recorded and the cross reference number is placed in the event of a cancellation should this happen at a later date. The reference code of the member of staff taking the reservation is recorded, in case of any mistakes or problems occurring, where the individual concerned can be identified. On the bottom line the reservation is given an individual number for reference purposes and the date that the booking was actually made is recorded.

Using the display menu in our integrated computer system allows the reservations clerk or receptionist to enter the information concerning a reservation very

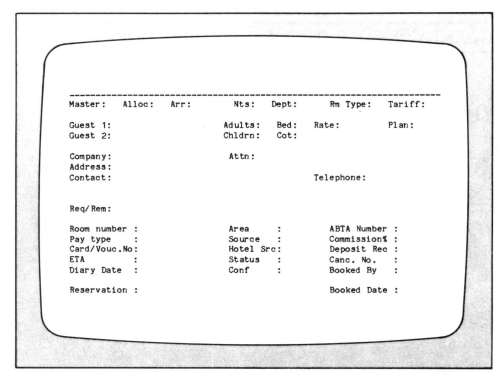

(a)

'Pay type' — payment types

CASH	Cash
CHEQ	Cheque
CRED	Credit
ACCO	Account room only
ACEX	Account to include extras
VOUC	Voucher room only
VOEX	Voucher to include extras

'Tariff' — tariff codes

RACK	Full rate
COM	Commissionable rack
S/OCC	Single occupancy
BBRK	Bargain break
BH/S	Business house rate
GRP	Group rates
CONF	Conference rates (24-hour)
TOUR	Tour
FIT	Fully inclusive tours
DISO	Other discounts
PROM	Promotions

'Plan' — plan

EP	English plan (Room only)
BP	English breakfast
CP	Continental breakfast
AP	American plan (inclusive)
MAP	Modified american plan (D, B and B)

'Area' — areas

LOC	Local/provincial
LON	London/city
UK	United Kingdom
I	International

'Source' — source

PRI	Private
CO	Company
AIR	Airline
TA	Travel agents
HBA	Hotel Booking Agents

'Status' — status

GU	Guaranteed
CO	Confirmed
UN	Unconfirmed
OF	Offer
CA	Cancelled

'Conf' — confirmation

RE	Request confirmation
SE	Confirmation sent

(b)

Figure 36   *(a) Typical reservation display for VDU screen   (b) Sample codes*

quickly and also helps to ensure that vital information is not forgotton. Once entered and stored the information should automatically update the occupancy figures projected for the day of arrival and be able to be recalled in a number of different ways. For example, it should be possible within our computerized reservation system to obtain a density chart in the form of a graphic display to show room availability in the future. Overbooking may be handled and controlled by the computer according to the managerial instructions entered for particular days while room allocations should be possible if this needs

Figure 37 *A typical VDU in operation with the check-list of codes visible on the right.*

to be done at the time that the guest books. Any number of alterations should be capable of being accommodated up to the level of a cancellation while rooms that have been taken 'off' should be recorded. Financially at the time of booking the reservation system should be capable of handling any of the complex tariffs and discount rates that will be found in a hotel that is the size of the International. This hotel will, after all, be dealing with a large number of tour and conference bookings so that the computer must be capable of handling block bookings as well as the more common individual reservations.

By the use of a screen-based integrated hotel computer system there is an added advantage that not only will there be a large saving in paperwork in the front office, as there is no necessity to produce a print out before analysing information, as necessary details are displayed rapidly on the screen, but the high stationery costs usually associated with computers that rely solely on printing information will be reduced. However, printers alongside certain terminals should not be discouraged as there is a definite need at times for permanent written output for reference rather than relying throughout on the VDU alone. One of the advantages, after all, of a computerized system is that it may be programmed to produce a confirmation letter or slip automatically for each customer saving considerably on secretarial work. Without printers or word processing facilities this would not be possible (Figure 38).

One major factor that should be borne in mind with computers that are to be used for reservations is that access to them is needed instantly if the picture of bookings is to be kept continually up-to date and if problems such as double-booking or uncontrolled overbooking are to be avoided. Consequently the reliability of the particular computer under consideration for reservations should be examined closely as the amount of 'down-time' must be kept to a minimum for the reasons already mentioned. It is always worth contacting previous purchasers of a system being considered to see whether the reservation system really is reliable or not. Also the ability of a computer to undertake a number of functions at the

```
                         UNCONFIRMED AND OFFER ARRIVAL LIST 3:08:
                                                                              1:08:__ 00:00

     ROOM   NAME          DATE    RES    ETA     NTS   ROOM   PNS    COMPANY            CONTACT      TEL.NO.
                          BOOKED  NO.    PAY           TYPE

            INNES MR/S D  1:08:-  22     18:00   7     FAMB   3      GULLIVERS TRAVELS   BARBARA
                                         VOUC                :CHILD AGED 5 YEARS

            REED MR/S p   1:08:-  19     14:00   2     FAMB   2
                                         CASH                :WILL CONFIRM BY MONDAY

            THOMAS MR W   1:08:-  18     19.30   2     SB     1      ICL LTD             MRS SHAW
                                         ACCO                :ATTENDING CONFERENCE
```

Figure 38 *A typical print-out that may be obtained showing unconfirmed reservations for a particular day*

same time must be examined. For example, in the diagram of a complete integrated hotel computer system it will be seen that there are many different functions that could be undertaken at any one time by various departments around the hotel. Many staff may be trying to use their VDUs or printers at the same time for widely differing reasons and the computer itself must be capable, certainly as far as reservations are concerned, of coping with multi-use. It is no good having to wait for an accounts run for example, to be completed in half an hour before reservations may be undertaken again. Some of the smaller systems suffer from this very problem, which means that the reservations staff have to rely on a manual system and then return to the computer when it is available to them again which is a very inefficient way of operating a computer.

In reservations the consequences of a loss of a large amount of information would be catastrophic to the business and so it is a good practice to take copies of the reservations information held in the main memory of the computer to guard against loss due to accidental or mechanical problems. Therefore at some time of the day information in the reservations and other parts of the computers main memory may be copied onto spare disks, or whatever the computer requires, to be stored in an alternative location so that if there were a major breakdown, which the back-up systems cannot cope with, information is not lost for ever. In some cases with smaller computers a simple power surge in the electrical supply could erase information and it is as well in this sort of case to have copies of the reservations detail elsewhere.

Up to now we have referred to reservations systems that by implication have utilized computers within the hotel itself but it is now very common to find that hotels within groups are linked together via major reservations and computerized information systems. Some large hotel companies with as many as 1500 hotels, boasting more than 250,000 rooms as well as twenty or more centralized reservations offices are linked via a central computer facility. A company might use its computer basically for reservations, but it may have other peripheral functions as well. Wherever a reservation is made, whether it be at a centralized reservation office or in an individual hotel, the information is transmitted via land lines to head office where the mainframe computer locates the appropriate

accommodation requested, records the information, informs the hotel concerned and produces a confirmation for posting or handing to the customer all within a matter of seconds. An excellent facility that is possible with some systems is that if a particular hotel were full and could not accept a reservation the computer would automatically furnish alternative destinations, thereby attempting to retain business which might otherwise be lost. In the hotel itself management information is continually transmitted to the centralized computer at head office as is the state of occupancy and especially any rooms that are taken 'off' for any reason so that an up-to-the-minute picture is maintained. Some companies are franchise operations and then the computer system is used to maintain contact with, and to collate management information from their constituent hotels so the computer system, which in each hotel may consist of a VDU screen, a teletype and a small memory and printer, is paid for from the franchise fee. The system may also be used just like a telex for written communication between the hotels themselves within the group.

Another use of a computer network as a reservations system is to interface it with telex, Prestel, airline networks and travel agents. As well as reservations a system may be designed to function as a general purpose message-switching and management information system able to handle accounting inventories and numerous other administrative tasks.

Some of the bigger systems are operated by the consortia which are marketing organizations on behalf of a number of independently owned hotels around the world. The central computer is linked to the rest of the company by having on-line access to its own satellite. This means that a specific reservation query or booking may have a reply from head office in an average time of five seconds or the time that it takes to enter the request on a terminal and obtain the information back on the screen. Handling reservations by satellite direct may be faster than using the phone and it is also more reliable.

The importance of correspondence

Whichever reservation system is used in a hotel a large amount of the paperwork involved will revolve around communication with the potential guest. This correspondence should not be ignored as not only might it be important legally that at a later date correspondence was composed correctly but it is an opportunity that should not be missed to make the potential customer feel like an individual rather than an occupancy statistic.

The first time that potential guests might contact the hotel is when they are researching hotels where they may wish to stay and one way or another may request copies of the hotel's brochure and tariff. Requests may have come in writing or from phone conversations and in either case this is the opportunity to impress customers that your establishment is better than the opposition. Indeed, if more care is taken over replies to enquiries a corresponding increase in occupancy is almost bound to follow. It is very easy to hurriedly place a brochure and tariff into an envelope with a 'With compliments' slip and post this off as the reply to the customer and to completely miss out on the opportunity of further impressing the potential customer. It may well have been that particular questions were posed in the enquiry that need answering. It is essential that questions are answered, as omitting to do so will indicate to customers that the hotel does not care about their wishes and they will almost certainly respond by taking their business elsewhere.

Analysts of the way offices operate have long since decreed that it is not only time-consuming but expensive to reply individually with a personalized letter to each reservation enquiry but in a hospitality industry such as the hotel and catering industry it is vital that guests are made to feel welcome and that they are going to be given a service when they arrive at the hotel. Consequently an individual reply to enquiries is essential and the repetitiveness and supposed expense may easily be overcome by the use of automatic typewriters or a word processing facility on a computer. What these two systems provide is a stock letter for various occasions that may be altered to suit, individual situations and which may then be personalized and printed so that the customers are unaware that the letter they receive had not been dictated personally by the manager concerned. Needless to say both systems print the letters extremely quickly and may therefore cope rapidly with a large amount of mail that is bound to be handled by the reservations staff in any size of hotel. The word processing facility on a computer is one of the commonest applications to be found and may easily be tailored to hotel reservations needs and, with the costs of computing coming down all the time, it is virtually essential in any size of hotel and could be utilized in our case by all three of our hotels. The end product of these systems is hopefully a reply to an enquiry that is personalized, giving the correct impression and that answers any questions.

It is not necessarily the case that the potential guest is going to select a hotel only on cost grounds or even the quality of the reply but another aspect that may be important is the speed of the reply. An enquiry should be answered as quickly as possible as there is no doubt that a quick reply will impress the guest and give an indication of efficiency. It is unfortunate that correspondence frequently takes a low priority where reservations work is concerned and letters sometimes take time to be replied to with consequential loss of business in the meantime. A conscientious accommodation manager will ensure that reservation enquiries are replied to as speedily as possible.

The next occasion that the reservations department will have correspondence to deal with is when a guest specifically requests accommodation and legally an 'offer' has to be sent back if rooms are available to initiate the first part of the law of contract. As far as the composition of the letter is concerned it is wise to make sure that not only are the exact dates of the reservation quoted but also the details of pricing so that there may be no opportunity for confusion. The ways in which service charges and VAT affect the pricing should be spelt out in the letter and again any specific requests should be noted and confirmed back to the customer. Do not forget either, to make sure that the exact type of room is stated in the letter and whether such items as views, balconies or private bathrooms are quoted if these have been requested. Every letter that is an 'offer' of accommodation to a guest should be compiled with the knowledge that it might have to be used as a legal document; therefore every care should be taken to ensure that any terms or conditions that are an implied part of the contract are not left to chance but are included so that the customer is aware of them. Only then may one be certain, as a hotelier, that one will succeed in the case of any legal action having to be taken in the event of the guest not honouring his or her part of the contract. It will also help in the event of a customer trying to claim that the hotel did not complete its obligations under the law of contract if it may be shown that every reasonable step was taken to both inform and help the customer.

As we have seen earlier in the chapter the guest has to 'accept' the 'offer' for a contract to be formed and it is polite to confirm back to a customer any acceptance, taking care once again to make everything legally correct. It is also polite to confirm receipt of any cancellation letters so that guests are aware that you know they are not coming.

One of the times that the reservations staff are put to the test with correspondence is when guests' requests for accommodation have to be turned down because the hotel is fully booked or when a similar problem stops them from being accommodated. Rather than lose sales a carefully phrased letter regretting the non-availability of rooms may persuade guests to change their dates of stay or to accept different types of rooms. If this is done in a tactful way business may be kept within the establishment rather than being turned away and lost for ever. After all, let us hope that our hotel has such a good reputation that guests will be clamouring to book in and therefore a change of date or type of room will be quite acceptable as other hotels will just not do.

It may be seen therefore that reservations correspondence should:

1   Impress the potential guest.
2   Be personalized as much as possible.
3   Answer all the guest's questions.
4   Be replied to speedily.
5   Be composed with the law of contract in mind.
6   Offer alternatives where necessary.
7   Convince the guest to stay at your hotel.

So far where correspondence has been concerned we have assumed that a letter is the best means of reply to a customer but it should be realized that some hotels prefer to issue 'tickets' which contain the same information and which are easily prepared by computerized facilities. The sort of layout that might be used is shown in Figure 39.

It should be emphasized that a ticket is a very businesslike way of confirming reservations but that the reverse side of the ticket shown should have the terms and conditions of the booking clearly stated so that there is no room for misunderstandings to occur.

The layout also allows for a window envelope to be used. This will reduce the amount of secretarial work required for typing; the method is consequently ideal where a computer is being used for reservations correspondence.

Another way in which reservations may be handled is by a pre-printed booking form which is sent for the customer to complete. This has the advantage over a letter in that the request for accommodation will return in a uniform layout and will therefore cut down on administrative work when information is having to be located from the reservation letters written by customers. If the form is compiled correctly it may go straight into our reservations system, or be transferred onto the computer, with comparative ease. It is important, though, to ensure that the information asked for is easy to understand by the customer so hotel jargon is avoided, as is shown in Figure 40.

The advantage of sending out the booking or reservation form at the time of an enquiry is that the customer completes the paperwork and gets over the psychological deterrent of having to compose a letter. If it is combined with the use of a reply-paid postage facility much of the time consuming worry that the customer might have in replying is removed and hopefully business will be won.

Once the exchange of correspondence has taken place it is important that it may be located as quickly as possible should it have to be referred to. Ideally the correspondence, which will include reservation forms, original and copy letters, telex and fax messages, travel agents' vouchers and many similar communications, will be filed in the reservations office by *date of arrival*. The consequences of filing all correspondence alphabetically, as is often suggested, is that a huge amount of paperwork has to be consulted should a particular letter have to be located; it is therefore much easier to file items by date of arrival initially. Of course within the individual files for each date it will be logical to keep correspondence in the alphabetical order of guest's names but it is essential initially to file by arrival date. The advantage is that when the day of arrival occurs the front desk staff may be equipped with a file of correspondence referring to that particular day which they will need to consult when guests actually arrive. Consequently they may come to the reservations office and take out the one file rather than having to sort through a large alphabetical

THE INTERNATIONAL HOTEL GROUP			DATE 30 JUL		TYPE OF TRANSACTION RESERVATION	HOTEL NO. 02	TICKET NO. E819

HOTEL NAME AND TOWN   INTERNATIONAL HOTEL, MELCHESTER AIRPORT, ENGLAND.   DATE OF ARRIVAL 14 SEP
HOTEL TELEPHONE NO.   041-646400   TIME OF ARRIVAL 18.00

NAME OF GUEST   MR BRAHAM   ROOM INFORMATION

FORM OF PAYMENT   OWNACC

ROOM TYPE	★	1B
NO. OF NIGHTS		3
NO. OF ROOMS		1
NO. OF ADULTS		2
NO. OF CHILDREN		
TARIFF TYPE	●	EP 2295
TARIFF		PER ROOM

RESERVATION AGENT   CALL OUT AGENT   HOTEL REF.

RESERVATION MADE BY AND ~~GUARANTEED BY~~

NAME   MR BRAHAM

ADDRESS   CORPS CORNER
29 BROWNSEA VIEW AVE
LILLIPUT
POOLE. DORSET.

ADDITIONAL INFORMATION

CREDIT CARD ACCEPTABLE

TELEPHONE NO.

SERVICE CHARGE   INCLUSIVE
TAX   INCLUSIVE

THIS TICKET HAS NO MONETARY VALUE UNLESS OTHERWISE INDICATED IN ADDITIONAL INFORMATION SECTION, AND IS SUBJECT TO THE CONDITIONS OVERLEAF.

Figure 39   *A 'ticket' reservation acknowledgement*

system. *All* correspondence relating to bookings should be retained, even details of cancellations, as it is vital to have everything to hand should customers query details and even forget that they had cancelled their reservations! To have the proof readily available will cool down a problem situation and establish whether the hotel is correct or not.

What are centralized reservation offices?

Up to now we have dealt with reservations that are being placed direct to a particular hotel by the customer but there are several ways in which reservations may be received from alternative outside sources. One of the most common is from a centralized reservation office (CRO) of which there are two distinct types.

First, there are the CROs operated by a particular hotel group which restrict the choice of customers using them to hotels within that particular company. Most of the main hotel groups possess their own CROs whose purpose is to supplement individual hotels giving an alternative medium through which rooms may be filled. It should therefore be made clear that if customers contact one of these CROs their choice will be restricted to establishments within that particular company.

The second type of CRO is that which is operated by a marketing organization who may draw member hotels from many different companies. In this case the marketing group passes on bookings to hotels that have contributed to their scheme and there may be several hotels within the same destination or resort town who may receive bookings from the same source. In some instances these CROs offer a wider choice to customers than those operated by specific hotel companies.

Having established that there are two types of CRO we should examine their use and why they are in existence. They are operated primarily to give customers a single source from which they may glean information about a large number of potential hotels. Customers may therefore book a stay or a series of stays at one or several hotels with a single phone call rather than having to carry out the costly task of phoning all those hotels direct. It may be that geographically the CRO is situated close at hand to the customers so that they may make local phone calls rather than long distance or international calls that may be costly. Some CROs deliberately market an easy to

The Ship Inn
Shipwrights Way
Southmouth

Telephone: 0317 - 26547 AA ★★ RAC

Booking Form

Please complete in BLOCK CAPITALS

Date of arrival . . . .   Date of departure . . . .

No. of adults . . . .   No. of children (under 14 years) . . . .

Type of room	Occupants (Mr, Mrs, Miss)	Age if under 14 years	Terms per week

Deposit enclosed, being £   per person, £ . . . .

or debit my Access/Barclaycard no. | | | | | | | | | | | | | by £ . . . .

Name . . . .   Have you stayed at the Ship Inn before? . . . .   Please leave blank

Address . . . .   If not, were you recommended? . . . .

. . . .

. . . .   If you selected the Ship Inn from an advertisement, please state which publication it was in:

. . . .

Tel no: . . . .

Date . . . .   Any other reason? . . . .

Figure 40   *A booking form*

remember Freefone number which in itself allows customers to contact the CRO free of charge. The advantage therefore to customers of using a CRO is that they receive a wide choice of hotel information very cheaply if they make use of the service.

It is also, of course, advantageous to the hotel receiving reservations from another well-publicized source so that it is not only the accommodation manager who single handedly has to find sufficient custom to fill the hotel. The CRO may well provide that extra number of bookings without which the hotel might not otherwise have been filled. The effectiveness of the relationship between the CRO and the hotel, though, depends entirely on the level of communication that takes place between the two.

There must be virtually instant communications between the hotel and the CRO otherwise there are reservation staff in two locations trying to sell the same rooms simultaneously. If they are both successful, and have not bothered to liaise, a large overbooking or double booking situation could arise. It is therefore essential that both parts of the system keep in constant touch so that mistakes do not occur. Undoubtedly the best systems are those which use linked computers so that every reservation clerk, whether in the CRO or at the hotel, receives an instant picture of the up-to-the-minute state of bookings. Where such sophisticated facilities do not exist the CRO should receive daily, from each individual hotel, an allocation of rooms that it may sell and when a room is sold the CRO should confirm this straight back to the hotel by phone, fax or telex. Without this liaison a CRO reservation system could dissolve into chaos. Where liaison takes place without computers it is also imperative that the people involved in the system have a code number or are able to identify themselves to avoid the possibility of 'rogue' reservations being inserted.

The CRO itself should be equipped to deal with all the potential aspects of reservations and enquiries that the individual hotel may be faced with normally. When a customer contacts the CRO by phone the reservation clerk answering must have ready access to information that will answer any enquiries that may be posed. When it is realized that questions could involve complex details about any single hotel of perhaps many hundreds covered in the system the staff must have to hand the relevant details and be given the most detailed of induction programmes to enable them to be familiar with all the operations of the hotels for which they may be responsible. In a computerized system the CRO reservation clerk should be able to gain access to a display concerning the details of each individual hotel and in a manual system a reference folder should be kept on each establishment so that potential questions may be answered. A typical display or reference might be as shown in Figure 41.

When a reservation request is received in the CRO the usual reservation information will be taken from the customer once it has been established from the manual records or by the computer that rooms are available. The customer will be asked by the reservations clerk to confirm his booking if there is time and as soon as possible the details are either passed direct by computer, faxed or telexed to the individual hotel so that the records may be updated there. The CRO will also be equipped to send out brochures and tariffs for each hotel and to deal with

cancellations and alterations on behalf of the hotel. The staff of the CRO therefore are just an extension of the hotel reservations staff but are operating at a distance from the hotel and therefore the close communication is essential.

Many company CROs have found that an application that may be added on to the reservations made by individuals is that of handling group and tour bookings through a separate part of the office. Indeed a centralized conference reservation office is a common feature of the CROs of the bigger companies and allows large conventions or tours to be accommodated in the facilities of more than one of the hotel company's establishments thereby gaining business that might otherwise have been turned away by a single hotel if it had been approached on its own. The CRO may therefore act as a co-ordinator of larger 'bulk' reservations.

Group reservations are essential to hotels

Reservations for large numbers of people or group bookings are very common in the larger hotels and involve several different techniques from those applied to reservations for individuals. Many hotels in fact specialize in group bookings and those for individuals are slowly disappearing in this kind of establishment.

The most common type of group that one may be accommodating in a hotel is a package tour of travellers who may be holidaymakers or persons attending a specific event, such as a sports match locally and who have been booked by a tour operator or a travel agent. Whatever the type of group being booked it is essential to gain just as much information as one would normally do when booking an individual, as all the customers on a group booking expect just the same level of service as would normally be given. Therefore the information one would obtain for an individual is taken on a 'bulk' reservation form and stored in the reservation system as normal. The way that the details may differ is the pricing, which will almost always involve discounts over the normal 'rack' rates, and the individuals names which may only come at the last moment in the form of a rooming list from the organizer. This list will match the numbers of rooms booked against individual's names and give details of any specific requests that may have

```
INTERNATIONAL HOTEL GROUP: CRO HOTEL REFERENCE DISPLAY
------------------------------------------------------
HOTEL CODE: 056 ST JAMES'S BEACH HOTEL BARBADOS
---------------  --------------------------------
```

ADDRESS: Coconut Way, Barbados,
-------   West Indies.
TEL: 21311   TELEX: WB225   FAX: 21312
---   -----   ---
CABLES: JAMESB

GENERAL
MANAGER: Mr MICHAEL WARD

ASSISTANT
MANAGER: Mr DONALD SMITH

LOCATION: Airport: 18 miles
          Bridgetown: 7 miles
          Shopping Centre: 1 1/2miles

HOTEL FEATURES:

-Built in 1981
-350 acre estate with own beach
-9 hole golf course and club house
 adjoins hotel
-Tennis courts-2 all weather, near
 golf course
-Tennis courts-2 all weather, in
 hotel grounds
-Open air swimming pool
-Table tennis
-Shuffle board
-Sailing/fishing
-Health club/solarium
-Water skiing
-Open air car park for 150 cars
-Card room
-Writing room
-English - speaking baby-sitter

GUEST BEDROOM INFORMATION

No. of rooms: 115
No. of beds: 217
No. of floors   3

Lifts serve all floors in new wing.

Rooms on ground floors: 40

BEDROOM BREAKDOWN

Singles: 13
Twins: 96
Penthouse suites: 6

Each suite consists of 2 twin bedrooms,
3 bathrooms, lounge, dining room and
patio, large terrace and fridge.

All rooms face the sea, have private
patios or terraces, are air-
conditioned and have telephones

Laundry/valeting service.

Check out time: 12.00

Voltage: 230 volts 50
                       cycle AC
Service charge: 15%

ENTERTAINMENT: Provided nightly throughout
--------------   the week
COCONUT ORCHESTRA plays 6 nights per week,
----------------- including Cabaret, Steel
Band, Calypso Singer, Trio and Singer.

A BARBECUE EVENING is held once a week,
------------------ with background music.

Other Entertainment includes:
Film shows-Weekly floor Shows-Disco

DINING FACILITIES: CAPACITY
------------------   --------

DINING ROOM: 130 ⎫
-----------   ⎬ 320
TERRACE: 190 ⎭

GRILL ROOM: 85 ⎫
----------   ⎬ 265
BEACH RESTAURANT: 180 ⎭

Breakfast: 07.00-09.30
Luncheon: 12.30-14.30
Afternoon Tea: 15.00-18.30
Dinner: 19.30-21.00

BREAKFAST AND LUNCHEON are served in the
BEACH RESTAURANT, with an extensive Buffet
Luncheon provided during the season:
December to April.

DINNER: Served by candlelight on TERRACE, or
in air-conditioned DINING ROOM

TABLE D'HOTE TARIFF:

Buffet luncheon: $20.00 US
Dinner: $35.00 US

Packed lunches are supplied by arrangement,
a la carte

LOUNGES:

MAIN LOUNGE: SEATING - 50

BARS:

BEACH BAR: 10.00-17.00

LOUNGE BAR: 09.30-01.00

TERRACE BAR: 19.00-24.00

POOL BAR: 09.30-17.30

RESERVATIONS/SHOPPING FACILITIES IN HOTEL:

-Men's boutique   -Duty free shop
-Ladies' boutique   -Woollen goods
-Perfumes   -Drug store
-Ladies' hairdresser   -Barber

There is a shopping centre 1 1/2 miles from
Hotel, with banks, Men's & Ladies'
outfitter and duty free shops

Figure 41   *A reference display*

```
INTERNATIONAL HOTEL GROUP: CRO HOTEL REFERENCE DISPLAY
------------------------------------------------------
HOTEL CODE: 056 ST JAMES'S BEACH HOTEL BARBADOS
----------------- ------------------------------
                    -----------------------------------
                    CONFERENCE/BANQUETING FACILITIES
                    -----------------------------------
CAPACITIES CHART:
----------------

                 ------------------------------------------------
                      MAIN DINING   SMALL MEETING  LOUNGE
                        ROOM           ROOM
                 ------------------------------------------------
        CONFERENCE      200             20           30
                 ------------------------------------------------
        BANQUET         320*            -            -
                 ------------------------------------------------
        LUNCHEON        320*            35           -
                 ------------------------------------------------
        DINNER          320*            35           -
                 ------------------------------------------------
        RECEPTION       300             60           60
                 ------------------------------------------------
        DINNER-DANCE    280             -            -
                 ------------------------------------------------


                 ------------------------------------------------
FUNCTION SUITE:  FLOOR SIZE: FLOOR AREA: CEILING HEIGHT: DOOR SIZES
---------------  ----------- ----------- --------------- ----------
MAIN DINING ROOM    30'X82'  2460 sq.ft (a)To beams:7'9"  5'x6'6"
                                        (b)To domed
                                           ceiling:11'
ROOF TERRACE adjoins
MAIN DINING ROOM    82'X34'  2788 sq.ft

SMALL MEETING ROOM  40'X17'   680 sq.ft                   5'x6'6"

LOUNGE              40'X25'  1000 sq.ft

*Main dining rooms and use of adjoining covered terrace, give maximum
number 320 persons for lunch or dinner

N B -The above rooms are on reception level.
    -Toilet facilities are on ground floor.
    -All rooms are centrally air-conditioned.
    -The MAIN DINING ROOM can only be used for a conference when all
     delegates are accommodated in the hotel. The hotel is therefore
     only geared for larger conferences if residential.
-------------------------------------------------------------------
EQUIPMENT:   STANDARD                        ON REQUEST
----------   --------                        ----------
        2 Lecterns         Plumber           Tape recorders
        3 Blackboards      Carpenters        Video cameras
        3 Easels           Painters
        3 Pointers         16mm projector
        1 Spotlight        Full size movie screen
        Secretarial services Video playback system (colour)
        Electrician        PA system
                           Copying machine

VOLTAGE: 230 volt AC : 13 amp points.
-----
```

to be catered for. One important item that must be gained from a group, especially if they are all travelling together, is the time of the party's arrival and departure. This will enable sufficient staff to be on duty to meet the group so that the large influx of customers is shown to their accommodation as quickly as possible without undue delay.

The acceptance of group bookings will be a matter of management policy and while large groups will be unlikely at our Ship Inn, the International Hotel by virtue of its market will cater for a large number of groups. The Majestic Hotel has the biggest problem for even though it may want the quantity of business associated with groups they may not fit into the luxury image that the establishment is trying to project and therefore only a percentage of total bookings will be allocated to tour or group business. As far as the accommodation manager is concerned he or she will be offering discount rates to groups to try to fill in the troughs of business. Often the holiday groups want to come in peak times such as the high season, and therefore a delicate balancing act has to be carried out so that discount group business does not take away revenue that could have been obtained from customers paying the full 'rack' rate in high season.

The reception staff will be involved in group bookings from conference delegates in all of our three hotels and will undertake the allocation of the appropriate bedrooms for the time specified. Conferences hinge around the meeting accommodation and it is unlikely that the reception staff will necessarily become involved as this will tend to be the responsibility of the manager or a conference manager as will the overall pricing policy. It may well be that in a hotel such as the International arrangements will be reached with airlines and business houses to keep blocks of rooms available for the use of their customers or staff. Quite often these rooms will not be used every night and therefore the reception staff are sometimes allowed to re-let these rooms to individual customers once it is established that they are not required by their usual inhabitants.

Many of the tours and groups will be booked by organizations such as travel agents who depend for their operation on commission given to them by the hotel. This commission is normally in the region of 10 per cent of the guest's bill. The policy for allowing commission is compiled by the management but it is important that the reservations staff handle the details of the booking, and particularly the 'travel agent's voucher', most carefully to avoid confusion. The agent will make bookings with the hotel in the normal way supplying the information that he or she is a bona fide agent and the commission rate applicable will be decided, in the case of a new contact, by the management. The travel agent will then send confirmation to the hotel which is one of the three parts of the travel agent's voucher. This details payments made by the customers and also any added facilities provided for which they will not be obliged to pay extra. This copy of the voucher must remain in the hotel's reservation correspondence as the guests will arrive on the due date with a carbon copy which must be checked at the front desk to make sure that it is identical to the original. It thus enables the customers' identities to be established. Inability on behalf of reservations staff to deal correctly with travel agent's vouchers may lead to bad guest relations and an impression of inefficiency at the front desk.

It may be seen therefore that group reservations are one of the complications that reservations clerks have to be able to deal with as they are unlikely to be aware, when they pick up the phone, of exactly what sort of business they are going to be faced with from one moment to the next.

The reservations clerk

The reservations clerk in a large hotel or the receptionist in a small establishment has a responsible job in ensuring that 'the right person is booked into the right room on the right night'. The systems that have to be operated and the detail that has to be gleaned in order to cater for the requests of customers is enormous and the smallest mistake may lead to a guest relations problem or, worse, a major complaint which may be laid squarely at the feet of the member of staff who took the booking originally. Other staff in the hotel may also have to take the blame for any mistakes made inadvertently at the time of booking; reservations staff must thus be carefully picked to ensure that they are fastidious enough to undertake the detailed task.

The wrong person in the position of accepting reservations may greatly influence the quantity of the business undertaken by the hotel and the correct person may help by his or her attitude to make the establishment achieve the projected occupancy levels. As a consequence reservations staff are normally paid slightly more than their front desk colleagues and will sometimes be on incentive schemes to encourage them to increase business. Not only will reservations clerks be recording the reservations as they come in and sending confirmations to customers but they must act as a salespeople and not just become passive sources of information. They have to show skills of diplomacy when it is impossible to fulfil the reservation requirements of guests and must be competent in ensuring that policies, such as those formulated by management to cater for overbooking, are rigidly applied. They must also of course use their common sense to overcome difficult situations. A reservations clerk must possess a perfect phone manner and voice as well as being able to use telex and fax machines and a computerized system if necessary.

Reservations are the lifeblood of the hotel and if the wrong person is entrusted with handling them then the profitability of the hotel will be greatly impaired and the reputation of the establishment adversely affected.

4 Communication

Why is communication important to a hotel business?

In any business organization communication is vital in order that all the many parts of that business may be co-ordinated and therefore effectively achieve the common aim. A hotel is no different in this respect from a factory or a large clerical office, because they all depend upon the communication of facts about the business to all the departments involved for there to be progress towards the conclusion of transactions.

Where a hotel does differ from other organizations is that there are a large number of minute details included in the transactions that may cause very personal problems for customers if they are not precisely communicated. There are also many transactions to be communicated, for in the larger hotels there may be thousands of individuals staying under one roof with a vast amount of information which needs to be communicated throughout the establishment daily.

The majority of information that has to be communicated around the hotel concerns the details of reservations; as a consequence the front office becomes the nerve centre of the hotel for communication as it is there, in the reservations system, that all this information is held. It is therefore a responsibility of the front office to make known to the other departments in the hotel all the information concerning individual reservations. Indeed, the staff in those other areas of the hotel depend upon this being carried out effectively to be able to undertake their services correctly for guests. It is no exaggeration to say that all the details of a hotel's customers are kept in the front office systems, so if this is not shared with the other areas of work in the hotel the level of personal service given to customers will be non-existent.

It should also be realized that guests expect communication to take place prior to their arrival and will be most distressed in certain circumstances if this has not happened. Guests will have given certain information to the member of staff who initially handled their reservations and will expect this information to have been acted upon by the time they arrive. Should they, for example, have asked for a certain type of diet they will expect the reservations clerk to have passed this detail on to the chef and the restaurant manager so that there is no embarrassment when they actually go to the restaurant and ask for their desired meal. Had communication not taken place on what externally may appear a trivial matter the guest would quite rightly feel it necessary to make a strong complaint. It should be realized that to become blasé about communication will lead to disaster as those items that may appear trivial in the context of a large business are by no means unimportant to the guest concerned, and the inability to communicate them properly may ruin a person's stay at the hotel and that customer may be lost for ever. It is often said that 'the best advertisement is a satisfied customer' and good communication within a hotel may lead a long way towards satisfying customers and the hotel will improve its reputation for giving a good, personal service.

A happy staff will also lead to guest satisfaction and one of the ways that management may make staff happier is to make sure that they are confident in their work. It is therefore necessary that all the staff in the hotel are informed of the details about the customers and the business that they need to know in order for them to carry out their duties to the best possible effect. Unfortunately many staff problems occur when detail has not been communicated effectively and members of staff concerned are in total ignorance about their responsibilities through no fault of their own. The management should therefore ensure that a good system of communication is installed.

The front office and reception staff are in any case looked upon as the experts in communication as it is generally there that the necessary communications equipment is situated. In the front office there will be the telephone switchboard, the fax machine and in many cases the computer, apart from all the clerical equipment needed to deal with written communication. The staff will be experts in dealing with communication both internally and externally using any of these items of equipment; they are a natural source of communication for the hotel. The system they are given to use for communication will depend entirely upon the size and needs of the type of hotel but they will be prepared and able to use any of those systems remembering that the written word is far more effective than communication by word of mouth.

It should not be forgotten that communication about the customers due to come to and then stay at the hotel is only one side of the story in a hotel. All their charges have to be collated and placed onto bills before they leave so there is a very important second part to the complete picture of communication.

It is fair to say, though, that communication is vital to the effective operation of any hotel and in this chapter we will examine the various methods of communication as well as the information that has to be distributed and also collected.

How to communicate the numbers of arrivals, departures and guests in residence

The most important operational statistic that every department in the hotel needs to know is the number of persons who will be staying in the hotel each night. The calculation of this statistic allows all the departments to cater for the expected number of guests and allows preparations to be made, particularly with regard to staffing, for busy and slack periods. Needless to say this information needs to be known some time in advance and it is therefore common to find that the front office and reservations staff will be asked to prepare an occupancy forecast for several weeks ahead so that departmental heads may make the necessary arrangements to meet the demand. This forecast will normally be presented in the form of a list for dates during a certain period, whether it be a month or a week, and will contain no detail whatsoever other than the total number of guests actually booked and expected on those dates. Needless to say the figures will be treated by the departmental heads only as a rough guide, for a more accurate figure may be achieved much nearer the actual date. The occupancy forecast is therefore a rough managerial guide as to the expected business in the hotel some time ahead.

The detailed information concerning guests will be collated and distributed only the afternoon or evening before the day that guests arrive and this will be in the form of an *arrival list*. Whatever the size of hotel and whether the arrival list is actually prepared manually or by computer the information it contains will be vital to all the departmental heads and their respective staff.

The reservation system is consulted for the relevant guest details which may be found, depending on the system used, in the bookings diary, bedroom book, conventional reservation chart, Whitney advance reservation rack or the reservation computer's memory. The information about each reservation will be conscientiously checked against the reservation forms and the correspondence to ensure that all the remarks and requests made by the customers are recorded. This is most important as the arrival list is the way that these details, given originally to the reservations staff, get through to the departmental staff concerned with their implementation.

Whatever the size of hotel the arrival list, as probably the most important single method of communication within the hotel, should contain similar information in detail and should not be skimped. Simple arrival lists tend to leave out information that may consequently have to be placed onto an alternative list and the more lists that are involved the higher the chance that details will be forgotten and customers mishandled.

Let us look at the information that each department needs. This will demonstrate the reasoning behind the suggested layout for an arrival list.

The person at the top of the circulation list each evening for the arrival list will be the *general manager*, who will be keen to see the details of the proposed business for the following day and will consequently examine the list in detail. Among other items sought are the names of guests due to arrive so that the manager may be available to greet any VIPs or take the necessary action if anyone is booked in who might have been a problem on previous visits. In the case of guests who may have been unreliable in settling their accounts in the past credit limits may be set or it may be stipulated that guests pay cash only for services provided. The general manager will be able to give guests who have been regular customers a greeting, having become familiar with their details from the arrival list and then the corresponding guest history card. The arrival list will therefore enable the manager to give a personal approach to customers as well as indicating the overall business within the hotel during the next twenty-four hours.

Reception staff themselves will need several copies of the arrival list as they will work from it the following day when greeting customers on their arrival. Provided the list is completed alphabetically each guest may be located quickly, as they arrive, on the list and the details of their stay checked off with them. Quite often it will be at this time that a room is allocated so the front desk staff will insert this onto the list. As far as greeting customers is concerned the priority for the reception staff is that the arrival list is prepared in alphabetical order with tours, conventions or business house customers listed under the name of their company or organization.

At the time of arrival the *head hall porter* will need a copy of the list so that appropriate guests may be shown to their correct rooms as long as these have been pre-allocated. The list will also give the head hall porter advance warning of the numbers of staff needed on duty at specific times to cope with peak time for luggage handling such as the arrival of coach tours. Quite often *enquiries* are also. handled by the porters but whether this is the case or not the staff involved in dealing with enquiries will see from the arrival list if there are any messages or items of mail in their possession awaiting customers due to arrive the following day.

In the food and beverage departments the *head waiter* will be able to gauge from the arrival list the numbers of guests in particular groups and therefore he may arrange the table allocation and plan in the restaurant should it be necessary to pre-allocate tables to specific guests. Like other departments it will also allow for the calculation of staffing levels and whether there is a need to bring in part-time staff to deal with coach tours or increases in business. The *head chef*

will be interested in numbers of guests, again for staffing reasons, and also for an indication of how much food to prepare. By looking at the tariffs that customers are paying the head chef will be able to gauge the expected totals of guests for each meal. For example, customers on full board will be requiring all meals, whereas those on half board may well not be in for lunch in a resort hotel. The arrival list therefore makes calculations much easier and will help cut down on any potential food waste. It will also facilitate catering for any specific dietary requests that customers have as already referred to at the start of the chapter.

The *head housekeeper* will examine closely the arrival list to see the number of rooms and sometimes the specific rooms, that customers will be occupying the following night. This will give an indication of the number of staff needed on duty for the servicing of rooms. The housekeeper will calculate the linen requirements, whether this be coming from a laundry or a linen hire firm, and will be able to cater for requests such as specific types of pillows, bedboards or extra beds and cots.

The *telephonist* will need a copy of the arrival list so that it is possible to tell callers whether guests will be in the hotel or not and also making it possible to put calls through to the correct rooms.

Where finance is concerned the *bill office staff* will be keen to open accounts for those guests who have arrived and from the arrival list will see the tariff that each guest is paying and therefore start the charging. The arrival list will also enable them to apportion charges made under specific guests' names to the correct room number.

These are the main departments that require a copy of the arrival list and the suggested layout is as shown in Figure 42.

On this layout a column has been added to show the 'booking status' which is necessary in those hotels which practise the release of rooms unclaimed by 6 p.m. The column shows those rooms that are confirmed in writing (CF), those that are confirmed verbally (VCF) and those that are definite (DEF) or in other words not confirmed but definitely coming. The front office manager will be looking at the status of bookings at 6 p.m. on 8 September to see whether there are any rooms that may be released to customers on the waiting list for accommodation. As the terms

Majestic Hotel				Arrival list for Saturday 8 September 19___			
Guest's name	Booking status	Room type	Number of persons	Date of departure	Tariff rate	Room number	Remarks
Aplin, D.	CF	Ix+ Ix-	3	10.9	Incl. £200	122/ 123	Regular
Case, A.	CF	+	2	9.9	R & B £60	309	Late arrival 11.30 p.m.
Dodd, E.	CF	=	1	23.9	R & B £60	246	
Duck, D.	NC	-	1	9.9	Incl. £80	232	Vegetarian diet
Headley, R.	DEF	=	2	10.9	Free	118	VIP tell manager Tour operator
Jarvis, R.	VCF	+	2	14.9	Incl. £120	217	A/C to minister hydraulics
Kung, F.	·CF	=	2	10.9	R & B £60	329	
Lacey, D.	CF	+	2	11.9	Incl. £120	251	
Loud, D.	NC	-	1	10.9	Incl. £80	237	Bedboard
Tanner, F.	CF	=	2	10.9	Incl. £120	318	Quiet room
Tisdall, A.	VCF	=	2	9.9	R & B £60	211	
Total number of arrivals			20				

Figure 42   *The Majestic Hotel's arrival list*

quoted are that rooms unclaimed by 6 p.m. will be released it is safest in law to release those rooms that are not confirmed (NC) and so rooms 293 and 232 should be used in this way. The tariff and rate column is used to show the total amount of money to be paid by the guests for each night of their stay as well as the tariff upon which they are staying as a help to the bill office staff as well as the *cashiers*.

It may be seen that the arrival list contains a large amount of information which is useful to many of the departments already discussed and it may easily be typed in this form for distribution around the hotel on the evening before the day to which it refers. The particular list for the Majestic illustrated would therefore be compiled by the reception staff during the afternoon of Friday 7 September and distributed that evening.

In a hotel the size of the Majestic the compilation of the arrival list into alphabetical order is quite a time-consuming process and may take a member of staff up to two hours to locate the information and type it out.

The example illustrated is for a Saturday evening, which is probably a quiet period in a city-centre hotel, and so the list is relatively small but during the week the list would be considerably larger and take much longer to complete. One of the advantages of the Whitney System is that the arrivals are already collated into alphabetical order so the list may be completed quickly, but the best system is undoubtedly to use a computer upon which a list, such as that shown in Figure 43, may be produced in seconds provided the correct program is used.

The computer-produced layout for the International Hotel shows a reservation made by Baker and Son for five family rooms and bath, all at single occupancy, and these are listed at the top under the parent company's heading. The other guests due to arrive on 3 August then follow on alphabetically including that for Mr Collins who is not in fact staying in his room but using it for a meeting during the day. A second line is used rather than a separate column for remarks and a variety are illustrated. The great advantage of this type

```
                         INTERNATIONAL HOTEL

                         ARRIVAL LIST 3:08:                              1:08:

      ROOM  NAME              STATUS  RES NO  ETA    NTS   ROOM   PNS   BD   CT   PLAN  RATE    DEPOSIT
            COMPANY           PAY                          TYPE
      --------------------------------------------------------------------------------------------------

            BAKER & SON       GUA     29      15.00  1     FAMB 5  5               EP    70.00   200.00
                                              :ALL ROOMS FOR SINGLE OCCUPANCY

            BAKER & SON       ACCO

            CASWELL MR P      GUA     29      15.00  1     FAMB    1                EP    70.00
            BAKER & SON       ACCO

            HOWELLS MR I      GUA     29      15.00  1     FAMB    1                EP    70.00
            BAKER & SON       ACCO

            KILROY MR I       GUA     29      15.00  1     FAMB    1                EP    70.00
            BAKER & SON       ACCO

            LONG MR W         GUA     29      15.00  1     FAMB    1                EP    70.00
            BAKER & SON       ACCO

            VARNEY MR A       GUA     29      15.00  1     FAMB    1                EP    70.00
            BAKER & SON       ACCO

            HUDSON MRS V      GUA     21      16.30  2     SB      1                EP    70.00   100.00
                                              BEDBOARD:DM TO MEET ON ARRIVAL
            BIRD TRAVEL BUREAU

            COLLINS MR T      GUA     23             0     SUIT    0                EP   100.00   100.00
                                              MEETING ROOM 9.30AM-5.00PM.LUNCH IN RESTAURANT FOR 6 PNS:
            COLLINS & CO

            EPSON MR A        GUA     20      16.00  5     SX      1                EP    82.00   300.00
                                              :TAKE CARE, DIFFICULT GUEST
            COM CORPORATION

            WILLIAMS MR P     CON     35             2     SB      1                EP    70.00    10.00
                                              :FLOWERS ON ARRIVAL
                              CRED

            YOUNG MR S        GUA     17      20.00  1     SB      1                EP    70.00   200.00
            THOMAS COOK TRAVEL VOUC
```

Figure 43   *The International Hotel's arrival list*

of computerized system is that the information may be accessed quickly both onto a VDU screen or into a printed list as illustrated. Provided the computer system has been programmed correctly lists could be obtained in many different orders such as lists of reservations for which deposits have already been paid, lists by company names, lists by room types or even guests with specific names may be located and listed. Communication may therefore be extremely swift if the correct computer program is utilized.

Having communicated the details of the expected arrivals to the various departments some also need to know the information concerning those guests who are due to leave the following day. Consequently the second part of the process of communication initiated by the front office and reception is the accompanying *departure list*. This list contains relatively little detail as it is compiled from information found on the reception board behind the front desk as well as that located on the conventional reservations chart should this be used. If a computerized system is in operation a listing of the rooms due to become vacant the following day should be easily accessed and printed. The layout that could be typed or printed may be as shown in Figure 44.

The departure list illustrated is deliberately compiled in room number order as it is by this method that guest's identify themselves when they come to check-out whether this be at the *reception* or at the *cashier's desk*. It therefore becomes easier on a departure list to locate a specific customer by their room number which will also, obviously, correspond with their bill. The list gives the cashiers warning of which rooms are going to be vacated the following day and therefore allows preparation work to be undertaken and enables the bills to be up-to-date by the time the guest leaves. This, of course, applies only to those accounting systems that do not keep guest's accounts ready for instant settlement. Any peculiarities that apply to the payment may be recorded in the 'remarks' column for the benefit of the cashiers as may any unusual arrangements for departure that may be of importance to the *porters*. Probably the department that makes most use of the

Majestic Hotel

Departure list for Saturday 8 September 19___

Room number	Guest's name	Number of persons	Remarks
101	SAVORY, Mr J.	1	Taxi at 9.30 a.m.
143	HOBDAY, Mr/s K.	2	Leave late, 3.30 p.m.
223	ROSE, Mr/s T.	2	Thomas Cook Voucher
206	BOWDEN, Mr P.	1	A/C to Costello Ltd
250	ANDREWS, Mr I.	1	
251	LOVELL, Mr/s D.	2	
216	FOWLER, Miss L.	1	VIP. Manager to see on departure
322	HAKE, Mr A.	1	
346	TILLIN, Mr/s T.	2	Avis car at midday
221	WILLIAMS, Mrs D.	1	Large amount of baggage. Two cases in store.
Total number of departures		14	

Figure 44 *A departure list*

departures list is *housekeeping* who rely on this information each evening to establish the work allocation for the following day. From the departures list the housekeeper will be able to inform the floor supervisors and maids of those rooms that need a complete change of linen as their occupants have left but she will also need a list of the guests remaining in residence from reception to complete the picture of occupancy in the hotel.

The third part of the communication system that reception completes from its records is a list of those guests who are remaining in residence or who are called 'stays' in hotel jargon. The *stays list* will be a straight listing of those rooms and the numbers of persons occupying them for the benefit of housekeeping so that they may check the actual occupancy of rooms against the list. The stays list also acts as a cross-reference that rooms are being utilized properly. A typical layout is shown in Figure 45.

The combination of the arrival, departure and stays (A & D) lists will give all the relevant information that the hotel departments need concerning arriving customers and will also allow an estimate of the total number of guests who will be in residence the next evening using the following equation:

$$\text{Projected number of guests in residence} = \frac{\text{total}}{\text{stays}} + \frac{\text{total}}{\text{arrivals}}$$

$$= 35 + 20$$

$$= 55$$

In some hotels where there are a large number of VIP guests a separate list will be circulated to the relevant departments concerning the intricate details surrounding these person's stay. VIPs may vary from celebrities, politicians or wealthy customers to business contacts or senior management of the hotel company who need special treatment at the hotel. Often the management of the hotel will personally supervise the arrangements for VIPs and compile the *VIP list* that needs to go to certain staff in the hotel. (See Figure 103.)

Majestic Hotel

'Stays' list for Saturday 8 September 19___

Room number	Number of persons	Room number	Number of persons
101	2	249	1
107	3	301	2
116	1	305	3
121	1	314	2
124	2	316	1
128	2	317	2
221	1	321	1
225	1	323	2
234	3	325	1
238	2	343	2
		Total 'stays'	35

Figure 45   *A 'stays' list*

It will become apparent that the communication concerning the following day's movement of guests may not be completely accurate on the day itself. With the lists having been made out the previous day a lot of the information may be overtaken by events. The lists will not take into account any cancellations that may occur or the large number of 'chance' guests that may arrive at the hotel. Some guests who are due to depart may decide to lengthen their stay while others may leave early. Customers may request to change rooms or there may be a multitude of reasons why the original arrangements may be altered, all of which have to be catered for in the process of communication. As reception and the front office is the department that will be aware of these problems first it is the staff there who have to have an alternative method of communicating the changes.

The system that keeps the departments up-to-date with the last minute movement of guests is the use of 'arrival and departure notifications' if a paperwork system is thought to be the best. These slips of paper are made out at the actual time that a guest arrives or departs and may also be used to indicate changes of room should this be the information that needs to be distributed. The notifications are printed with enough carbon copies to allow for one copy to go to each relevant department and are usually stamped with serial numbers, so that it is apparent to a department head if one has gone astray, and may even be on different coloured paper for each department. Each head of department will therefore receive a stream of notifications throughout the day listing firstly the departures during the morning and then informing him of all the arrivals, including chance guests, during the evening, so that a complete picture is built up of the occupancy of the hotel. A typical layout of an arrival and departure notification is shown in Figure 46.

The notification itself, although designed only to cope with arrivals, departures and changes of room, may also be used to explain cancellations, extensions of stay and any other alterations provided this is clearly stated in the remarks section. Each head of department will therefore be able to update constantly the arrival, departure and stays lists so that they are instantly in touch with the business as it is happening in the hotel.

You will realize, though, that a small mountain of paperwork is created by the use of lists and notifications and that in many cases an individual member of staff, either a receptionist or porter, has to physically distribute the paperwork throughout the day to the various departments. Unless a vacuum tube system is installed at the time that the hotel is built there will be an inevitable delay before notifications arrive at their desired destination. In the larger hotels the volume of arrivals and departures, as might be experienced at our International Hotel, is such that a paperwork system is an impossibility to operate while it may be a perfectly adequate system for a hotel of the size of the Majestic.

In many hotels the best method of distributing this information is to have a VDU terminal in each department which allows the head to ask the computer for information on recent arrivals, departures and changes. This detail may be readily accessed from the computer's memory and will save a considerable amount of time and paperwork. In some systems the computer may be automatically used as a message switching device within the hotel so that the relevant information is in fact printed in the departmental offices so that a written message awaits the head of department.

In a hotel the size of the Ship Inn it is probably sufficient for the small number of heads of department to call in at reception and ask the current situation regarding arrivals and departures as long as the individual requests made by customers are not forgotten. Whatever system is used it is therefore necessary to have a written record of the detail concerning arrivals and departures going at various times to all the relevant departments and, if communication is to be effective, 'word of mouth' alone must never be relied upon as this will lead to mistakes severely affecting guest satisfaction.

What other written forms of communication will reception handle?

Reception tends to be the department which collates information on behalf of other departments and an example of this is the method by which requests for early morning calls, newspapers and early morning teas are handled.

All these three items are important guest services and the reception staff at the front desk will handle the requests for these usually by completing a sheet which

```
                                                    Serial no. 90953

                              Majestic Hotel

                   Arrival/Departure/Change*notification


    Date ......................... Time .........................................

    Room number: ....................................   Change to: ...................................

    Guest name/s ..............................................

    ....................................................................   Number of persons: ...............................

    Date of departure ........................................

    Tariff/rate ...............................................

    Remarks ...................................................

    .........................................................................................................

    .........................................................................................................




    Signature ................................ Receptionist/cashier*


    *Delete as necessary
```

Figure 46   *An arrival and departure notification form*

details the requirements of each customer. It is important that the hotel staff fill in the details themselves: to leave the sheet open for guests to complete on their own behalf is a temptation to those customers who revel in practical jokes! Provided there is sufficient space for the information to be inserted the best policy is to lay the sheet out with relevant columns for each service against particular rooms as shown in Figure 47.

From the information collated on the call sheet at the Ship Inn the porter will be able to compile a list of early morning calls and their times as well as an order for newspapers from the newsagent. The housekeeper will also be able to give a list of those rooms that require early morning teas (EMTs) to the relevant maids who will be able to arrange and distribute the trays at the appropriate times. Reception has therefore been instrumental in preparing this information which may be collected in an identical manner at both the Majestic and International Hotels for whichever services are provided.

Communication by phone

Probably the most frequently used method of communication in a hotel is the phone, which may be used for conversations both internally and externally. The manner with which it is approached by the staff will affect greatly the impression that customers receive of the efficiency of the organization.

In many cases customers wishing to stay at a hotel will contact the establishment by phone and literally the first time they receive any impression at all of the hotel is when the telephonist answers. It would be very revealing to many managers of hotels if they were to simulate this situation themselves and ring into the hotel from outside, pretending to be a customer. They might receive a very different impression of the

Ship Inn
Call, early morning tea and newspaper sheet
for morning of:

9 September 19____

Room number	Call/ time	EMT no./time	Newspapers	Room number	Call/ time	EMT no./time	Newspapers
10	8.00	2 @ 8.15	TELEGRAPH	24	9.30		MIRROR
11				25			
12				26		2 @ 8.00	SUN, MIRROR
14	7.00	2 @ 7.30	EXPRESS, TELEGRAPH	27			
15	6.30	1 @ 6.30	TIMES	28			
16				29	8.00		TELEGRAPH
17				30			
18				31	8.30		EXPRESS
19				32	7.30	1 @ 7.45	GUARDIAN
20	6.00	1 @ 7.00	STAR, TIMES	33			
21				34			
22				35			
23							

Figure 47   *A call sheet*

organization rather than relying on what happens when they use their own well known, phone from their office.

It is very important that the right equipment is used as well as the correct staff being hired to make sure that the operation of the hotel is beyond criticism. If one or other of these two components of the phone system is faulty then untold harm may be done to the business. Let us look at the staff first to see what they may do to improve the impression given of the hotel, no matter what the size, to customers.

The staff who use phones frequently, such as the switchboard operators, the receptionists and the reservation clerks, must be selected for their good tone of voice which must not only be clear but must convey a feeling of interest and welcome to the caller. While it is preferable to avoid staff who have strong dialects a clear soft voice is ideal as is the ability of the member of staff to be able to converse in more than one language in the event of calls being originated from abroad. The staff, particularly on the switchboard, must have the ability first and foremost to keep calm under pressure and to be courteous whatever the circumstances, using their common sense when faced with difficult situations. If the switchboard operator or telephonist has these abilities the first contact that a guest has with a hotel by phone will be good and part of the battle is won in trying to persuade them to stay at the hotel.

Some good procedures must be followed by the telephonist so that calls are handled as efficiently as possible. First, the calls being received should be answered as quickly as possible; to keep customers hanging on a long time before being answered will almost certainly convince them to place their business somewhere else. It is also important to identify the hotel in the first sentence so that callers know that they have reached the correct number. Phrases such as 'Good morning, Majestic Hotel, may I help you?' or 'Thank you for calling the International Hotel, may I help you?' will establish the identity of the hotel and start the phone process off in a courteous, good mannered way. Already customers will feel that unlike many hotels there is someone on the line who is interested in them and willing to help.

Once the caller has indicated his or her requirements the telephonist will almost certainly have to transfer the caller to another department such as the reception or reservations. The polite way to carry this out is to say to the customer 'I am putting your call through to reservations. Will you hold on, please,' and then ring the correct extension number. It is then imperative that the member of staff being called answers the phone in the same courteous way and again identifies the location by saying 'Good morning, this is reservations, may I help you?' so that the good impression is maintained. Should it be clear to the telephonist that the extension the caller requires is busy the caller should have this explained to him or her in a phrase such as 'I'm afraid reservations are busy but I will be able to connect you in a minute. Would you mind holding the line?' Hopefully the extension will come free fairly quickly but it is good manners never to leave the caller for more than twenty seconds without saying 'I'm afraid reservations are still busy. Do you mind holding or may I take your number and call you back?' The last phrase is always useful as reservations may then call the customer back at the earliest possible time and the caller is also saved the considerable expense, and sometimes annoyance, of hanging on for a long time to a call that is not completely connected.

Some procedures that creep in as extremely bad phone technique are the temptations, to stop phones ringing, of taking the receiver off the hook and laying it down without answering it. Sometimes the receiver may be lifted and quickly replaced, thereby disconnecting the call or the switchboard operator may accept the incoming call but not answer it for sometime. All of these techniques should be rigorously avoided and discouraged as they are extremely aggravating to guests. Another source of complaints is where staff unused to phones are left to deal with them as is sometimes the case in departments such as room service. It is essential here also that staff are trained in the correct methods of using the phone so that complaints from customers or errors are kept to a minimum.

In order to cope with the many calls that occur in peak periods telephonists must have certain items near them all the time so that they do not have to leave the phone at all. They should have to hand a wide selection of *directories*, including Yellow Pages and Thomsons, so that they may locate numbers for guests or help with general enquiries. There will almost certainly be a large amount of numbers that are called frequently by both staff and guests which it would be time-consuming to look for every time in a directory. These more common numbers should be listed on a board alongside the switchboard so they are always at hand. They should include such numbers as the suppliers of foodstuffs to the hotel that the chef or storeman will phone each day, the other local hotels, the head office number and emergency numbers such as that of the hotel doctor. A list should be relatively easy to compile and will save a lot of time in originating calls. A list should also be to hand of the names and extension numbers of all staff should they be required on the phone or, in the case of the senior staff, the code for their electronic location devices or '*bleeps*'. Apart from a *rough pad* for jotting down numbers there should be a *message pad* for callers who wish to leave communications for guests or staff who are not readily available. The pre-printed pad should act as a check-list reminding the telephonist to obtain the name of the caller, the detail of the message and the name of the person for whom the message is intended. The completed form will then be placed in an envelope and left in the pigeon hole for the appropriate room. Often calls will be coming in for customers and therefore an *alphabetical guest list* will be most useful to refer to so that the location of each customer may be found quickly. A copy of the *A & D list* may suffice for this.

The telephonist should also be aware of the managerial policies regarding 'reverse charge calls as to whether they are acceptable, which is unlikely unless the person for whom they are intended is willing to pay. The telephonist must also be aware of all the services that the telephone service is able to provide such as the A D & C service ('advise duration and charge'), which may be needed for costing some guest calls or the arrangements for both local and international telephone enquiries.

The telephonist should also be aware of the accessory equipment that is near the switchboard and what to do in the event of any being utilized. For example, the switchboard is usually one of the few places in the hotel that is manned constantly and therefore it is the place where fire alarms and smoke detector display boards are commonly located. Should the alarms be sounded there may be a set of instructions for calling the fire brigade and these should be followed rigorously. (In some fire systems the fire brigade is contacted automatically.) Also there may well be a Tannoy system for calling guests or staff to the phone and this must be operated carefully so that inconvenience or embarrassment is not caused to customers. We have already mentioned that senior staff will have bleeps or small electronic radio devices which may be operated from the switchboard when a particular code is punched into the transmitter. These should be used when trying to call a senior member of staff to the phone and in some cases a conversation may be possible.

Having examined the staffing requirements and some of the procedures involved in good phone technique we should look at the improvements that have taken place in the design of phone equipment recently and how these have made the telephonist's work considerably easier. Until comparatively recently all phone calls coming into and going out of a hotel had to go via the switchboard so that the telephonists, of which there were considerably more than there are now, were involved in originating and receiving every phone call. The method of charging for outgoing calls was what really took the most time as a meter on the switchboard was used to record the number of units incurred in every phone call, which then had to be written onto a slip along with the room number and sent through to the bill office for the staff there to cost and add to the guest's bill. A mountain of

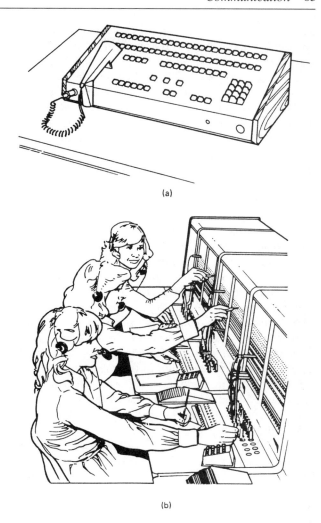

(a)

(b)

Figure 48 *(a) The Ship Inn's phone-call connect switchboard*
(b) The Majestic Hotel's old multiple position private manual exchange

paperwork was therefore involved in phone call charging apart from the fact that mistakes occurred when the telephonists were under pressure.

With the arrival of direct dialling from the guest's room many of the phone calls were taken away from the telephonist altogether and individual meters for each room were placed in reception so that at the end of a guest's stay a total calculation of the number of units incurred by each room could be costed and added to bills. While this took pressure off the telephonist it did not stop complaints from customers about the detail of bills which were often disputed with no record of numbers called or who had made the call. It could be argued, after all, that the maid had made the calls when the guest was out of the room.

The introduction of microprocessor technology, in common with phones being normal equipment with direct dialling facilities in each bedroom has resulted in the reduction and elimination of many of the problems encountered previously. All charges, using a computerized system connected to the switchboard, can reach the guest accounts quickly by overcoming many of the previous meter inaccuracies. Manual calculations and arithmetical errors are eliminated and guest disputes are reduced with a consequent faster check-out time. Individual call details can be substantiated along with an improved operator service to guests and a reduced administrative time and therefore cost.

A simple computerized phone billing and management system connected to a computerized switchboard will list the date and time of each call, the number dialled, the duration of the call, the number of meter units incurred and the total cost of the call at the rate charged by the hotel. This may be posted directly onto the guest's account or displayed in a room audit as shown in Figure 49.

Not only are guest phone calls logged instantly using this automatic system but costs incurred by each individual administrative extension may be monitored so that only vital calls are made by staff in the peak cost morning period, long duration calls are kept to a minimum and personal calls are discouraged. The very costly use of phones within a business is therefore closely monitored. The system may be programmed to provide quick management information on the total revenue from guest phones as well as those of the hotel staff; they may even monitor the unanswered number of calls showing how efficient or otherwise the telephonists are at their work.

The sort of phone logging system that we are referring to may be fitted to any manual (PMBX), Automatic (PABX) or computer controlled (SPC) switchboard and is a great step forward in the sometimes very costly business of charging for phone calls. The telephonist is therefore left free to deal with incoming calls or any enquiries that residents in the hotel may have concerning the phone operation.

What are telex and fax machines?

While most people are familiar with the use of a phone many are unfamiliar with telex and fax machines, unless they have actually seen them in operation. Phones are installed in most domestic homes, but a telex or a fax, because of their use, are generally only seen in commercial premises.

A telex machine is essentially an electronic typewriter which may be connected into an international communications network of landlines and satellite links thereby allowing messages to be sent to any other telex machine in any country. The old telex system used lines very similar to phone lines and was operational twenty-four hours a day so that it was a most useful means of communication between businesses. More recent telex systems, based on personal computers, use ordinary phone lines by the use of modems. In just the same way as for the phone there are telex and fax directories which give the numbers of all the other machines installed throughout the country; there is also access to a local as well as an International Enquiry office. Consequently it is

		INTERNATIONAL HOTEL			ROOM 226
DATE 18/06/	TIME 13-43				REF. NO. 0038
LINE	START TIME	DIALLED	DURATION MIN-SEC	METER UNITS	COST
1	11-20	880814	0-54	1	£0.10
3	22-24	019594168	33-56	170	£18.15
4	12-00	0480523693	0-54	6	£0.60
1	12-21	0986752214	4-43	24	£2.56
1	12-27	7483561	2-02	2	£0.20

					£21.61

Figure 49   *A guest's room audit*

possible to contact any other machine and, provided it is not already in use or switched off, for a message to be sent on our machine which is instantly reproduced on the machine at the other end. It is therefore similar to using the phone with the difference that a written message is sent rather than a verbal one.

The way that telexes and faxes are paid for is like the phone with units of charge being incurred for time and distance. A large number of reservations are placed in many hotels, by the use of the telex and fax as it is possible to receive an immediate written reply rather than having to wait for a communication to come through the post. This is particularly useful if a last minute reservation is being made and a confirmation is required quickly as it may be sent by telex or fax virtually immediately. As businesses are the possessors of the majority of these machines, if a hotel is catering for the business market it is virtually essential to possess a telex and a fax machine as they are a very convenient method of communication.

Two useful facilities that telex machines have are, first, that a message may be pre-recorded onto a punched tape and then fed through very rapidly once contact has been made with the desired machine. The speed that the message may be transmitted using the tape is far faster than it is possible to type and therefore the cost of transmission may be considerably reduced. The second great advantage is that a message may be left on an unattended machine even if the business being contacted is closed which, of course, cannot be done by methods of communication such as the phone. Both telexes and faxes may also be used for sales by sending round advertisements using the machine to one's regular customers as a very personalized method of drawing attention to items such as reduced tariffs or special packages for business customers.

Figure 50 *A telex machine*

Telex and fax machines are therefore vital pieces of communications apparatus for the majority of hotels and especially those who specialize in the accommodation of business, convention or tour customers (Figure 50).

To explain fully, facsimile or fax machines allow exact copies of documents to be sent through the telephone network. In effect they are photocopiers that convert an image into electronic data and then transmit it to another fax machine that then decodes the data and presents it in the form of an exact copy of the original image.

Fax machines have become invaluable in the business situation and are being increasingly used in the domestic market as prices reduce. They have the great advantage of allowing an exact copy of a document, whether it be handwritten, typed or totally pictorial, to be sent to a receiving fax machine very swiftly indeed. For confirmation handling in the reservation situation they are extremely useful.

5 Check-in

As stated in Chapter 1, the purpose of the reception desk is to receive guests and to make them welcome to the hotel, and the moment of arrival or check-in is therefore the *raison d'être* of the whole department. To be able to make a new guest feel at ease on arrival is an art in itself and involves the merger of a large number of separate functions within the department.

In discussing the check-in it should be made clear that the personal approach and social skills of staff are only one part of the process, albeit the vital part, as for a guest to feel comfortable on arrival also involves an air of efficiency to pervade the atmosphere. It is no good having the most personable staff possible if the actual arrangements for check-in are chaos. The reception staff therefore must be well prepared with all the relevant check-in information to hand in order for everything to proceed smoothly.

The reception area or foyer itself should be laid out in the most efficient manner, and the front desk be ergonomically correct, so that guests follow a logical flow during the course of their arrival. The staff should obviously be accommodating, as already mentioned, and formalities such as registration should be undertaken using the most suitable method within the law to the hotel. The receptionists should have received all the relevant information concerning the status of rooms that are free to let; consequently they should be able to allocate rooms to customers immediately without their having to wait around in the foyer; they should also be aware of the security arrangements for ensuring that customers will not leave without paying. Liaison will have to be undertaken with the other staff often involved in the guest's arrival, namely the uniformed or portering staff, and often both groups will have to have contingency plans capable of dealing not only with individual arrivals but also large numbers such as those involved with coach tours.

The short time taken over the check-in is the period when guests build up a mental picture of the hospitality that they are going to receive at the hotel. Hopefully the friendly welcome and the efficiency with which they are treated will put their minds at rest, but this will happen only if the organization is perfect and the many factors affecting check-in are competently co-ordinated.

What is the sequence followed during a typical check-in?

Let us assume that some customers approach the reception desk at the Majestic Hotel who have no previous booking, and follow the sequence of events that has to be successfully concluded for the guests to have received a favourable impression.

Presumably guests will arrive at the main entrance and if they have any baggage a porter will help them with this and escort them across the foyer to the front desk. In this instance the ice will already have been broken by the porter who will have been trained in the use of social skills in order to put the customers at ease, but the receptionist will all the same greet this 'chance' arrival and, having passed the time of day, will ask whether they have a reservation or not. As they have not the receptionist will establish what type of rooms are required and then consult the computer terminal to see whether there are any appropriate rooms available. If the answer is in the affirmative the guests will be handed registration cards to complete, in order to conform with the law and also to occupy them, while it is recorded into the computer that the particular rooms have been let and for how long. The computer will already have been furnished with information from the housekeeper concerning the rooms that have been completed as regards to cleaning and will therefore be available for immediate occupancy. The receptionist thus knows that a room number given to reception by the computer means that the room is immediately available to the guest.

Having recorded the guests' details into the computer and been assured that the information concerning the guests has been distributed to the various terminals in the relevant departments that need to know about arrivals, customers will as a matter of hotel policy be asked for a deposit by the receptionist. This is to ensure that should these 'chance' customers, who have not been accommodated in the hotel before, intend to walk out without paying then at least a considerable proportion of their potential bill has been paid in advance. Should an arrival list be in use the guests will be recorded on this; the registration card should now have been completed and the receptionist will take it back and check that all the items are clear.

The receptionist will then complete 'key cards' which have the effect of being identity cards for the guests during their stay and which will have to be produced in order for them to receive their room keys.

With the formalities concluded the receptionist will inform the porter of the room that has been allocated and the baggage will be taken to the guests' rooms using the baggage lift. It is the duty of the receptionists at the Majestic to escort the guests to their rooms and during the journey in the lift will have been trained to point out the various facilities within the hotel to which attention should be drawn. On arrival at the rooms the doors should be opened to reveal the baggage already delivered by the porter and the guests will be given their keys and wished an enjoyable stay.

On returning to reception the receptionist will check all the paperwork undertaken on the arrival of the guests and make sure that the computer details are correct in order for the guests' accounts to be produced, less a deposit, on headed bills.

This may be the sequence followed during a typical arrival at the Majestic and from it may be seen the various elements of the check-in process. By no means every hotel requires receptionists to show customers to their rooms but otherwise the sequence followed is typical for a chance arrival. The main variation to this sequence is for a guest who has booked in advance for which it is essential to check carefully the details held in the reservations correspondence so that any possible problems or errors that might have crept into the

system are erased at this early time rather than surfacing later during the guest's stay.

How should the reception be planned and equipped to aid the check-in?

The reception desk is deliberately situated in the front office near the main entrance so that it is easily visible on arrival by guests who do not know their way about the hotel. It must be obvious so that the nervous customer may spot the desk, reducing any time taken to locate reception prior to checking in. There is another very important reason for the reception desk to be overlooking the front door: any guest is easily watched either arriving or leaving. An entrance that is unsupervised is an open invitation to guests to walk out without paying or to smuggle extra customers into their rooms so the location of the desk in close proximity to the main entrance will help to discourage these practices. The same argument applies to the porter's lodge which may well be an extension of the front desk so that guests may be supervised and any that are seen struggling with luggage are helped by a porter as quickly as possible.

The desk itself will be well lit, so that the many pieces of paperwork being exchanged between the receptionist and the guest may easily be read. The lighting levels must be controlled so that eye strain does not become a problem for the front office staff. The desk itself will be situated so that it forms part of a well-defined flow of guests during their arrival and departure. The sequence that guests using the departments of the front office on arrival is generally started with a visit to the porter's lodge, then to reception and finally to the lifts. Reception should therefore be situated between the porter's lodge and the lifts or stairs in order to allow the customer to check-in in a logical sequence.

In order to make the check-in process as comfortable as possible the desk itself should be about 112 cm (44 in) in height so that the receptionist standing behind it may be able to fill in paperwork conveniently without having to stoop or stand on tip-toe. The desk itself should have every item required to deal with an arrival readily accessible without the receptionist having to turn away from the customer. Leaving a customer during check-in will give them time to worry so the desk should be equipped with everything that is needed. The registration cards should be in a drawer along with all the correspondence referring to the day's reservations and arrivals. A copy of the arrival list should be to hand so that guest details may be checked. Room allocation and occupancy may well have a 'reception board' set into the back of the desk or the terminal connected to the computer. A selection of stationery will help deal with arrivals such as the important 'key cards' that are needed to identify the guest when they return to collect their key throughout their stay. Do not forget to have an adequate supply of pens, preferably chained to holders fixed to the desk, available for the use of customers when registering and signing documents.

An unusual arrangement for the front desk, but obvious if major security problems are to be overcome, is to place the key and mail rack into the back of the desk which itself must be wide enough to stop guests helping themselves to keys. This is preferable to having the keys in neat pigeon holes behind the receptionist on the wall as in fact most already do, for if the key rack is visible to the general public a key hanging up under a room number means that the room is currently unoccupied. All a potential thief has to do is to select a room of a wealthy-looking customer and wait for that room's key to appear on the visible rack. Keys can then be obtained, making it an easy job to break into the room and even lock the door afterwards. To have a key and mail rack from which guests are encouraged to help themselves to keys is similarly asking for trouble, with thefts from rooms being carried out with ease. The first rule, therefore, of designing the reception desk is to ensure that the key and mail rack is obscured from public view and preferably set into the rear of the front desk; this allows staff to locate keys conveniently without turning away from the guest.

If the traditional lock and key is used on a guest's bedroom door then a duplicate keyboard will be needed close at hand so that there is always a key available for each room. Replacements are constantly needed as keys frequently disappear with guests who forget to hand them in.

The plan of the new Majestic Hotel reception (Figure 51) shows a typical layout with all the equipment that is usually found necessary to deal with the various jobs. Note the office equipment needed to back up the communication responsibilities of the

reception such as the photocopier, the spirit duplicator and the electric typewriter, all of which are obvious but frequently forgotten essentials in reception.

Notice also in the plan that this particular reception at the Majestic has been computerized and that there are a large number of facilities around to handle the technology. First, an old management office has been converted into a computer room, which some suppliers of computers do not deem to be essential, but there is no doubt that if the central processor and its ancillary storage units are kept in an atmosphere that is free from the dust and humid atmosphere of the front office itself the incidence of breakdowns may be significantly reduced. The computer and its relevant files will therefore be kept in this isolated room, making it easier for maintenance to be carried out away from the activity of the front desk which would otherwise be a great source of inconvenience with some computers. On the front desk itself there are two VDUs and two printers, thereby overcoming one of the most common problems experienced in setting up a front desk computer system. At peak check-in and check-out periods one VDU or printer may not be sufficient to deal with more than one guest at a time. Consequently it is almost essential to have a number of terminals, depending upon the size of the hotel, otherwise the initial aim of speeding up check-in and check-out procedures may well be destroyed. Notice also that in the back office there is another computer terminal and printer for administration applications which will probably be utilized most for recording reservations but also for any 'Electronic Office' facility especially word processing.

Security problems will be discussed later but notice the two safes situated in the front office for general and managerial use. The accommodation manager has access to a separate computer terminal so that supervisory tasks may be carried out, keeping up to date minute-by-minute with the progress of business.

Having examined the layout and equipping of the front office we should next move on to the important primary task of registering guests.

Many hotels unwittingly break the law regarding guest registration

It comes as a surprise to many hoteliers that the process of registering customers at their hotel is

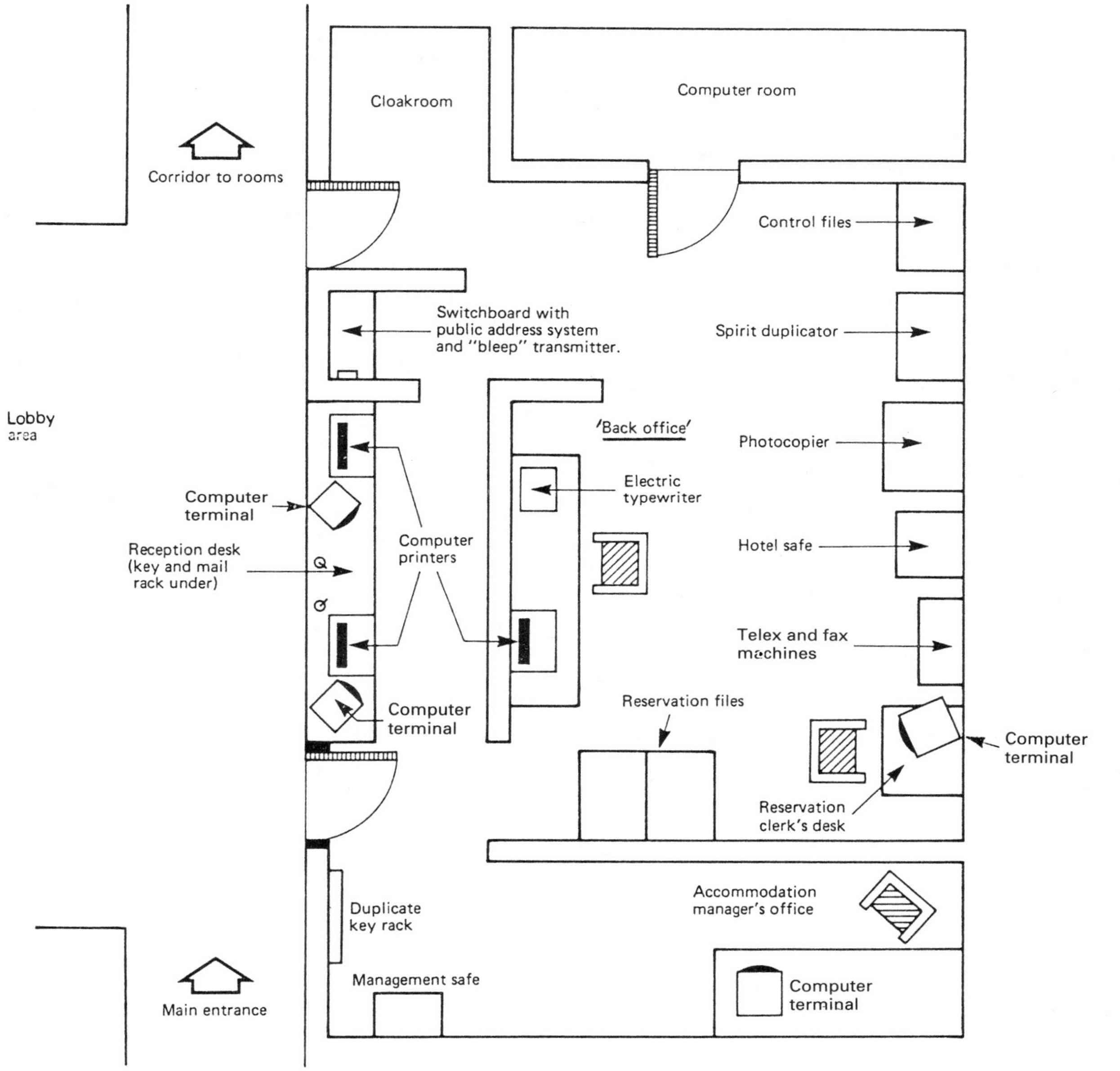

Figure 51 *The new reception at the Majestic Hotel*

controlled quite rigidly by specific items of legislation and that failure to comply with these could, in extreme cases, lead to substantial fines or even imprisonment. Consequently accommodation managers and their staff should be aware of the implications of the various items of legislation and select the method of guest registration which is best suited not only to comply with these but also to complement the type of business in which the hotel is engaged.

The moment that a guest arrives at the reception desk is not only a time for ensuring that the legal implications of the registration legislation are complied with but also an opportunity to undertake some basic market research and we shall examine both these registration requirements thoroughly.

The laws regarding registration were originally introduced as a basic method of trying to record the movements of aliens, or people other than British passport holders, when they stayed in hotels in this country. The Aliens Orders of 1953 and 1957 therefore require the hotelier to establish who is an alien and who is not and for this purpose every person who is of sixteen years of age and older who stays for one night or more in an establishment where accommodation is offered for reimbursement shall on arrival at those premises furnish details of his or her *full name and nationality*.

Legally, a non-alien (the reasoning for this title will become apparent later) only has to give his or her full name and nationality and the law has no requirement for any other information, such as an address or signature, to be provided, which is a common misunderstanding. It is true to say that the date of arrival should be recorded but in several types of register, as we shall see later, this is done automatically and therefore it is not a requirement that the guest has to fulfil. It is a common misconception of registration to believe that because we ask customers to 'sign the register' that a signature is required by law but this is not the case even though it may well be a good practice to ask for this as a proof of identity for situations that may occur later during their stay. It is certainly a good practice to ask for addresses of customers in case a problem becomes apparent after they have stayed at the hotel, but do not forget that anyone intending to deceive the hotel is hardly going to furnish a correct address.

Looking very carefully at the phraseology of the legal terminology it will be seen that every customer has to complete the registration details if they are sixteen years of age or older. It is therefore legally necessary for both husbands and their wives to fill in the register separately as well as any adolescents in the group who may fall into the age range. In case there should be a misunderstanding the law is quite specific that only guests who are staying for 'one night or more' are required to fill in the register, but it is also a requirement that the register is completed on arrival so that, for example, should the police inspect the details those relevant to guests still in residence will be readily available.

With regard to 'full name' the law becomes rather ambiguous, asking that all the guest's forenames and surname should be recorded but allowing an assumed name to be used. This is only provided that the assumed name is not being used with the intention of defrauding the hotel.

By this initial process of investigation it should be clear to the staff whether a guest is an alien or not. If he or she proves to be an alien, in the eyes of the law, they are then obliged to furnish the following information:

1   The number of their passport or registration certificate.
2   The place of issue of their passport or registration certificate.
3   Details of their next destination and if possible their full address there.

The information required from aliens is therefore quite straightforward as it may be found in their passport or registration certificate where the first two items are concerned. It may be difficult for guests on business or on a touring holiday, for example, to know at the time of their arrival exactly where they will proceed to next. It may therefore be necessary, in order to find out the details of the next destination, to place a reminder with their bill so that they may be asked for this information at the time of their departure. Presumably most guests will know at this time where they are going. Even if they cannot be specific regarding an address an area or town might satisfy the law.

The major difficulty facing receptionists is the method by which they establish who exactly is or is not an alien. This is not merely limited to those customers without British Passports; it is not quite as simple as that. It is in fact easier to say who is not an alien. This category takes in British passport holders who are citizens of the United Kingdom and Colonies as well as citizens of the Irish Republic or Eire. Commonwealth citizens and members of the armed forces of NATO countries who are based or serving in this country are not regarded as aliens. Under the Diplomatic Privileges Act of 1964 foreign diplomats, envoys and their staff are not aliens while another category of non-alien is the overseas national serving with the armed forces of the UK. It can therefore be seen that the recognition of an alien is not as easy a process as it may initially seem.

Meldevordruck für Beherbergungsstätten
(Vom Gast handschriftlich auszufüllen)

Ankunft Date of arrival / Date d'arrivée	Bezeichnung des Betriebes	**Bemerkungen:**
Abreise Date of departure / Date de départ		

Name Name / Nom	**Vorname** Christian name / Prénom

Postleitzahl, Wohnort, Straße
Residence / Domicile

Staat (bei Wohnort im Bundesgebiet - Bundesland)
State / État

Begleitet von

Ehegatte: Name, Vorname, Geburtsname
Marital partner: Name, christian name, maiden name / Épouse: Nom, prénom, nom de naissance

Kinder Children / Enfants	**Reisegesellschaft**
Anzahl Number / Nombre	**Anzahl und Staatsangehörigkeit der Teilnehmer**

Unterschrift Signature

....
(Vor- und Zuname) / Christian name and Surname / Prénom et nom

Hoteldruck Rick, 5300 Bonn 2 - Nr. 100 NRW

Figure 52 *Similar information is required from guests registering in hotels in Germany but, unlike the UK, a signature is obligatory*

Up to now we have assumed that guests are obliged to complete the register themselves, but which discounts such customers who may be disabled or blind. It is therefore quite permissible for either a friend or the receptionist to ask for the information and complete the register on the guest's behalf and illustrates again why the law does not require a signature to be given. It is also quite legal for a courier of a coach tour or a conference organizer to give a list of registration details concerning their group to the receptionist, provided it is all correct, so that guests themselves need not register individually. This speeds up the check-in of groups of customers.

The Aliens Orders put two more obligations on to the hotelier in that the registration details must be kept in a written form for a minimum period of twelve months. This means that they must be available for inspection for at least a year after they have been completed. The second obligation is that the register must be produced should an officer of the police or a representative of the Secretary of State for the Home Office so request. Needless to say those people who are entitled legally to examine the register must show their warrant or identity cards to demonstrate their authenticity. It should also be remembered that a register contains customer details that may be regarded as confidential; so any records concerning customers are protected and only those persons mentioned have a statutory right to examine them. Private detectives or enquiry agents have *no* right to examine the registration details and access should be refused, should they ask, on the grounds of protecting the privacy of customers.

Bearing all these legal obligations in mind the hotelier has to select the type of register which will best fulfil his requirements as well as facilitating the best possible office practices.

Which is the best type of register?

There are several different types of register in use, all of which have certain advantages and disadvantages in certain types of hotel. With the legal requirements in mind we shall examine each one individually.

When the term hotel register occurs the first picture conjured up is of a book which is open on the reception desk in which customers record the relevant details concerning their background. The *book register* is in fact the most common type of register in use and is frequently found in hotels of the same type as the Ship Inn where there are a limited number of arrivals over a fairly long period of time. The book is most useful in this size and type of hotel because once in use only one person can use it and anybody checking in at the same time has to wait. It would therefore be useless in a hotel the size of the International. The book is usually leatherbound and may be obtained from most catering-orientated stationers but care should be taken to see that it contains the information required by law. It is surprising how many are not printed to make allowance for the legally required information and which therefore require supplementary forms to be

used for aliens. If one cannot be obtained which is correct it is worth having one printed up to the hotel's specification including appropriate space for the aliens' information. Twenty or thirty entries on each page of the register is relatively cheap per entry but what it gains in cheapness is lost in privacy because all the previous guest entries may be witnessed by the person 'signing in' so is by no means ideal. The book also tends to get very untidy after a while so some hoteliers prefer a system that presents a better image. It does though have the advantage that all the entries occur in the chronological order of the date and time of arrival; provided this is known entries are relatively easy to locate. There is no opportunity, though, when compared with other systems of register to rearrange the entries into alphabetical order, and while the register is in use it cannot be referred to for any administrative reason or by the police. However, despite its disadvantages, it may be seen that the book register is very common in smaller hotels where there is no pressure of arrivals. A typical layout is shown in Figure 53.

Some of the disadvantages of the book register may be overcome by using a *loose-leaf register* which is very similar in design. Loose-leaf pages are kept in a binder at the reception desk and if more than one customer wishes to register at a time separate sheets may be handed out, thereby speeding up the check-in. Unfortunately this advantage does not outweigh the problem of lack of privacy and entries tend to get out of sequence if separate sheets are distributed. Loose-leaf sheets are also easily lost although those

Ship Inn						For foreign visitors		
Surname	Forenames	Nationality	Address	Car reg. number	Signature	Passport number	Place of issue	Next destination

Figure 53   *Book register layout for Ship Inn*

completed may easily be added to by staff behind the scenes with only those currently in use needing to be available for the customer. The loose-leaf is probably the type of register seen least in use in hotels.

A registration system that could be used almost universally by any hotel is the *card register* which has major benefits over the registers already discussed. An individual card is completely private with the guest using it unable to see any other registration details at all. It is easy to design the card to take into account the information required from aliens and any other details that may be required. Being used by one guest only there is little opportunity for it to become soiled and therefore presents a clean and efficient image that many hoteliers prefer. There is no limit on the number of customers who may register simultaneously and should a whole coach tour arrive at the same moment they may all be given a card and be allowed to complete their details separately. An individual card may easily be kept in a filing system in any particular order and the reverse side may be utilized for a 'guest history card' enabling an economy of printing costs.

The registration card may therefore become part of any file whether it be the VIPs file, the black listing or the listing of regular guests. Cards may even be produced on the return visits of regular customers and provided their new date of arrival is added may enable them to disregard registering for a second or subsequent time. The only drawbacks to the cards are that being relatively small they are more easily lost than the other systems and the printing cost 'per entry' is high but this is heavily outweighed by the advantages. A sample layout may be as shown in Figure 54.

Computer-assisted registration is popular in the larger hotels such as the International where the benefits of the cards may be supplemented by the use of the computer. This further illustrates the point that no signature is legally required on arrival on the register as provided the information is retrievable all the requirements of the Aliens Orders may be dictated to a receptionist who may then enter the information into the computer where it may be stored. Should the police require access to the information it may easily be recalled and presented to them in print-out form or,

Majestic Hotel

Registration Card

Surname .... Date of arrival ....
(in capitals)

Forenames ....

Home address ....

....

Nationality ....

Room number ....

Car registration number ....

Purpose of visit ....

....

Signature ....

The following information to be given by a guest who is *not* a British subject:

Number of passport ....

Issued at ....

Next destination, and full address there, if known ....

....

....

....

Figure 54 *Registration card for the Majestic Hotel*

Registration Form

GUEST REGISTRATION

Names				
BRAHAM B.R.V.				
Address: 12 AMBERLEY ROAD, CANFORD CLIFFS, POOLE, DORSET				
Date of arrival	Time of arrival	Date of departure		
3:08:	15:00	4:08:		
Room type	Nos.	Rate	Adults/child	Deposit
FAMB	5	35.00 R	5 0	200.00
Nationality				
FOR FOREIGN VISITORS				
Passport no.	Where issued			
Country of residence	Next destination			
Special requirements				

INTERNATIONAL HOTEL GROUP

Room no.

HOME ADDRESS (if different from adjacent)

Car registration no: ______

Have you stayed here before? Yes/No

Please indicate how you intend to settle your account:

☐ Cash ☐ Cheque ☐ Company A/c ☐ Voucher

☐ Credit card: type. ______

No. ______

Accounts may be paid by cheque presented in sufficient time for clearance within 3 working days.

SIGNATURE ______

OFFICE USE

Area:		Commission %		
Source:	CO	Tariff:	F3	EP
Hotel source:	1	Booking no.:	29	
Status:	GUARANTEED	Date booked:	1:08:	
Conf.:		Pay by:	ACCO	

Checked in by: At:

'WHITNEY' OR RECEPTION CARD

Dep. date

Room no. ______

Name ______

Arr. Date

Figure 55 *Registration form for the International Hotel*

as is often their wish, individual names, nationalities or aliases may be searched for rapidly and the relevant information retrieved.

In many cases the registration forms or cards are completed with whatever information that is relevant to registration before guests arrive so that as soon as they are located on the arrival list they may be given their partially completed form to be checked and finalized. The assistance of a computer is excellent for this as may be seen from the example (Figure 55) which also has the addition of a Whitney slip carefully allowed for on the computer's continuous stationery. This is an excellent example of combining traditional records with the help offered by a computer, thereby eliminating much of the tedious paperwork and allowing the receptionist to devote more time to the customer.

Many hotels make use of the registration systems to glean some extra details not required necessarily by law from their customers for it is the one time that guests will answer questions about themselves. This elementary market research will enable conscientious accommodation or sales managers to compile some interesting statistics about the clientele for which they are catering. Asking for an address will enable a picture of the geographical location of the customers to be established and if plotted onto a map will show areas where marketing has been successful or areas which should be concentrated upon. Car registration numbers will indicate how many customers come by car and therefore whether it is worth advertising in the relevant motoring organizations' publications. The purpose of a guest's visit, if asked, will enable the manager to establish accurately whether the hotel is catering for a business or tourist market and may be quite revealing. It is important not to ask too much so that the guest is overloaded at the time of arrival but this useful source of market analysis information should never be overlooked as it exists already in most hotels.

Once the guest has completed the registration process it is important that the receptionist checks that the items required by law have been completed satisfactorily and, if not, that the guest is asked to do so. Should the receptionist be suspicious of any individual guest then the management and subsequently the police should be consulted.

The obligatory process of registration is useful to the receptionist at the time of the check-in as for a few minutes guests are occupied filling out their details. The receptionist may make use of this time to complete the necessary paperwork concerning the guests' arrival and also to allocate rooms if this has not been done already.

How to establish room status to enable room allocation

We have already discussed in an earlier chapter the importance of reception communicating information to the other departments in the hotel and now we come to an instance where reception itself is very dependent upon the information received from the housekeeping department.

In order to allocate rooms or even to be able with confidence to send a guest to a bedroom on arrival, reception have to be kept up to date with the current situation of rooms and their ability to accept customers. It will be realized that every bedroom is thoroughly serviced and cleaned after a guest has left and before the new guest is accommodated and guests should not be shown rooms that are still being serviced. Equally it should be checked that the previous customer has already left and is not still in residence. To avoid these complications an agreed communication system has to be initiated so that customers may be sent to their rooms in the knowledge that they may occupy them immediately and gain the privacy that they require.

The term 'room status' is given to the information that the receptionist needs to know, which basically is knowing whether the particular room is free to let or not so that when the guest arrives at the reception desk a clear course of action may be taken.

The simplest form of communicating room status is for the housekeeping staff initially to check all the rooms on their floors twice a day. One check will take place during the morning and another during the late afternoon and the results of these two checks should immediately be communicated to reception. Reception will look for any anomalies between their room records and those presented by the housekeeper which may be rooms found vacant that should have been occupied and vice versa. By this method guests who have walked out without paying may be discovered, or more beds may have been occupied than paid for or that some guests have decided to stay on without asking reception if this is possible. Whatever the outcome, by receiving what is called a 'housekeeper's report' in reception twice a day there is a regular opportunity of keeping a doublecheck on the status of rooms to see whether they are let or not.

The next vital information requires very swift communication: that is an up-to-the-minute indication from housekeeping of which rooms have been cleaned and which have not. In the smaller hotels like the Ship Inn this communication may simply take the form of a phone call to reception when each of the small number of rooms has been cleaned, whereas in the Majestic and International this would not be possible with the large number of rooms involved and the number of staff concerned with their preparation.

In the bigger hotels each floor of bedrooms will have a floor housekeeper in charge who checks the work of each one of the maids who probably cleans twelve to fifteen bedrooms each working day. A room is not cleared for occupation until the floor housekeeper has personally agreed that the room is up to the required standard and only then will it be indicated to reception that the room is satisfactory. In many of the larger hotels the housekeeper will send a list of completed rooms down to reception but a quicker, although complex and costly, system is by operating the room management system in each bedroom.

A room management system is a somewhat glorified term for the guest facilities commonly found in the headboard of the bed in each guest bedroom. There will be controls for the television and radio, a phone with message light, a baby-listening microphone, an early morning call facility and a fire alarm system in some of the more common versions. Of immediate interest to us, though, is that there may well be a seemingly anonymous 'jack socket' which is for the use of the floor supervisor or housekeeper. When the housekeeper has checked and agreed that a room is ready to let a jack plug that is carried is placed into the socket, thereby completing an electrical circuit to the cashier's office, the reception and the housekeeper's office. In each of these locations there will be an electronic board with bulbs alongside every room number; and in reception the green light will come on to show that the particular room is ready to be occupied. The receptionist, should that room be

needed, will therefore know the moment when it becomes available. Some systems take this room status one step further so that a flashing red light shows that the room maid is currently servicing the room and therefore that guests should not be sent up until the green appears. There is no reason why, and in fact this is commonly done, the jack plug cannot send the same information direct to the computer, hotel's and then the computer will only offer rooms that are free to let to customers. This saves a lot of time and also negates the use of small electric bulbs which are notoriously unreliable. Another system allows the room telephone, by virtue of a dedicated number that is dialled, to communicate room status directly to the computer.

By one or other of these methods the room status may easily be communicated to reception in a large hotel. The next problem is to record this information and then utilize it to allocate rooms if the hotel is not fortunate enough to have a computer programmed to do this.

In most traditional hotel systems part of the back of the front desk itself is used to locate what is called a 'reception board'. This is generally an aluminium rack which possesses a slot for every room number in the hotel and into which a card is placed to show when a guest is occupying that room. The card that is used may show the details of the customer in residence and will be removed when the guest leaves, thereby showing that the room is not occupied.

In order to cut down on paperwork and printing, cards already in existence in our systems could be used such as the registration card that the guest has been asked to complete or the Whitney card should we have this system in operation. Indeed, a compatible reception board (or as it is called in America a 'room rack') is an essential part of the Whitney system and allows the receptionist to see at a glance those rooms that are currently occupied or empty (Figure 56). This is a common advantage of all reception boards which are generally found most useful to the receptionist who can see at a glance, as the room types are clearly displayed on the board, a suitable room for the guest checking in at that very moment. Should an electric bulb system of indicating room status be in operation it would be logical for these to be mounted alongside the slots on the reception board so that all the information the receptionist needs is in this one place.

A computer is of great assistance to the check-in if it

Figure 56 *A reception board set into a front desk*

carries the correct program because many of the decisions may be taken away from the receptionist when it comes to allocating rooms. When the customer arrives at the desk the computer may very quickly be consulted as to whether rooms of a particular type are available and if not it will be able to offer alternatives. In many hotels the tariff may differ from one side of the hotel to the other, depending upon such items as views and balconies, and charges may differ between rooms which are low down in the hotel, and consequently more subject to traffic noise, and those high up in the hotel which will be quieter. Even if the charges do not differ guest preference may be for different requirements regarding noise and view. Whatever they may be these can be fed into the computer which will then offer a choice of rooms if possible; the computer may be programmed to offer the best rooms (be that defined by price, location, etc.) first. Once the guest has agreed, the room allocation will be executed automatically within the computer and all the necessary departments informed. A properly programmed computer system may therefore be invaluable to a large hotel as many of the decisions are made automatically for the receptionist provided the housekeepers have completed their part of the communication chain by keeping the computer up-to-date with room status.

The whole point of room allocation is to get the customer to the room of his or her choice as quickly as possible and a computer aids this particularly in a hotel the size of the International. It should not be assumed,

though, that every guest is allocated a room on arrival as the system will also have to cope with special requirements for individual rooms, such as suites, as well as the needs of VIP guests. There will also be problematical rooms that have proved unpopular with guests in the past and these will always be the last to be let; also there will always be the rooms taken out of service for redecoration or repairs. All these must be catered for in the system that will deal with room allocation. The system of room allocation must always be flexible enough to take care of individual guest wishes which is why the conventional reservation chart used to allocate rooms in small hotels becomes unwieldy and inflexible if care is not taken. It is a part of the trade, though, in this type of hotel to have to cater for a large number of specific requests for individual rooms unlike the larger business hotels.

The allocation of rooms becomes problematical at 6 p.m. each evening in a hotel particularly if it is the policy to re-let unclaimed accommodation after this time. This is why in the bookings diary that a careful note is made of those customers who have confirmed their reservations and those who have not.

The problem facing the accommodation manager is how to fill rooms and yet keep within the law of contract even though there may be a waiting list of customers wanting accommodation. Legally it is always best, if rooms are going to be re-let, to select those customers who do not have a contract or who apparently have not bothered to confirm. In law they will cause the least problems should they arrive and find no accommodation available. Guests with a confirmation are legally obliged to receive the accommodation they have booked and consequently their rooms should always be retained as should those for customers such as VIPs who are guaranteed to arrive. The best policy is always to ensure in all reservations correspondence that a 6 p.m. release time is quoted if it is going to be enforced. Customers may always advise the hotel of their late arrival and the room will be kept for them should this situation arise.

Another problem that may entail looking for extra rooms is when overbooking has been incorrectly calculated. In this case rooms may have to be found, and those unconfirmed reservations will be the first to be sacrificed. Legally customers, if they cannot be accommodated, are entitled to similar accommodation of the same standard at no extra cost, at a hotel nearby.

Consequently the customer may have to be sent by taxi to another hotel and any price difference or travelling costs paid for by the original hotel where the customer was overbooked.

Having examined some of the room allocation problems concerned with the check-in we should next move on to the security problems concerned with the front office.

The receptionist must be constantly aware of possible fraud

Because a hotel is a public place it is open to many different types of fraud or security problems which receptionists who are alert may often play their part in preventing.

At the time of check-in the main problem that a receptionist has to be aware of is that the guest, and particularly the chance guest, is not allowed to leave without paying. In many cases it is the least obvious people who 'skip' or 'walk out' and therefore the management may introduce sensible procedures or policies which may take the onus off the receptionist. The best policy is to ask *all* guests to pay a deposit on arrival so that in the event of their departing without paying a part of their bill may still be covered. Liaison with the porters will help as they should be primed to watch out for guests with small amounts of luggage which is often a sign of a potential 'skipper'. If all guests are treated in the same way and asked for a deposit one cannot then run into problems of 'favouritism' which is a charge sometimes levelled against a receptionist who asks for a deposit.

It should be remembered that legally a hotel is obliged to accept every traveller who arrives and the only grounds for refusing a person a room is if the hotel is already full or if it is felt that the customer is unfit to be received. By unfit the law could mean a person who is drunk or who is a known prostitute. In either case, rather than risk confrontation, it is sometimes better to simply say that the hotel is full and to make sure that this 'cover story' is maintained while the refused customer is around.

There will also be a large number of details and photographs circulated to hotels by the police concerning the names and aliases of persons they want to interview or criminals who have a known speciality in defrauding hotels. The receptionist should therefore be vigilant to ensure that if any of these people try to stay at the hotel they are apprehended, by calling the management and police, on their arrival.

One of the biggest security problems facing a receptionist is that of issuing room keys, because if these fall into the wrong hands they may make it extremely easy for a thief to break into a bedroom. At the time of check-in the receptionist will therefore issue what is called a 'key card' which is basically a proof of identity which customers show to identify themselves when they want to pick up their keys during their stay. In most cases this stops a thief being able to ask for a room key without having to produce any identity. A typical key card may be also used to act as a small information sheet about the hotel and consequently grows into a sizeable booklet in some establishments. A common design of key card is as shown in Figure 57.

To combine two security problems, it may be necessary if the spending capability of a guest is unknown, or for convenience of billing in a large group, that the guest is allowed to incur items only as long as they are paid for at the time of purchase. In other words, every meal or drink must be paid for immediately and not put through to the guest account; this is a common system for tours especially overseas. Here the fact that credit is not allowed should be told to the guest on arrival. A polite reminder could be placed on their key card as the example shown in Figure 58 illustrates.

Unfortunately not even a key card overcomes the problem that either it or the key to which it refers may be dropped or accidentally lost or even removed by a thief who is also a pickpocket. So high has the incidence of burglaries of rooms been that yet again computers have been installed to help overcome the problem.

The problem of keys is compounded by the fact that mechanical locks on doors in many hotels are old and easily picked or slipped by the use of plastic cards and in some hotels even the master and section keys have been lost. It has even been known for staff to steal from rooms, while other guests 'rob' themselves in order to falsely claim off insurance companies. Consequently computer-controlled locks are now common in many hotels, their being impossible to pick or slip, and any keys unaccounted for may automatically be invalidated. A good system will even

Figure 57   *A typical key card*

record the time, date and identity of the keyholder every time a lock is used and invalidated keys or an attempt at forced entry will automatically sound an alarm and page the security officers. Staff may be issued with a single key and people such as contractors may be given timed personal keys which only allow them access to specific rooms. As far as the guests are concerned, they may retain the key for the duration of their stay and if it is accidentally taken away when they leave it does not matter as the 'combination' will be changed anyway. Interestingly, some systems will even allow a special key given to the floor supervisor to indicate to reception that a room is ready to let, helping with the room status communication as mentioned earlier in this chapter.

While some electronic key systems utilize cards others use replica plastic keys and there may be as many as 250 million combinations possible for the locks. The systems are operated from terminals in the reception office and may or may not be connected direct by wires to each individual lock. Quite simply the key is prepared virtually with a random code that the lock will 'read' each time a new guest arrives. With each lock capable of operating on eighty different combinations in many systems, the chances of a key being used again by a returning guest or a thief are remote indeed. Compared with the risk of a traditional key when it is lost, it is not surprising that electronic keys have significantly cut down the number of thefts experienced by hotels who previously used traditional lock systems.

Having examined some of the security problems experienced by reception at the time of check-in, we should now turn our attention to the actual time that the complete check-in system is put severely to the test.

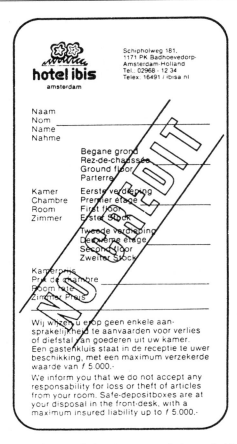

hotel ibis
amsterdam

Schipholweg 181,
1171 PK Badhoevedorp-
Amsterdam-Holland
Tel.: 02968 - 12 34
Telex: 16491 / ibisa nl

Naam
Nom
Name
Nahme

Begane grond
Rez-de-chaussée
Ground floor
Parterre

Kamer   Eerste verdieping
Chambre   Premier etage
Room   First floor
Zimmer   Erste Stock

Tweede verdieping
Deuxieme etage
Second floor
Zweiter Stock

Kamerprijs
Prix de chambre
Room rate
Zimmer Preis

Wij wijzen u erop geen enkele aan-
sprakelijkheid te aanvaarden voor verlies
of diefstal van goederen uit uw kamer.
Een gastenkluis staat in de receptie te uwer
beschikking, met een maximum verzekerde
waarde van f 5.000.-

We inform you that we do not accept any
responsability for loss or theft of articles
from your room. Safe-depositboxes are at
your disposal in the front-desk, with a
maximum insured liability up to f 5.000.-

Figure 58   *A key card showing no credit is available*

The arrival of a tour or large group puts severe strain on reception

Many hotels put undue emphasis on the arrival of large groups or tours, putting unnecessary strain on the reception and front office staff, when there are several clear-cut guidelines that may be followed. The type of group commonly encountered by most hotels is the coach tour when as many as fifty people and their baggage arrive at one moment at the hotel and all expect to get to their rooms as quickly as possible. Where a tour is concerned the way to handle this group is to make sure that the courier or tour company does the majority of the work.

Registration of a tour group through the check-in process may be the problem but a sensible hotel will ask for a list of the guests' details in advance. Provided their full names and nationalities and any aliens

information is provided, this may be sent to the hotel or brought by the courier so that there is no necessity for each customer to register individually, thus removing any necessity for a lengthy registration process.

Room allocation might appear to be a problem but most coach companies will indicate well in advance the numbers and types of rooms required and provided all the tour group are given rooms close to each other there should be no problem in apportioning room numbers in advance.

A problem in some hotels is giving out the room keys and issuing key cards to customers. A good idea here is to make up a package on the morning of arrival consisting of a clearly labelled envelope containing both the room key and the key card as well as any supplementary information the guest may require. Rather than requiring the receptionists to try to locate people they have never met before, the packages may be placed into a container and given to the courier, who in most cases will be all too pleased to extend their personal service to their customers. A typical envelope for the package might be as shown in Figure 59.

For reasons that should be obvious the practice that some hotels have of leaving the keys for a group arrival in the doors of the rooms prior to a tour's arrival should be discouraged.

Luggage is the next problem and while it may be acceptable to some hotels for guests to carry their own bags up to their room once they have been unloaded off the coach it is a necessary service that the porters must carry out in the hotels with higher star-ratings. The porters must therefore be equipped with a rooming list so that once their luggage is allocated they will quickly be able to apportion rooms. The first principle is to ensure that the tour company has informed its customers to clearly label all cases. If this is done the porter may easily fix labels or chalk room numbers on the sides of cases so that the luggage porters may take the bags to the correct rooms. The porter will, of course, have spotted from the arrival list that there is a need for extra staff to be on duty to meet the coach and therefore there will be plenty of luggage porters available to distribute the bags quickly.

The principles used to check-in a coach tour may also be used for the arrival of other types of group. However, a large group, such as that consisting of

Figure 59   *An envelope for the key and key card*

convention delegates, may all arrive independently. In this case it is better for the organizers to be allowed to set up their own convention reception table or office in the foyer so that they may deal separately with their 'flock' while the hotel's receptionists concentrate on normal arrivals.

Having overcome the problems concerned with the arrival of a tour it is time we looked in detail at one group of staff who are vital to the smooth check-in of customers and who are often taken for granted as members of the foyer staff. These are the 'uniformed staff'.

The uniformed staff are essential for a smooth front office operation

The uniformed staff is a term given in hotels to those more usually identified as the porters and really refers

to the fact that the porter's uniform is usually more distinctive than those worn in other departments. The term uniformed staff therefore applies to those who wear a 'liveried' uniform which usually carries the name of the hotel in its design or at least a distinctive style peculiar to the hotel.

The work that the porters undertake in a hotel is often underestimated and for the satisfactory operation of the front office it is essential to have both sufficient members and staff of the optimum quality. The porters are often given a large amount of responsibility so it is important not only to recruit the correct type of person initially but to ensure through strict supervision that this trust is not misplaced. There is nothing more detrimental to a hotel operation than a dishonest porter and there are various ways of safeguarding this possibility.

The first essential to a hotel of any size, such as the Majestic or the International, when recruiting for the position of head hall porter, is to engage a person who is capable of instilling some professional pride into junior staff. One of the best ways of ensuring this is to recruit porters who are members of the 'Société des Clefs d'Or', which, literally translated, means the Society of the Golden Keys. This society is a long-established organization similar to a guild which exists to promote the quality of porters in the hotel industry throughout the world. Not only will membership of this society indicate the professional quality of porters but will also ensure that they are people who are both capable of and interested in giving an excellent personal service to customers. The society will allow only porters of proven quality in the form of experience and impeccable references to join and retain membership, so when recruiting porters current membership is a good indication of honest and trustworthy members of staff who are interested in carrying out their work to the best of their considerable ability. Members of the Société des Clefs d'Or may be recognized by the crossed golden keys on their lapels which only current members may wear. Many customers will look for this emblem and regard it with a great amount of trust, calling them by their first name.

Apart from an indication of professional competence the society provides many benefits to the hotel lucky enough to employ a member. The first of these is that a useful communication system is constantly in operation between the members across the world each member will receive a list of their fellow members and will help them out whenever possible, thereby giving the best possible service to customers. For example, the society member of the International Hotel will often be faced with the problem that guests are arriving having lost their baggage which has accidentally been sent to the wrong destination. It is a common service offered by society members that lost baggage may be traced and forwarded back by a member in the other destination thereby taking a lot of worry off the mind of the customer concerned. Equally the International head hall porter may well disappear to the airport terminal nearby to help send lost luggage to the correct destination on behalf of society colleagues elsewhere. Without the society the guests might be faced with a long and arduous problem in reclaiming their baggage or in sorting out a large number of potential problems which might occur elsewhere. Another benefit is that society members will often recommend customers in their hotel on to hotels which employ fellow members, knowing that the level of personal service they have instigated will be maintained by their colleagues. This may well be a very useful source of bookings to a hotel especially as the guests are personally recommended.

The Société des Clefs d'Or therefore gives the hotel that is employing a member a good quality *head hall porter* who is equivalent in status to a concierge overseas. Head hall porters are often regarded as members of management especially in the very large hotels where they may be responsible for up to fifty staff in their departments. The porter's lodge in a large hotel will undertake many of the jobs undertaken by reception in a small hotel like the Ship Inn, being responsible for enquiries, security, keys and the distribution of luggage among many other duties dependent upon the organization of the particular

establishment. The head hall porters will supervise their staff and are often personally involved in their hiring and firing and they will make out their rotas so that peaks of business, such as the arrival of tours, are adequately covered. They will also be responsible for distributing the 'Tronc' or pool of tips that the porters receive, if such a system is in operation, and makes sure that a log book of all the events and services carried out by their staff is kept in case of queries or complaints at a later date. As so many personal services are involved for customers the log book will ensure that nothing is forgotten for customers especially when different shifts of porters change over.

The staffing of a very large hotel's uniformed staff department would be as shown in Figure 60.

The head hall porter is therefore in overall control, having to ensure that the Porter's lodge is manned throughout twenty-four hours and the assistant is normally called the *hall porter* who will take over when the head hall porter is off duty. The hall porter is therefore capable of supervising or undertaking any of the other jobs in the department and sometimes has the particular responsibility of making sure that customers are collected from the station or airport using the hotel's courtesy transport.

In the bigger hotels such as the International there will be separate courtesy coaches running from the airport terminals to the hotel and back as well as into the city-centre with separate drivers or *chauffeurs* employed to drive them. In many hotels of a smaller size a mini-bus or a limousine may be utilized as courtesy transport and in these cases the hall porter may drive them for guests.

Quite often the uniformed staff are those members of the hotel's staff who meet and greet the customer initially and the *linkman* is probably the first, being responsible for the front door area of the foyer and greeting cars and taxis. A linkman's job is to act as the

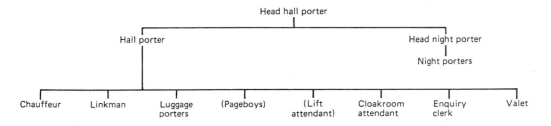

Figure 60

commissionaire, ushering guests into the hotel and seeing them out when they depart. A linkman will quite often be equipped with a distinctive uniform boasting a top hat and will be responsible for seeing that the front door and main entrance of the hotel are kept clean and free from leaves and snow and for ensuring the swift flow of guests both in and out. Should it be raining he will usher the guests in and out under an umbrella if there is no awning and among the uniformed staff he is the one who receives the most tips. In fact in some of the Park Lane hotels in London the linkmen pay the hotel for their jobs because of the amount they earn in tips. A quite unusual situation where hotel employment is concerned.

The linkman is unlikely to have to carry any bags as there are normally a large number of *luggage porters* whose task this is. They will collect the bags from the cars and taxis and having checked with reception will take the bags up to the customer's room. Under the traditional methods of arrival the bags will be taken by separate luggage lifts to the floors so that when the receptionist reaches the room with the guests their bags, impressively, will already be waiting for them. In recent times economies have meant that it is generally unlikely that the receptionist shows the customer to the room so the luggage porter has the job instead. On departure the luggage porter will be sent to the guests' rooms to collect the bags and take them back to the entrance and quite often will require a 'luggage pass' from the cashier before being allowed to take the bags out of the hotel. This ensures that guests have paid their bill and that the luggage porter is not unwittingly helping them to walk out without paying.

Two jobs are listed next which for various reasons are gradually being phased out. Both the *pageboys* and the *lift attendants* have largely been replaced by new technology in the form of public address systems and automatic lifts respectively. The pageboy's job used to be filled by young school-leavers who were the apprentices of the uniformed staff department and embarking on a career leading to an eventual post as a head hall porter. Their job was to run messages and to 'page' customers to the phone, sometimes using small blackboards and chimes. In some hotels this service still survives but it has frequently been eliminated for economy as has the job of lift attendant. When lifts were much less safe than they are now, with

latticework gates, it was essential to staff lifts and, indeed, it was a job frequently undertaken by disabled staff as it could be carried out from a sedentary position. With the advent of easy-to-use automatic lifts the job has gradually disappeared but those who are still employed tend to be in the more luxurious of hotels where they come under the auspices of the head hall porter.

The uniformed staff frequently supply the *cloakroom attendants* in the large hotels where they are responsible for looking after the hats and coats of those guests who are attending functions or banquets. Sometimes, they come under the responsibility of the head housekeeper and, like the *valet*, it depends on the particular hotel organization as to which department they report to. The valet, if a member of the uniformed staff, is responsible for the dry cleaning and pressing of guests' clothes but it is more usual these days to make use of a local laundry and dry cleaning service.

In hotels where there is no separate enquiry desk the complicated tasks of dealing with guest enquiries is undertaken by the uniformed staff and their *enquiry clerks*. We shall examine this work more fully in the next chapter.

Some of the most important members of staff are the *night porters* who are sometimes given heavy responsibilities as, in medium-sized hotels like the Majestic, they are frequently the only staff on during the night. The night porters receive higher remuneration than their daytime colleagues because of the unsocial hours that they work which only a certain type of 'nocturnal' person finds possible to maintain. They will frequently come on duty at 10 p.m. and leave at 7 a.m. thereby covering the time that the reception may not be manned in the type of hotel where there are only two straight shifts. Before starting work they will be given details of any late arrivals and rooms that are free to let by reception so that they may take on reception duties during the night when this is their responsibility. They therefore have to be capable both of checking in customers and checking them out should they leave early in the morning, so reception work is one small part of their responsibility. While referring to their reception tasks they will be manning the switchboard during the night and therefore must be capable of operating this piece of equipment perfectly. Quite often their work will take them away from the front desk and the porter's lodge and frequently they will be equipped with a 'bleep' which is automatically activated by the switchboard should a call be received so that they may return to deal with the call or any emergency that might occur.

The job that invariably involves the night porter leaving the foyer is the security fire patrol that is often insisted upon by the insurance companies of licensed hotels. This patrol is carried out using a night watchman's clock that is activated by strategically placed keys around the hotel. These record the time that each key has been inserted into the clock and therefore in the morning by examining the tapes in the clock the assistant manager may see that the hotel has been constantly patrolled during the night. The tapes are usually pasted into the night porter's report book so that a permanent record is on file for the insurance company should they require to examine it. During the patrol the night porter will be watching out for undesirable persons as well as shutting any windows that may be left open and turning off unwanted lights.

A hotel is obliged to provide refreshment for residents during the night and if there is no separate room service department the night porters will have their own stocks of sandwich-making materials and liquor to serve guests in rooms and in the lounges. It is essential for control purposes that they have their own stock so that they do not have access to bars or the chef's fridges which may lead to ambiguity in these areas if stocks are ever found to be short. Prices charged should be the subject of spot checks by management to ensure that overcharging does not take place after hours. In some hotels the night porters pick up the breakfast order cards from the door handles of bedrooms and distribute the continental breakfasts while in many, shoe-cleaning is also a recognized night porter service. Where possible machines are taking this service over but to obtain certain star-ratings hotels must provide a personal service; if this is the case the night porters are responsible. Another service frequently undertaken is the ordering and distribution of newspapers, so the night porter keeps a close liaison with the local newsagent.

In conference hotels the night porters frequently set up the banqueting and convention rooms for the following day and will almost certainly do the vacuuming and other cleaning of the public areas that are free of customers during the night.

From this long list of possible jobs it may be seen that the night porters in some hotels have a particularly busy time and it is therefore essential that reliable and honest staff are employed who are capable of undertaking the responsibility without succumbing to the considerable temptation of falling asleep!

6 The guest in-house

Once guests are safely installed in their rooms in the hotel it is sometimes assumed that the work of the front office and reception has come to an end until the customers check out on departure. While it is true that administratively the front office works towards the presentation of the bill to guests at the end of their stay there are still a large number of reasons for which the customers will wish to come and make use of the facilities in the front office. The assumption that guests are largely forgotten while staying in the hotel is therefore incorrect.

It is quite possible for guests to stay in a hotel and meet only the staff of the front office as there is no obligation on them to partake of the services of the other departments such as the restaurant or the bars. Indeed, many customers meet only the receptionist on arrival and the cashier on departure in hotels where the minimum length of stay is short or business customers are catered for. Because the front office is the department that has to be involved with every guest who is residing in the hotel it is this familiarity that guests have with the front office staff which leads them to perceive the department as the 'gateway' to the management of the hotel or the 'source of information' concerning any requests or problems that they might have.

The front office therefore becomes the department that deals with all the guest enquiries that may occur and carries out guest liaison should the guest have reason to complain about any specific facet of the hotel's operation. The front office staff therefore have to become mines of information as well as being able to converse on a friendly basis with customers. These abilities may often be tested in the case of any irate customers who have complaints that they want solved.

In this chapter we are therefore going to examine the work of those staff in the front office who are most likely to come into contact with guests during the course of their stay.

How to provide guest information and answer enquiries

It will be the responsibility of the front office staff in any size of hotel to deal with information that guests request and to answer any enquiries. The front office staff are ideally situated to be able to deal with the multitude of questions but it will depend upon the particular establishment as to which member of staff is asked to deal specifically with information and enquiries.

The point should be made that all the staff of the front office, regardless of size, should be able to deal with enquiries. For a member of staff to tell a guest that it is not their responsibility, thereby initiating the 'not my job' syndrome, may be disastrous to guest relations. Even if the question being asked is obscure, the guest should be listened to and every endeavour made to find the answer for them even if the member of staff concerned is not called an enquiry clerk on his or her job description. In fact it will be in only the larger hotels, such as the International, that there will be a separate enquiry desk with specialist staff dealing with general enquiries. In smaller establishments like the Majestic, it is often the responsibility of the uniformed staff either to operate an enquiries desk or to answer enquiries as part of their normal duties. In the very small hotels, such as the Ship Inn, as one of many responsibilities it will be the receptionist who undertakes the guest relations and who is therefore best situated to deal with general enquiries. The volume of enquiries, of course, diminishes the smaller the hotel, but it still means that the member of staff with this responsibility has to have access to a vast amount of information that has been gathered through either practical experience or personal knowledge. There must be a readily available reference source close at hand to provide answers to the more obscure questions.

It is probably best to look first at the work of specialist enquiry clerks at a hotel like the International. In this size of establishment with the sheer volume of customers using the hotel's facilities every member of staff has to take on specific responsibilities. The receptionists, for example, are so specialized that they will be dealing with only the welcoming, room allocation and registration of arriving customers and will not have time to deal with individual guest enquiries. Therefore a separate desk has to be set up with full-time enquiry clerks.

The enquiry clerks in this type of hotel are probably faced with the largest number of possible enquiries the majority of which, due to the hotel's close proximity to an airport, will involve questions about methods of travel. It is possible that the clerks will administer the courtesy coach service which fetches guests from the airline terminals as well as taking them back there on departure. Indeed the courtesy coach that the hotel owns may well have a well-time-tabled route between the airport terminals, the hotel and the centre of the nearby city. Most hotels will give this service free of charge to customers, advertising a first-come-first-served arrangement. Other hotels may charge for seats on specific coaches and therefore a complex booking and fare-charging system has to be administered. Many of the travel problems of guests may be solved should the hotel provide a courtesy coach service and in a large hotel this is often best administered by the enquiry desk staff.

Travel, of course, is not just restricted to local arrangements as at a hotel like the International guests will be enquiring about the times of flights and in some cases even make reservations. This in itself is a complex business as even though the enquiry clerks will have a large number of airline time-tables they all have different layouts and are frequently updated. Extreme care should be taken by the enquiry clerks in dealing with airline reservations as the smallest unintentional error may lead to major problems for the guest should arrangements go wrong.

The enquiry clerks should have an extremely good local knowledge as well as knowledge of the hotel because many of the questions that are asked will concern the hotel and its facilities. While this information should always be part of the induction programme for all the front office staff, as mentioned in an earlier chapter, there should always be a check-list close at hand at the enquiry desk should a quick reference be required. The enquiry clerks should be aware of everything that is going on in the hotel and the surrounding area and will be capable of arranging a large number of tours or giving detailed advice about the facilities available in the locality. Sightseeing tours may be arranged by the staff, with a local coach owner or using the hotel's own transport; advice on shopping may be given or details of places of historical interest distributed. Should the guest want to go to a show or visit the cinema the staff will be able to advise and obtain tickets, while stately homes, museums and churches will be recommended to customers wanting to make individual trips or visits. It will be apparent that should our hotel be situated in a resort then the enquiries staff will be more orientated towards recommending leisure pursuits and holiday arrangements rather than the travel information which is the most common request in a business hotel. In the larger hotels the enquiry clerk will almost certainly be called upon to converse with customers in various languages and may well even have to act as an interpreter. Overall he or she must be capable of answering any question at all.

In dealing with enquiries it is important to keep in mind the local sources of information, so should a guest's question not be answerable from the hotel records there are always other sources of information. One of the most useful is the local Tourist Information Office whose staff are experts in dealing with the queries of travellers and holidaymakers. If close liaison is maintained with this office it is likely that there will be very few problems that their staff or the hotel staff themselves cannot solve. Also the local council will probably be responsible for compiling the town guide and the local government officer in charge of this publication will be able to supply further information if required.

However, there is a large amount of information that may be answered in-house if the enquiry desk and the hotel itself is equipped with some basic reference works. It is very easy to keep an up-to-date library of reference books that will be able to solve the vast majority of queries. The books in this small library will be useful in sorting out a large number of enquiries and will help the staff themselves deal with most problems in-house. First, a collection of reference books capable of answering problems about people is essential, ranging from telephone directories for addresses to be located, to major reference works such as *Who's Who*, which gives details of celebrated people, allowing VIPs to be identified and addressed correctly. In order to deal with problems about travel and various places of local interest a large number of maps and time-tables are of use as well as hotel guides and the local authority's town guide. Of general help in answering any obscure questions will be reference works such as an encyclopaedia as well as books like the Post office Guide. A suggested listing of reference books to keep in the enquiries desk is shown in Figure 61.

Apart from providing information for guests a large amount of the enquiry clerk's time is spent supplying information about guests. The enquiry desk situated in the foyer is the obvious place for someone to enquire whether a friend is in the hotel or not. In order to answer enquiries about guests in residence it is therefore necessary for the staff concerned to be kept up-to-date all the time with details of arrivals and departures. These notifications and lists should be sent through to the desk and an *alphabetical guest index* kept on which the staff will be able to establish which guests are actually in the hotel and the particular rooms. Quite often a rotary display of guest names is used which when arranged alphabetically will enable the enquiry clerk to locate a particular surname very quickly. However, the best system is undoubtedly to have access to a computer terminal which may be used to search for guest names and will establish for the clerk if the person requested is in the hotel or not. If the answer is negative the computer will search to see whether that guest has left or is in fact expected at a later date. A well-programmed mainframe computer set-up will therefore prove essential to an enquiry clerk in a large hotel such as the International.

Should the guest requested be in residence the enquiry clerk will contact the room by phone or have the guest paged using the public address system or a pageboy depending on which is used. It is of course up to the guest whether he or she wants to see the caller or not and security arrangements must be borne in mind

People
Army List
Black's Titles and Forms of Address
Burke's Peerage
Classified Telephone Directories
Crockford's Clerical Directory
Debrett's Peerage
Directory of Directors
Law List
Medical Directory
Thomson Local Directory
Who's Who
Yellow Pages

Travel and Places
AA Guides
A-Z Guide
Bartholomew's Atlas of Greater London Bartholomew's Gazeteer
Bartholomew's Road Atlas of Great Britain
Bus Timetable
Cook's Internation Rail Timetable
Egon Ronay Guide
Fodor's Guide to Europe
Hotels and Restaurants in Great Britain
Kelly's Street and Trade Directories
London Underground Map
Michelin Guide
Oxford World Atlas
Ordnance Survey Map of immediate vicinity
RAC Guides
Rail Timetables
Town Guide
Ward Lock Red Guide
What's On for locality

General
Chambers' Encyclopaedia
Concise Oxford Dictionary
Encyclopaedia Britannica
Foreign dictionaries and phrase books
Keesing's Contemporary Archives
Pears Cyclopaedia
Post Office Guide
Roget's Thesaurus
Whitaker's Almanack

NB The above list is by no means complete as there may well be many local publications and timetables that are peculiar to the business undertaken in a specific hotel. This list should therefore only act as a basic guide which may be added to.

Figure 61 *Essential reference sources for an enquiry clerk*

should the guest be a VIP. In many cases although the guest is resident he or she may not be in the room and therefore the enquiry clerk must have a system for taking and recording messages ensuring that they get passed on to guests on their return. A good message system was mentioned in Chapter 4.

In the hotel a floor-plan is most useful in directing callers to rooms and in dealing with many enquiries about the accommodation if it is displayed in a prominent place in the front office. It is always easier to describe to a guest the location of a bedroom or a hotel facility by referring to a floor plan, so the ideal position for it is on the top of the desk itself under a glass cover. If it is mounted facing the customer it will then be very easy to direct guests.

The floor plan itself should contain details of the various public areas of the hotel that a guest might want to find as well as the numbering and situation of all the hotel bedrooms. Should the building be an old one then probably a separate plan of each floor may be required but in the more modern establishments where floors are similar a master floor plan is satisfactory.

In the example shown in Figure 62 the floor plan is unusual in that the public areas of the hotel are separated from the bedrooms and the hotel is surrounded by a large car park which in itself is a facility that should be shown on the enquiry desk plan. All the major areas of interest to a guest are shown with all the room numbers similar on each of the three bedroom floors. The first number only is different, which is why the numbers on the plan run from 01 to 62. The layout of rooms is identical on each of the three floors.

In order to deal with general enquiries it may well be necessary to have hotel literature available that will answer most problems. For example, it is common to be asked questions concerning the menu in the restaurant or opening times of the various bars so it is essential to have a copy of the day's menu to hand so that a customer may actually read what is available. Menus should be presented in as clear a way as possible, giving the correct impression of the establishment. A bad example is shown in Figure 63 to illustrate what might happen if the management is not vigilant.

The first menu might deter customers from using the

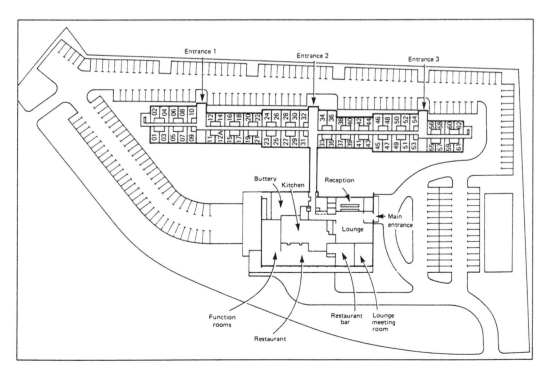

Figure 62   *Enquiry desk plan*

Dinner

Sardine Salad
French Onion Soup
Fruit Juice

Roast Leg of Pork with Apple Sauce
Braised Beef Chasseur
Cod and Chips
Salad

Roast Potatoes
Buttered Cauliflower

Apple Pie and Custard
Ice Cream
Cheese and Biscuits

Guests are requested *not* to pay for drink in the Restaurant.
A signed docket will be added to guest's account.

Figure 63   *A bad example of a menu*

hotel restaurant, as little care has been taken in its presentation. The time and trouble taken over the second menu serves to attract customers whose curiosity is aroused, so if possible the enquiry desk should be equipped with menus like the standard of 'Le Restaurant' (Figure 64).

The provision of information and the answering of enquiries should be organized to encourage 'in-house' sales. This basically means that the facilities of the hotel itself should be offered before any suggestions are made for other competing establishments. The two menus illustrate the positive way in which this might be carried out and items such as these menus may be placed on display in prominent positions or in the hotel's lifts in order to encourage guests to use the hotel and its many services. Where 'in-house' sales are concerned the staff themselves will, of course, be trained to recommend their own hotel facilities in preference to others.

One way of taking pressure off the staff dealing with enquiries, especially in small hotels where the receptionists may be also responsible for this service,

le Restaurant

Situated on the third floor
Opening hours from
10.00 a.m. till 11.00 p.m.

STARTERS

French onion soup	Crab cocktail
Cream of tomato soup	Mushrooms with cream and herbs
Mussels 'Paris style'	Mushroom paté with a green herb sauce
Avocardo with shrimps and whisky sauce	Smoked ham with melon

SPECIAL DISHES AND GRILLS

Fried trout with almonds	Sweetbread of veal with mushrooms
Fried salmon steak with asparagus	Mixed grill with a herb sauce
Fried sole with mussels or picasso style	Grilled sirloin steak with sauce choron
Schnitzels choice of: – Wiener schnitzel – Holsteiner schnitzel – Zingara schnitzel	Fillet steak with a pepper sauce
Fillet of pork with a cream sauce	

DESSERTS

Fresh fruit with a cold sabayon sauce	Vanilla icecream with a peach
Pudding with rum sauce	Vanilla icecream with a hot chocolate sauce
Coupe Colibri	Cheese platter

Daily 'table d'hôte' menus
Special menus for children
Ask for our lunch/snack card

BAR 'CLOUD NINE'

*International bar open
from 4.00 p.m. till 1.00 a.m.*

VISIT OUR

HAPPY HOUR

from 6.00 till 7.00 p.m.

*ALL DRINKS HALF PRICE
FREE SNACKS*

The bar is situated on the groundfloor

NIGHT RESTAURANT

GRILL SPECIALITIES

- HAMBURGER
- FILLET OF CHICKEN
- SIRLOIN STEAK
- FILLET STEAK
- T-BONE STEAK

*All dishes are served with:
BARBECUE SAUCE AND
GARLIC BUTTER
COLESLAW AND FRENCH
FRIED POTATOES*

Open from 11.00 p.m. till 6.00 a.m.

Figure 64   *An example of good menu presentation*

is to print a detailed 'room information sheet' which details some of the most likely questions. Normally a folder in each hotel bedroom will house the information sheet and it is essential to ensure that the housekeeper replaces any that might be taken by guests or damaged. The days of leatherbound folders have disappeared, as these expensive items rapidly became 'fair game' for 'souvenir' hunters and it is more likely that a specially printed plastic wallet will be placed in most rooms so that guests may automatically be informed of the many details of the hotel and its facilities. In order to attract the attention of guests to their information sheets a lively layout should be used and one such imaginative suggestion from a hotel in Paris is shown in Figure 65.

In many hotels the enquiry desk or reception itself acts as the co-ordination point for many types of sundry service provided to guests, including the provision of packed lunches. The main item of importance to remember here is that close liaison over requests is maintained with the restaurant manager and the head chef so that lunches are not forgotten. Guests are often encouraged to order in advance via the information sheet in their bedrooms and a typical example, in this case called a 'carriage hamper', is illustrated in Figure 66.

The successful handling of enquiries and information will go a long way to making a guest's stay at a hotel both enjoyable and memorable and it is a service that should never be underestimated. For the staff concerned it may lead to a large amount of job satisfaction if there is evidence that the help given to guests has made their holiday or trip more enjoyable or if a guest has been helped out of an otherwise awkward situation. Accommodation managers should therefore always remember to select their enquiry staff carefully so that only people who are interested in customers and their well-being should be considered for this important work.

Throughout the discussion on enquiries and information we have referred to the bigger hotels such as the International where there is a separate enquiry office or desk, but in the smaller hotels either the uniformed staff or the receptionist is going to be responsible for answering queries. In these sizes of establishment the receptionist is able to maintain a much more personal level with customers and may even be regarded as a 'family friend' by guests. It is also possible for the receptionist to follow the same basic principles when answering enquiries in the larger establishments. These principles are:

1 To be ready to answer any question a guest may have.
2 If not immediately able to find out the answer for the guest, to have to hand all the necessary information to be able to answer forseeable enquiries.
3 To be interested in the guest and his or her problems.

Why might guests use the front office during their stay?

Undoubtedly the answering of questions and queries is the main reason that guests make use of the front office departments during their stay but in the big hotels such as the International it will be obvious that there are many other services offered from the various departments situated around the foyer. See the plan of the International's front office in Chapter 1 (Figure 15).

In the types of hotel such as the International much use of the floor space in the foyer is made not only to increase the income for the hotel but also to increase the services offered to guests by encouraging outside companies to lease various units. In the plan of the International's foyer, for example, there is a bank, a luxury gift shop, a news kiosk, a shop and a rent-a-car desk. There could also have been a beauty parlour, a flower shop or a travel agent. It is obvious that these are specialist services which it is not possible for the hotel to offer to guests itself so it will be relatively easy to encourage these specialists to lease specific sites in the knowledge that there is a large 'captive' market of hotel customers to which they have exclusive rights. These other services are also of tremendous value in attracting custom to the hotel. Most are now expected of a hotel the size and quality of the International. They may also take pressure off the existing hotel-run departments whose staff may have sufficient work to do at peak times. A prime example is that the bank may, at the time of check-out, be encouraged to undertake foreign currency transactions to help save the time of the cashiers.

It should also be remembered that the foyer and front office are a focal public point in the hotel and that

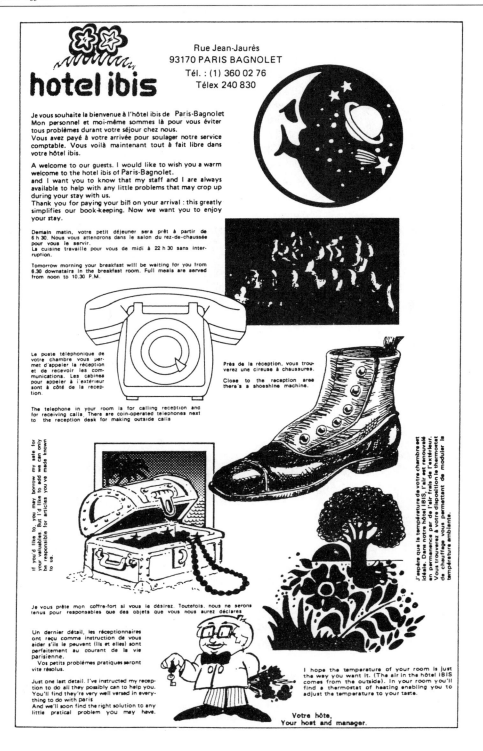

Figure 65   *An information sheet*

Carriage Hamper

Please choose your 3 course meal from the following à la
carte menu by ticking one box in each section.

Appetisers
Prawn Cocktail ☐
Country Paté ☐
Fresh Grapefruit Cocktail ☐

Main Course
Cold Roast Beef with Salad ☐
Cold Chicken and Ham with Salad ☐
Peeled Prawns and Tuna Fish with Salad ☐

Desserts
Fresh Fruit Salad with Cream ☐
Chocolate Roulade with Cream ☐
Cheddar Cheese with Celery and Biscuits ☐

All carriage hampers contain Coleslaw Salad, Thousand
Island Dressing, French Bread and Butter and Apple Juice.

Children's Munch Box
Chicken Sandwiches, Biscuits, Banana
Crisps and Apple Juice packed in our
special Munch Bunch carry case, to
keep for future use ☐

**One order form per person,
please return to reception.**

Name _____ Room _____

Date _____ Time required _____

Signature _____

Figure 66

consequently guests will rendezvous there to meet
friends, business contacts and fellow travellers as well
as using the foyer as a lounge area awaiting transport
away from the hotel. Every opportunity should
therefore be used to make guests as comfortable as
possible should they be waiting in the foyer, with
lounge chairs and coffee tables strategically placed to
provide the necessary comfort.

In a small hotel the same principles will apply but in
many cases there will not be the range of services on
offer to guests in the foyer. Rather than shops there
may well be display cases that are let-out for rental to
local shopkeepers or organizations and often goods

will be offered for sale through the reception.
Reception may even have a stock of goods in various
sizes which are sold on commission on behalf of the
various shops. In this case a careful check must be kept
not only of the money taken but also the stock of goods
available so disputes do not occur between the
shopkeeper and the reception staff.

There are thus several very good reasons for guests
to make use of the front office departments including
reception during the course of their stay.

What happens when a customer complains?

One of the unfortunate problems that does occur in
reception is that due to the familiarity that customers
have with the department they will bring their
complaints, both major and minor, to the staff in
reception as this is where they expect to gain access to
the management. It is frequently the case, therefore,
that the reception staff receive complaints that have
arisen through no fault of their own. There are specific
tactics which may be adopted to lessen the impact on
staff of these problems.

Before going into detail it should be made clear that
the way in which a specific complaint may be dealt
with at the front desk depends heavily on the
personality and experience of the receptionist
concerned; every confrontation has to be handled
according to the severity of the problem. Textbooks
deal in generalities while the individual, whose
experience and social skills are best suited to tackle a
particular situation, is faced with the problem. This
book therefore will try to give only very basic
guidance, for the majority of the solutions are always
left with the receptionist 'on the ground'.

The point should also be made that complaints occur
only if a hotel is run and co-ordinated inefficiently.
The sort of complaint that involves reception even
though beyond their control is even rarer; however 'it
is impossible to please all of the people all of the time'
and therefore a small percentage of total customers
will undoubtedly find cause for complaint. Many
guests are remarkably resilient and will endure a lot in
a hotel before complaining, while others will flare up
at the slightest provocation over something that may
on the surface appear trivial. In many cases the
complaining guest may have a justifiable problem that
needs sorting out but there are also the 'professional'

complainers who are merely trying to obtain a free meal or stay. Every complaint has to be judged on its individual merits.

Most customers are seeking an easy and a peaceful life and it is therefore totally out of their nature to seek a confrontation in the form of a complaint and thus demonstrate a cool and calm approach. However, there are customers who feel so justifiably aggrieved by the problem that has occurred that they are literally furious so the techniques offered by this book have to include both ends of the complaints spectrum.

In all cases of complaint at the front desk, whether it be the receptionist's fault or not, customers must be given time to explain their problems whether this be calmly or vociferously. At this early stage junior receptionists will be unable to tell whether the complaint refers to the reception or not or whether a manager should be called, so the best policy is to make it apparent that they are willing to listen and comprehend the extent of the problem. To interrupt or try to argue back at the guest at this early stage will only serve to aggravate the problem, so by far the best policy even with the most abusive of customers is to listen, keeping a calm but firm appearance. Once the guest has been listened to and the extent of the complaint has been understood the relevant action that is going to be taken should be explained, and even if there appears to be no 'real' problem an apology should be offered. It can be to the effect that the receptionist is sorry that the guest has felt it necessary to have had to complain. The golden rules are therefore to:

1 Listen to the guest.
2 Apologize.
3 Explain the action to be taken.

The room rates, the size and location of guest's rooms and the levels of service are the areas which cause the most complaints brought to the staff in reception. In some cases there is a just cause for complaint over which the guest may reasonably feel aggrieved. For some really serious problems the duty manager or at least a person in authority should be called in immediately as it would be entirely inappropriate for a junior receptionist to handle the problem. In some situations the receptionist may be quite capable of moving a guest to a different room to solve the situation but whatever the course of action to

be taken complaints should never be taken lightly. If the receptionist uses both tact and persuasion this will overcome most situations quite easily but the wrong attitude, such as indifference, will only serve to aggravate and irritate the guest further and may well cause the problem to snowball out of all proportion.

While they are very few in number when the total business of the hotel is considered the angry and the aggressive guests are the types of complaining customer that the receptionist fears most. Angry guests present a great problem to the receptionist as their judgements and statements may for the moment be clouded and they may well become quite irrational with the evidence of the complaint presented. With this situation, particularly if abuse is used, it is very difficult for some personalities not to retaliate. This, of course, must be avoided at all costs as it will only further irritate guests. The only policy is as already explained: to listen and to be sympathetic, thereby showing that there is a genuine interest in their problems despite their exaggerations brought about by emotion.

Should a member of the front office staff be involved with an angry or aggressive complaining customer he or she should remember to try to follow these recommendations:

1 Remain objective.
2 Keep cool.
3 Sympathize.
4 Try to give assistance, especially if the complaint appears justified.
5 Be tactful.
6 Make the right decision.
7 Call in the management where necessary.

One important item to remember when dealing with complaints is to keep a record of the decision taken so that should the problem arise again in correspondence at a later date then a clear reminder of what actually took place will be close at hand. A 'complaints book' should therefore be kept so that potential and past problems are clearly recorded. An illustration of how a clear perspective of a complaint may be gained will become apparent when the following real-life situation is explained. First, a copy of the entry in the complaints book is reproduced in Figure 67(a) which should be compared with the letter of complaint

MAJESTIC HOTEL
COMPLAINTS RECORD BOOK: 3 September 19—

Mr J. Smith of Smith and Jones has been looking for trouble and Duty Managers should keep an eye on him. The night porters advised me that he had been in the bar threatening to his representatives that he was going to have a showdown with the Majestic's management. The source of the trouble appears to be that he had wanted to eat from the main restaurant's a la Carte menu in the coffee shop and was put out when this proved not to be possible. Even if a change of policy had been agreed the main restaurant is not open on a Sunday evening and the Kitchens are closed down. The Food and Beverage manager explained the situation to Mr Smith who was not sympathetic.

The Conference Room for Smith and Jones was laid up by the night Porters in accordance with the instructions received in detail in the correspondence. Mr Smith, even though he had been shown the room the previous night, decided that he wanted a complete change in seating style only five minutes before his conference was due to start. As duty manager. I therefore took two porters with me and we were met with abuse which was hardly becoming of a company director. Mr Smith referred to the general manager as 'an idle swine who should get off his backside' Even though both I and the two porters took exception to this abuse we set the room up as quickly as we could. Both porters expressed their distaste to me afterwards at the exhibition that Mr Smith made of himself.

Mr Smith later in the day endeared himself to the porters when he was discovered trying to remove our lectern which he maintained was the property of Smith and Jones Ltd. The lectern was recovered from the boot of his car.

Signed............G. Guy Deputy Manager 3rd September

(a)

To: The Manager   6 September 19___
    Majestic Hotel.

Dear Sir,

I must point out that over the past few months my company has been very dissatisfied with the Majestic Hotel. In every instance the accounts that have been rendered have proved incorrect and amendments have been necessary.

In the case of our Sales Conference, we were extremely dissatisfied with most aspects of the hotel. Our Conference Room was not ready when we arrived, the table covers were dirty and ripped, we were given only one barman at lunch time to serve 45 people, which resulted in queues and frayed tempers. The attitude of the majority of your staff was one of complete indifference.

Our representatives have been staying at the Majestic since our Company was formed and recently have reported back to me that they were very unhappy and did not wish to stay with you again. It would seem very unfortunate that we have reached this state of affairs, since our relationship with the Majestic, in the past, has always been at a very high level.

I hope you are able to sort out these various problems and look forward to hearing some favourable comments from you.

Yours sincerely,

J. Smith
Director - Smith and Jones Ltd

(b)

Figure 67 *(a) An entry in the complaints record book (b) A letter of complaint received at the hotel*

(Figure 67(b)). The names have obviously been changed to preserve anonymity.

The fact that we are now referring to a complaint that has arrived at the hotel in writing shows that complaints need not necessarily be made in person at the front desk. In many cases it would have been better for the eventual outcome if they had been aired at the time that a problem had occurred, but in many instances the first that a management of a hotel knows about a complaint is when a letter arrives some days or weeks after the event. It is consequently difficult then to rectify the actual problem that occurred as this is now a matter of history. A meal or a room could have been changed at the time but now all that is on offer is a reduction or refund of the bill.

Where a complaint is received in writing at the hotel it is essential that a reply is sent by the manager straight away with the intention of regaining the goodwill of the customer. This letter should always apologize and state what remedial action has or is going to be taken. The best course of action should a complaint be justified is to offer a refund where appropriate or an invitation to revisit the hotel at the hotel's expense might suffice. In serious cases a personal visit or a phone call may be called for particularly if the customer is local.

Both the Majestic and the International Hotel are units of larger groups of hotels and a common problem here is that complaint letters are sometimes sent to the head office. While companies usually prefer complaints to be handled by the individual, clients are not discouraged from writing to head offices. The fact that they have taken the trouble to write to the head office shows that they believe that the company is able and willing to remedy the defects which have caused the complaints. Often complainants' letters are addressed to the managing director, who acknowledges them and passes them on to the general manager of the hotel concerned who will investigate and reply to the complaint. The managing director will request a copy of the reply sent to the customer to ensure that the problem has been overcome.

What action should a receptionist take in an emergency?

There are several security problems that might occur in a hotel in which the receptionist and the front office staff will have specific duties. Should a *fire* occur or a *suspect package* be discovered the receptionist must have specific and well-rehearsed contingency plans to put into action especially if, in the extreme, the hotel has to be evacuated.

Fires, unfortunately, are a common occurrence in hotels but in the vast majority of cases they are minor and may well only involve the use of a fire blanket in the kitchen and easily overcome. Regrettably when the fire alarms sound in reception there is no way of knowing whether it is another false alarm, or indeed, if a major fire has broken out. Fires do not happen to schedule and therefore every fire alarm has to be treated seriously by the staff until it is apparent that the threat is over. Because hotels cater for the public there are unfortunately many ways in which customers and staff may inadvertently start a fire apart from electrical or other faults, so the front office staff have to be constantly on their guard.

It is a requirement of the Fire Precautions Act (Fire Routines, Hotels and Boarding Houses) 1971, that the owner of the hotel is obliged to maintain adequate fire precautions. Fire protection equipment must be tested and the staff trained as well as adequate information given to guests staying in the hotel in the action to be taken in the event of a fire.

Appropriate steps have to be taken to ensure that information about the action to be taken in the event of fire is readily available to all guests. This is generally satisfied by the display of a prominent notice in each hotel bedroom (Figure 68).

The staff in the front office should be adequately trained and instructed as to their actions in the event of fire, which may involve fire-fighting and the use of the relevant equipment, and a written fire routine should be followed. On hearing the alarms it will normally be the telephonist's duty to dial '999' and alert the fire brigade while action is taken in the hotel to delay the spread of any fire. The management will decide if it is necessary to evacuate the building and in this situation staff will be allocated to specific areas to make sure that guests are cleared. It should be made very plain that staff should not put themselves at unnecessary risk. As regards specific actions required of the receptionists it is sometimes suggested that their priority is to make sure that all the monies in their possession are taken out of the hotel. The hotel's finance is in fact very secondary to taking the hotel

FIRE PRECAUTIONS

1   If you discover a fire immediately raise the alarm. The
    nearest alarm callpoint to your room is . . . .
    . . . .

2   On hearing the fire alarm (a continuously ringing bell)
    leave the building via the nearest available escape route
    and assemble at . . . .

3   Do not use the lift/ s.

4   Do not stop to collect personal belongings.

5   Do not re-enter the building until told it is safe to do so.

    NB   Make yourself familiär with the escape routes from
    the building *now*.

Figure 68   *Notice for guest bedrooms*

register and details of rooms allocated to guests which may be given to the fire brigade on their arrival thereby informing them where guests might be trapped. In the event of a full evacuation of the hotel, especially at night, staff must remain calm in order that the customers may hopefully follow their example. It will also be necessary to deal with complacency as many guests will only have a sense of urgency if a fire is very evident for they may think that it is yet another inconvenient false alarm. Staff at night will also have to overcome the problems of 'sleeping pills' which many guests take and which make them oblivious even to fire alarms. It may therefore be necessary to rouse some guests from their beds.

In order that the staff are aware of their responsibilities in a fire situation exercises should be carried out at least once every six months. In small premises where a limited number of staff are available, such as the Ship Inn, the exercise could take the form of a walk over the escape routes, checking of fire doors, the positions of fire alarm callpoints, fire equipment and, where appropriate, emergency lighting. In larger hotels, such as the Majestic and International, the exercise should include a simulated evacuation drill with the assumption that one escape route is not available. In order not to involve the public, the exercise should be started by a predetermined signal (not the full operation of the alarm) and the whole premises should be checked as if an evacuation were in progress.

In addition to all the preparations involved in compiling a fire routine for the hotel suitable notices indicating the action to be taken in case of fire should be prominently displayed adjacent to each fire alarm callpoint (Figure 69).

Fires are by no means the only reason that may require a hotel to be evacuated as another potential hazard that may necessitate this is the ever present worry over suspect packages that might contain an explosive device.

It is an unfortunate fact that at times hotels are targets for terrorist bombs whether actually placed in the hotel or sent through the post. Where this type of security problem arises the front office staff must always be alert to suspect packages. While precautions will be instigated by the management to stop luggage or parcels being brought into the hotel that might be confused for suspect devices, fixtures and fittings will be designed to minimize the effects of any device actually exploding. If a telephone threat is received or

FIRE ROUTINE

1　If you discover a fire, immediately raise the alarm by operating the nearest fire alarm callpoint.

2　On hearing the fire alarm (a continuously ringing bell) leave the building via the nearest available escape route and assemble at . . . .

3　Do not use the lift/ s.

4　Do not stop to collect personal belongings.

5　Do not re – enter the building until told it is safe to do so.

Figure 69　*Notice for display in staff areas and at fire alarm callpoints*

if a suspect letter bomb is received the front office staff will become most involved should the hotel have to be evacuated.

Virtually the same drill is used for evacuation as would be initiated in the case of a fire, although it is wise to route guests away from public areas as this is the most likely place for a bomb to be placed. Equally it is dangerous to make guests congregate in the car park as this may be the place that a car-mounted device has been planted. Generally guests should be moved as far away from the hotel as is practicably possible.

The telephonists are often the first people to be made aware of any potential bomb threat and they have to treat every call as if a bomb has actually been placed and not regard it as a hoax at the outset. As soon as it is clear that the caller is making a bomb threat they must be allowed to finish their message *without interruption*. If any response is required at all, it should be confined to one or two words and while they are talking the message should be written down *exactly* and also a note should be made of the following items which will enable the police to gauge the strength of the threat and to see whether the call is similar to any others received from the same source by other organizations. The caller's sex and approximate age should be listened for as well as any noticeable condition affecting their speech such as drunkenness,

laughter, anger, excitement or incoherency. Any peculiarity in the speech such as a foreign accent, mispronunciation, speech impediment or pitch of voice should be noted down as should any background noises audible during the call such as music, traffic, talking or machinery. This when given to the police will give a great number of clues as to the seriousness of the bomb threat.

When the caller has completed the message the telephonist should try to keep them in conversation and ask them the following key questions but *only after* they have *finished their message*. They should be asked where the bomb is located, what time it will explode, when it was placed and the reason for it being placed. As soon as the call has been completed the exact time of its receipt should be noted and the member of management be informed who is responsible for security (the duty manager) as should the local police. The message should be repeated to the police *exactly as it was received* and then any further details added.

Whether it is thought to be a hoax or not the police will attend and assist in a search of the building but police officers should always be accompanied by a member of staff who recognizes those items of furniture, fittings and, for example, luggage, that might be out of place. If a suspect package is found the problem will be handed over to the bomb disposal squad and *under no circumstances should hotel staff try to move it or tamper with it*.

Suspect letter bombs may be another problem encountered by hotel staff particularly if a large number of VIPs or dignitaries stay at the hotel, but it should not be forgotten that even someone with a grudge against the establishment might send one of these devices so the staff handling the post must always be vigilant.

A letter bomb might be any parcel, package or letter delivered through the post or other similar organization that contains sufficient explosive to make it explode on opening. In practice large parcel bombs are unlikely but packages the size of a book, calendar, photographic album or thick letter are more likely. Some envelopes may be as small as 15 × 10 cm (6 × 4 in) weighing between 50 and 75 g (2 and 3 oz), but most are likely to be rigid or semi-rigid. It is quite safe to assume that any device that has been delivered through the post has been handled quite roughly during its journey and therefore it is possible for a trained person to remove it from the premises in some safety. Special care, though, should be taken if the package is damaged, crushed, bent or distorted by handling and dropping or if it has become damp in the rain. In all cases suspect letter bombs are best left where they are found and *no attempt must be made to open them*.

If in doubt about a package the person to whom it is sent to should be asked if it is expected and, if affirmative, the problem may be resolved. It should be remembered that some parcels take a long time for delivery so memories should be 'jogged'. If the package is not expected the package should be left in a safe, dry place away from inflammable materials and people should be kept away from the immediate vicinity. It should ideally be left in a room with substantial walls and the *police should be sent for*.

There is a remote chance that VHF or UHF radio transmissions might detonate a letter bomb so it should be kept away from radio or 'bleep' equipment which must be at least 10 metres away from the package which equally *must never be placed in water*. The package *should not be carried round the building* but a note should be made of its franking mark, approximate size and weight together with any written features in case it should explode before there is an opportunity for it to be examined.

Whenever possible, responsibility for the initial handling of mail in a hotel should be limited to a small number of persons who are aware of the risks of letter bombs, and who are constantly employed on this task, particularly in large hotels.

Despite all the security problems mentioned, luckily there is still only a small risk that something might actually happen; but, rather like wearing a car seat belt, one should always be prepared in the unlikely eventuality that fire breaks out or should a suspect package be located. The management will be keenly involved in compiling the relevant policies and instructing the staff so that nothing is left to risk.

For dealing with emergencies in the hotel a major problem that may frequently occur is of a guest or a member of staff being taken ill. It is therefore essential that the receptionists are qualified in first aid, which is usually covered in their professional qualifications, so that they are able to cope with a situation before professional help arrives. While it is not the intention of this book to enter into specific treatments the methods of handling burns, breakages and abrasions should be known as well as how to deal with a heart attack or someone who might choke on their food in the restaurant. The methods of helping an unconscious person through the 'recovery position' should also be known but in all cases a formal qualification in first aid is preferable.

7 Accounting

While guests are staying in the hotel they are incurring items all the time that will have to be added on to their bills for payment when checking out of the establishment. They will be eating meals in the various food outlets, partaking of drinks in the bars, making phone calls and having newspapers delivered to their rooms as well as making use of many other hotel services all of which have to be charged for prior to their departure. It is often forgotten by people unaware of the work of the front office staff that a major part of their time is taken in ensuring that guests are presented with bills for all the items that they have purchased during their stay.

The hotel is, of course, in business to make a profit and it is therefore essential to operate an accounting and billing system that leaves as few opportunities for errors as possible, for the establishment can hardly be successful if the bills presented are inaccurate. Indeed, the guests will as a matter of course expect their final bills to be accurate, because if they are incorrect, it would reflect badly upon the efficiency and businesslike approach of the operation. Rest assured that if guests have been overcharged on their bills they will point out the error extremely rapidly and a major complaint may well be initiated that might involve the management. Equally if guests have been inadvertently undercharged for their stay they will still, as with an overcharge, think that the hotel is inefficient but it is less likely that they will point out the error. They may well leave, having got away with a cheaper stay than they expected. The primary aim of accounting then is to make sure that the guests are billed accurately for the services and charges incurred; anything else will greatly affect the reputation of the hotel. The number one rule of guest accounting is that guest billing should be 100 per cent accurate.

All the money and payments that are received for hotel services will at one time or another pass through the front office either for the compilation of guests' bills or for recording with the aim of letting the management know whether the hotel is making a profit or not in its various departments. A secondary aim, but no less important, is to produce up-to-the-minute managerial records that will show the success or otherwise of the various departments within the hotel.

In order to cope with these two aims the staff in the front office, or the reception in a small hotel, must demonstrate an ability to cope with financial accounting. Great mathematical ability is not necessarily an essential quality of a receptionist, but a basic numeracy is a distinct asset as is competence at handling money. Up to now the work of a member of the front office and reception staff may have seemed glamourous but a considerable amount of arithmetical work has to be undertaken in order for guests to be charged correctly and for managerial accounts to be produced. The apparent glamour may well wear off when hotel accounts fail to balance and the receptionist is still trying to trace an error at one o'clock in the morning before being allowed off duty!

A lot of assistance may be given to the front office staff to enable them to carry out their accounting work more accurately and efficiently by a management which is up-to-date and willing to install modern accounting systems. While in small hotels it is still common to find handwritten accounts, billing machines are used for the same purpose in some older establishments and very few hotels now operate without access to a computer programmed to undertake guest billing and financial accounting. New technology has the benefit of taking much of the tedious arithmetic out of the accounting process, but whatever the system the front office staff rely on accurate information being received from other staff in the hotel in order to produce a correct bill.

For guest billing the front office depends on the accuracy of staff in other departments

Most hotels, and even those with computers, utilize a paperwork system that enables the front office staff to know what charges are being incurred in other departments. It should not be forgotten that the front office staff are not clairvoyant and although they may well be blessed with a large amount of common sense they cannot guess what charges are being run up by guests in departments such as the bars and restaurants. Physically the office where guests' bills are compiled may be divorced from the part of the front office where the guests themselves are visible as well as the other departments of the hotel, so the staff concerned are totally dependent upon information being received from the staff in these other departments.

It may be surprising to learn that a paperwork system of collecting guest charges is even necessary where many computers are concerned, for, with terminals at each point of sale transmitting information directly to a computer that holds the bill details there would seem no need for any paper at all. This argument might be regarded as quite logical until the moment that a guest queries the amount being charged for a specific service. Unless a signature is produced as proof that he or she signed for the service – for example, a restaurant meal – he or she will be able to argue, possibly quite legitimately, that he or she did not eat the meal. Consequently even though computers apparently reduce the amount of paperwork involved in compiling information for bills it is not, as some computer manufacturers insist, eradicated completely. A proof of identity of the guest is always needed to sort out disputes at the time of check-out.

It will be seen therefore that in most hotel accounting and billing systems there is a necessity for information to be passed from the staff in the various departments to the staff compiling the bill with the detail of the various charges as well as a proof of identity of the guest concerned. These pieces of paperwork are normally referred to as 'vouchers' and take many forms and designs as well as colour and shapes but all have the purpose of explaining to the front office staff the amounts that guests have incurred for specific services. They are, though, all filled in by the staff concerned giving the service in specific departments and are then forwarded to the front office,

reception or bill office staff to allow the items to be placed or 'posted' onto the guest's bills. They are not thrown away, for in the case of a dispute arising the signature of the guest may well have to be checked to see if a particular charge was incurred or not.

In order to demonstrate the voucher system in the following illustrations we have listed the sequence of compiling a guest bill in a German hotel.

First, a restaurant voucher (Number 41583) in Figure 70(a) has been compiled by the restaurant cashier for a total of 59.30 Deutschmarks. The voucher having been presented, the guest has provided proof of his room number (349), by showing his key card, and has signed his own name at the bottom of the voucher. At the end of the meal the cashier has taken the voucher through to reception who have posted it onto the bill shown in Figure 71.

Looking at the bill, the next two items are the amount for the room itself on two successive nights which is a total of 105 Deutschmarks each night and then a fax charge has been added for 3.60 Deutschmarks. The 'voucher' for this is a totally different shape and in this case no signature has been required (Figure 70(b)). With the addition of another night's room charge the total bill comes to 377.90 Deutschmarks which has been paid to the front office cashier (*kasse*), leaving the bill total at zero.

From this very simple bill it may be seen how the universal system of vouchers may be used to compile a bill.

Having seen the way a voucher is used by the departments to tell reception the charges that should be posted on to guest accounts the one weak link should be discussed. Luckily in the example we have chosen the restaurant voucher was made out with the aid of the restaurant cashier's billing machine and the details were easy to read but in the case of the fax voucher there are many potential problems. In fact this voucher mirrors the problems found in voucher systems in many hotels.

As may be seen from the voucher itself it depends upon accurate information from the fax operator. The first omission is any proof that the fax transmission was requested by the occupier of room 349. Without a signature of confirmation it could be difficult other than by faxing the number and checking, to establish whether the actual guest wanted the fax transmission made. The handwriting of this particular member of

WALLDORF - HEIDELBERG

Holiday Inn®

INTERNATIONAL

Nr. 41583

6909 WALLDORF-HEIDELBERG
Telefon 0 62 27 - 6 20 51

Rechnung
Invoice

Kellner Waiter	Datum Date	Pers./Tisch Pers./Table
08 5842	22/09/	2/16

	3.00	APPL		
	3.00	#004		
	3.50	PILS		
2/	39.00	WIEN		
6	48.50	SALD	48.50	SJ 7
2/	10.80	KU 1		
9			59.30	SJ 7

Restaurant

Im Endbetrag sind ____ % MWST = DM ________ und das Bedienungsgeld enthalten
Inclusive Service and Taxes

Nur die von der Registnerkasse gedruckten
Beträge gelten als Quittung
Only printed amounts are valid

TOTAL: 59.30

Zimmer-Nr./Room-No.: 349

Unterschrift Gast/Signature Guest

Unterschrift Kellner/Signature Waiter

(a)

Fernsprechgebühren-Rechnung incl. MWSt

GEBUCHT

Datum Uhrzeit	Zimmer Nr	*)	Gespräch mit Amt	Vorwahl Nr.	Teilnehmer Nr.	Betrag	dankend erhalten	Betrag auf Hotel-rechn.
25.9	349		Fax — Nancy					3.60

(b)

Figure 70 *(a) The restaurant voucher which could also be used as a bill for a cash transaction for a non-resident (b) The fax voucher*

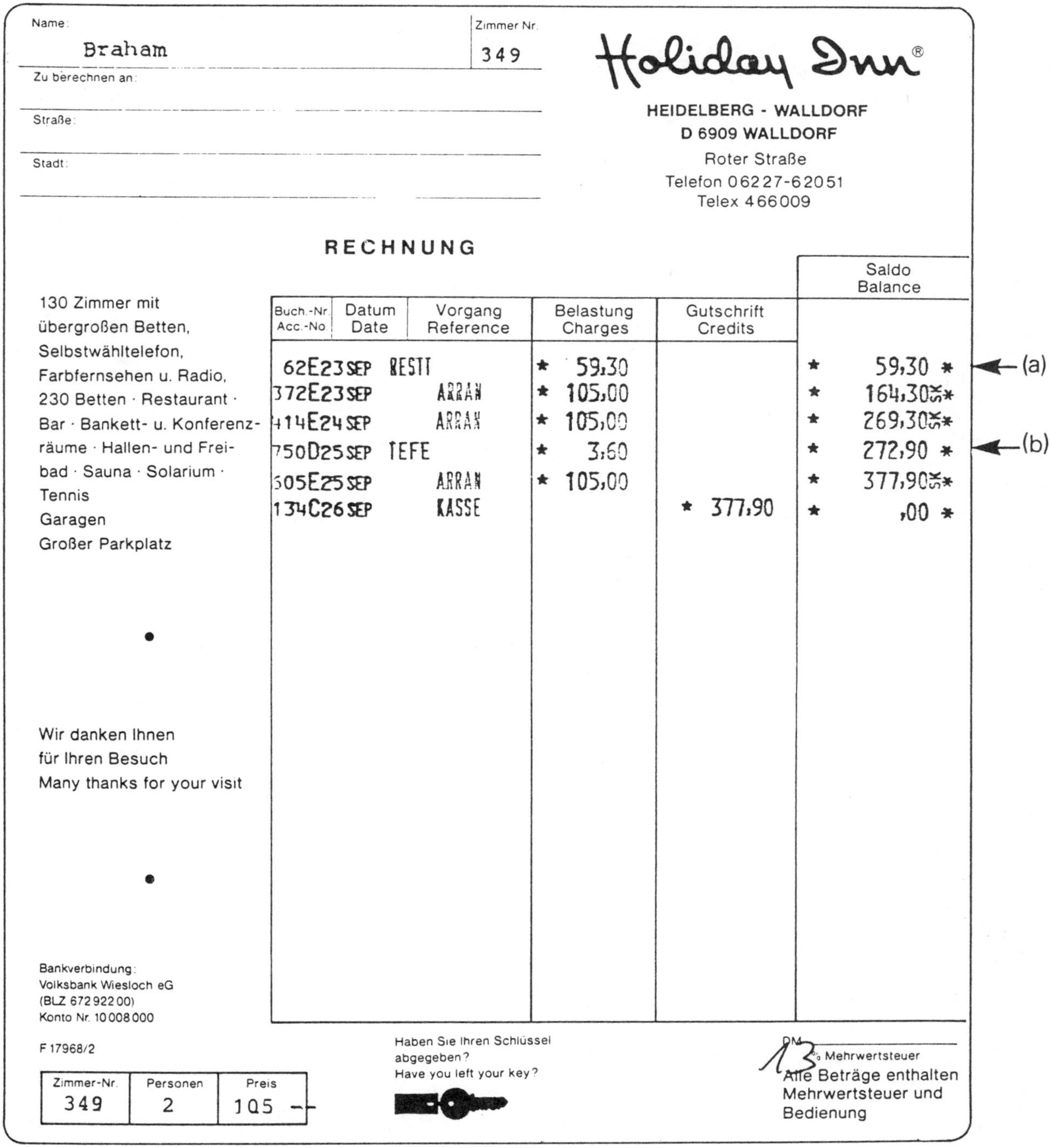

Name: Braham

Zimmer Nr. 349

Zu berechnen an:

Straße:

Stadt:

Holiday Inn®

HEIDELBERG - WALLDORF
D 6909 WALLDORF
Roter Straße
Telefon 06227-62051
Telex 466009

RECHNUNG

130 Zimmer mit übergroßen Betten, Selbstwähltelefon, Farbfernsehen u. Radio, 230 Betten · Restaurant · Bar · Bankett- u. Konferenzräume · Hallen- und Freibad · Sauna · Solarium · Tennis
Garagen
Großer Parkplatz

Buch.-Nr. Acc.-No.	Datum Date	Vorgang Reference	Belastung Charges	Gutschrift Credits	Saldo Balance	
62E	23SEP	RESTT	* 59,30		* 59,30 *	(a)
372E	23SEP	ARRAN	* 105,00		* 164,30 *	
414E	24SEP	ARRAN	* 105,00		* 269,30 *	
750D	25SEP	TEFE	* 3,60		* 272,90 *	(b)
505E	25SEP	ARRAN	* 105,00		* 377,90 *	
134C	26SEP	KASSE		* 377,90	* ,00 *	

Wir danken Ihnen
für Ihren Besuch
Many thanks for your visit

Bankverbindung:
Volksbank Wiesloch eG
(BLZ 672 922 00)
Konto Nr. 10 008 000

F 17968/2

Zimmer-Nr.	Personen	Preis
349	2	105 --

Haben Sie Ihren Schlüssel abgegeben?
Have you left your key?

DM
13 % Mehrwertsteuer
Alle Beträge enthalten Mehrwertsteuer und Bedienung

Figure 71 *The bill as presented to the guest. Line (a) shows the entry of the restaurant voucher (Figure 64(a)) and line (b) the inclusion of the telex charge (Figure 64(b))*

staff is not a problem – the figures are quite clear – but what could have happened had they been in a hurry or under great pressure? It would be very easy for a wrong charge or a wrong room number to be entered or for these to be difficult for the receptionist receiving the voucher to read. It is by no means unknown for vouchers to be made out and the room number or name of the guest concerned to be forgotten. In order to make the books balance in a case like this a disreputable fax operator might put any customer's room number on the voucher. In extreme cases a customer who had previously upset the member of staff might even be selected for this treatment. In their innocence the front office staff will post the details given to them and unless customers spot mistakes on their bill when they are checking out it may well go undetected.

With many vouchers being made out throughout the hotel by a wide variety of staff, with varying degrees of handwriting, there are plenty of opportunities for mistakes, deliberate or otherwise. It is therefore obvious that the front office staff may have acute problems deciphering vouchers and may inadvertently pass on errors given to them by other hotel staff.

From Figure 72 it may be seen that during a typical stay in the hotel a single guest bill could have contributions in the way of charges from vouchers added to it from a myriad of different sources and staff. With so many charges coming from all over the hotel to those staff compiling the bill there are many opportunities for the miscalculation or mis-reading of vouchers and the consequent undercharging or overcharging of guests. Some people might suggest that it is virtually a miracle that any guest's bills produced are completely accurate, but provided *all* the hotel staff are trained properly it is possible to be accurate in the vast majority of cases.

Which type of guest billing system should I use?

There are basically three types of billing system that a hotelier may contemplate, all of which facilitate the detailed recording of guest charges thereby allowing a guest bill to be produced which also gives the management an analysis of the revenue being earned in each department daily. The three types of billing

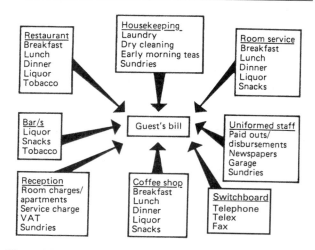

Figure 72   *The information process involved in compiling a guest's bill*

system available are the *tabular ledger* or *transcript*, the *billing machine* and *the computer*. The one selected depends largely on the type and size of hotel to which it is being applied.

A small resort hotel of twenty-five rooms such as the Ship Inn is the largest of hotels in which a manual ledger could be used. With modern technology available consistently reducing the cost it is pointless to continue with the tedium of a system like 'tab' relying on handwritten accounts in hotels larger than twenty-five rooms. Indeed many hotels as small as or even smaller than twenty-five rooms now make use of personal computer systems to handle accounts. With business in the Ship Inn being generally for prolonged periods and with a large number of those customers staying on inclusive tariffs there will be relatively little in the way of calculations to carry out on each guest's bill. As the majority of customers check-out on the Saturday 'changeover day' bills will be prepared in readiness and there will be little requirement for guest accounts to be instantly available at other times. In this size of hotel the handwritten manual tabular ledger system of guest accounting is quite adequate.

The Majestic Hotel, on the other hand, with 150 bedrooms and providing the full five-star service to guests staying for many differing lengths of time will have to utilize a much more complex system of guest billing. This is the type of hotel which may make adequate use of a billing machine relying on a microprocessor but is more likely to use a fully computerised accounting system. Not only will a multitude of vouchers be arriving in reception from a large number of departments but being a five-star hotel there will be a wide variety of complex charges that have to be recorded. Guests will be coming and going throughout the week and therefore there is a requirement to have their bills instantly available especially as a large number of businesspeople are accommodated. Businesspeople are notorious for changing their arrangements at a moment's notice and therefore the billing system has to be both quick and adaptable. There is little point in utilizing a 'tab' which is certainly not known for its flexibility or speed; therefore a computer would be very helpful to accommodate the Majestic's business.

The Majestic is the size and type of hotel that lends itself to computerization and in many similar establishments this very solution to guest billing has been taken. A personal computer or network might be utilized to compile guests' accounts. The International Hotel, in contrast, is the size of establishment that of necessity requires a complex mini-computer system. This 600-bedroomed hotel with an average guest stay of one or two nights needs an extremely efficient system capable of dealing with an almost total turnround of customers within twenty-four hours. Needless to say, a mini-computer is virtually essential but so reliant will the hotel be upon the computer that there will be a necessity for it to be totally reliable. One cannot, after all, ask one's customers to stop checking out and to come back later when the computer is back in service so it will be common for there to be a standby system to take over in the event of the main computer breaking down. This tandem system of operation will be essential in a hotel the size of the International, with all its guests billing.

The Ship Inn's tabular ledger billing system

The Ship Inn's tabular ledger is typical of handwritten billing systems that may be found in many hotels of a similar type and size and is ideally suited to this type of establishment.

The tabular ledger itself, as its name suggests, is a piece of paper on which all the financial transactions that are carried out by reception during the course of a single day may be tabulated or recorded. It is important to realize that each individual sheet of the ledger carries a single day's business in the hotel. The ledger system, though, is continuous as it has to be able to record the charges incurred by guests over a period of time. Yesterday's charges for each guest are therefore recorded in the 'brought forward' column and the total of today's business will be placed into the 'carried forward' column to be transferred onto tomorrow's tabular ledger in its 'brought forward'. The process of recording a long stay and all its consequent transactions is therefore continuous. This is illustrated in Figure 73.

The whole concept of the tabular ledger is that entries are made against the particular room numbers and under the headings which best describe the transactions that have been undertaken on behalf of the guest. Therefore on the right-hand side of the ledger there will appear each night the running total of each guest's bill and along the bottom will be the total amounts of money that have been 'taken' in each department during the day. The two main principles of an effective guest billing system have therefore been accommodated.

As illustrated in Figure 74 it should be realized that the tabular ledger will balance arithmetically whatever the financial amounts recorded on it. While a ledger will always balance it does not necessarily mean that

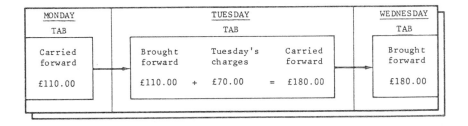

Figure 73

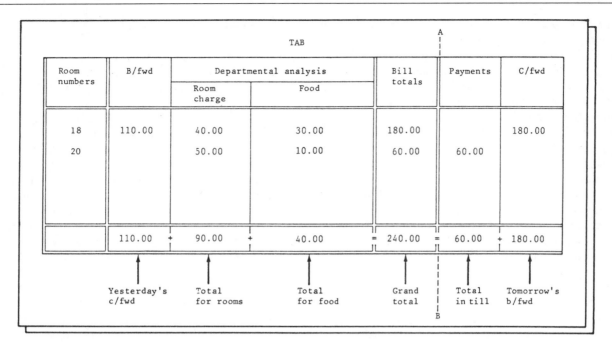

Figure 74

the amounts that have been placed onto the 'tab' initially were correct. There is no excuse though for the ledger not to balance arithmetically.

From Figure 74 it will be apparent that the all important balancing figure is the £240.00 which may be achieved by adding the bill total downwards and also by adding the total amount of the brought forward column to the totals of the departmental analysis thereby allowing the grand total to be a double check. Do not forget that this figure should always agree mathematically even if the initial entries are incorrect. It will also be seen in the illustration that for the first time we have introduced payments in the column after the grand total. Every day some guests may leave and there will therefore be no reason to have a carried forward figure for them as they have paid and left. As a consequence the tab will allow for the payments to be shown as well as the carried forward figures for those guests who are staying on. As a mathematical check the grand total as well as the individual bill totals should always balance with the entries on the right-hand side of line A-B and it may be seen that this is in fact the case as they do indeed add back to £240.

There is very little more to explain about the basic idea of apportioning charges to the appropriate departmental analysis and room number as the relevant vouchers come through to the receptionist at the Ship other than to say that cash transactions, such as the money taken in the Ship's bars, may also be recorded onto the tab using a departmental description rather than a room number. This may be carried out as shown in Figure 75.

The takings from the lounge bar have therefore been added in as could any other financial amount not apportionable to individual room numbers, such as 'chance' meals in the restaurant or amounts for conferences or meetings. All that is needed is an appropriate description in the initial column. Where the payments are concerned it may be seen that in this example we have differentiated between cash and ledger as regards methods of payment. In practice this means that any payment which we can pay into our bank account immediately will be recorded in the cash column. Methods of payment included here would be sterling and foreign currency, postal orders, current account cheques and travellers cheques. The ledger is reserved for credit payments by which the hotel does not in fact receive payment immediately. Items included here would be credit cards, company or ledger accounts and travel agency vouchers. These

TAB

Room numbers	B/fwd	Departmental analysis			Bill totals	Payments		C/fwd
		Room charge	Food	Liquor		Cash	Ledger	
18	110.00	40.00	30.00		180.00			180.00
20		50.00	10.00		60.00	60.00		
Lounge bar				100.00	100.00	100.00		
	110.00	90.00	40.00	100.00	340.00	160.00		180.00

Figure 75

amounts would be transferred to the ledger clerk, or, in this case, the Manager at the Ship, who would receive payment at the end of the appropriate accounting period whenever that may be. This extra analysis is necessary to be more specific within the accounts.

The basic principles behind placing entries onto the tabular ledger should now be clear and it will be realized that the ledger itself is the accounting record that remains in the possession of the hotel. The bill that the guest receives is made out separately from the figures produced on the 'tab' and in most cases is copied from the 'tab' unless a system such as the Kalamazoo is utilized. In this case the bill is provided automatically as it is literally a carbon copy of the tab with all the paperwork lined up on a board, by means of the specially located perforations. As the tab is completed so is the customer's bill underneath.

You will see from the two tabular ledgers reproduced in Figures 76 and 77 that there are two different types of layout commonly referred to as the 'horizontal' tabular ledger and the 'vertical' tabular ledger with selection depending upon personal preference. In Figures 76 and 77 the Ship's tab is a horizontal layout and the Hotel and Catering College of Technology is a vertical example as well as being an illustration of the Kalamazoo system (Figure 78).

Mathematically they both follow the same principles.

It will also be seen that a lot of detail is shown on the ledgers where the departmental analysis is concerned and again this is dependent totally upon the needs and preferences of particular hoteliers and the level of analysis or detail that is felt to be necessary.

While it is apparent that the tabular ledger is an adequate billing system for the Ship Inn it would be foolish to try to use it in a bigger hotel or a hotel where the business was substantially different. For the Ship the tab is a relatively cheap system as there is only paper involved with none of the heavy overheads necessary to operate any type of electrical system. As far as the single receptionist is concerned the tab is a simple system with relatively few complications. It also does not require the receptionist to have any specialist skills or involve any lengthy training.

There are problems though with the tab, many of which occur if it is used in any type of establishment larger than the twenty-five bedrooms of the Ship. First, the opportunities for making errors are enormous especially if the system used involves copying figures from the tab onto a separate bill. Just the act of copying offers several possibilities that may lead to time-consuming mistakes. Time is another factor with the tab in that even with the aid of an adding machine or

The Ship Inn   DATE 26 SEPTEMBER

Room no.	Name	Rate	B/f	Apartments	Pension	Breakfasts	Lunches	Teas	Dinners	Early teas	Beverages	Wines	Spirits and liqueurs	Beers	Minerals	Telephones	TOTAL	Cash	Allowances	Ledger	Balance c/f
24	MR F. BETTS		112 82	30 00	28 00			48		40						90	172 60				172 60
10	FLT LT/MRS PHIPPS		38 90				25 40			60							64 90	64 90			
33	MRS JOHNS		177 46	34 00	36 00			96		40						2 00	246 82				248 82
26	MRS COWBURN		99 18							40							99 58			99 58	
21	MR/S L. SMITH		69 12	42 60		7 50	20 70	1 44		1 20							142 44				142 44
29	REV. J. SMART		60 44							40							61 04	61 04			
18	MR/S JENNINGS		43 52	34 00	36 00			96		80							115 28		20 00		95 28
16	MRS BOWLES		68 24							40							68 64	68 64			
34	MR/S JACKSON		238 44	35 00		6 00	25 40	96		80							306 80				305 90
32	DR D. CLARK		265 78	28 00	7 00			48		40							301 66				301 66
23	MRS SMITH		60 00							40						3 06	63 46	63 46			
15	MISS M. CARRUTHERS		62 00	20 50		2 60	22 70	48		90						4 70	123 68				123 68
11	MR/S B. HALLOWS			34 00	36 00			96									70 96				70 96
20	MR/S B. HORN			38 00		5 00	25 40										68 40				68 40
28	MR/S GILLESPIE			34 00	36 00												70 00				70 00
	RESTAURANT																				
	LUNCHEON						147 84					43 20	51 12	5 64			214 80	214 80			
	DINNER								47 44			151 04	73 80	63 40	14 62	10 76	777 60	662 24		115 26	
			1296 30	340 00	179 00	20 00	267 44	6 72	47 44	7 00		194 24	88 92	72 04	14 62	10 76	2948 58	1136 08	20 00	214 84	1400 66

Figure 76   *The Ship Inn's horizontal' tabular ledger*

calculator a substantial amount of time is required to balance the mathematics, even with as few rooms as twenty-five. In some cases hoteliers expect the receptionist to balance the tab without outside aid and then the mental arithmetic involved is tremendous and in itself leads to errors. If one is copying figures there is unnecessary duplication of work which is again time-wasting and as far as many staff are concerned adding figures sideways or 'cross-casting' is very difficult and again leads to possible errors. In columns like the 'phone' there is very little room for more than one entry to be made and if several are consequently squeezed in this may lead to difficulty of reading and therefore balancing the tab. All through the system one is reliant upon the receptionist using perfectly legible figures but often misreading handwriting is a source of mistakes. Handwriting is also important when the bill is presented. Some hoteliers do not like handwritten bills as they appear amateurish and unless the staff write perfectly are often untidy (Figure 79).

The opportunity for errors has been adequately demonstrated and even in the well-presented bill from the 'Hotel garni Gunther' it will be seen that there are places where the figures could be misread and a wrong total reached. Errors or mistakes will eventually lead to the accounts not balancing correctly and this in itself is a source of great aggravation to reception staff. Invariably they have to start again to try to trace an error.

It is often the case that the accounts are being balanced late at night after all the money has been paid in from the various departments in the hotel. Needless to say the receptionists are keen to go off duty and this is not the time that they want to be faced with serious accounting problems. It is therefore not surprising that they will be preoccupied during the day with making sure that their tab balances, as this will necessarily enable them to finish work as quickly as possible. This preoccupation may well become an overriding priority and in some cases this will obviously detract from the personal relations that they have with customers. An arriving customer might well be ignored, for example, until the all-important tab calculation is completed. The system itself therefore may have criticism levelled at it compared with other systems of guest accounting that we are shortly to examine. There is no doubt that once embarked upon balancing the tab the receptionist will not take kindly to interruptions but in a busy reception office these are bound to occur whether in the form of an enquiring guest or with a phone needing answering. The tab, although entirely suitable for a small resort operation where customers stay a long time, is therefore not a system to be utilized in any establishment of more than twenty-five rooms especially if guests are short-stay.

The only exception to this rule is when the billing machine or computer in a larger hotel has broken down and a manual system has to be reintroduced. An accommodation manager must then know the way in which a tabular ledger is compiled and operated in case of emergency when he needs a back-up guest accounting system.

The Majestic Hotel's old billing machine for guests' accounts

When the Majestic was first built it too used a tabular ledger system for recording the charges that guests incurred during their stay and to produce the bills for guests on departure. Not only were a considerable number of staff employed to enable this system to be accurate in recording the charges for 150 rooms but it was often felt by the progressive management that there must be a more efficient system of guest accounting. When billing machines were introduced in the 1950s the Majestic was one of the first hotels to invest in what was then a major advance in modern technology – an electromechanical billing machine – and straight away the service to guests improved and the number of staff needed in the reception was reduced.

Electromechanical billing machines have long since been overtaken by newer technology but they may still be found operating in some hotels especially as many are now microprocessor based – and really all that we need to know is that they differ from more modern machines in that their 'memory' for accounts totals is a series of gears and cogs powered by an electric motor. They perhaps did have the advantage that if they were deprived of electricity in a power cut they could be used manually be means of a handle that enabled them to be cranked by hand, but they were very noisy and not suited to being situated in a quiet foyer. The noise of the clanking gears could be most off-putting to guests in a sober atmosphere encouraged in a large hotel foyer.

It is a fair comment to say that the manufacturers of

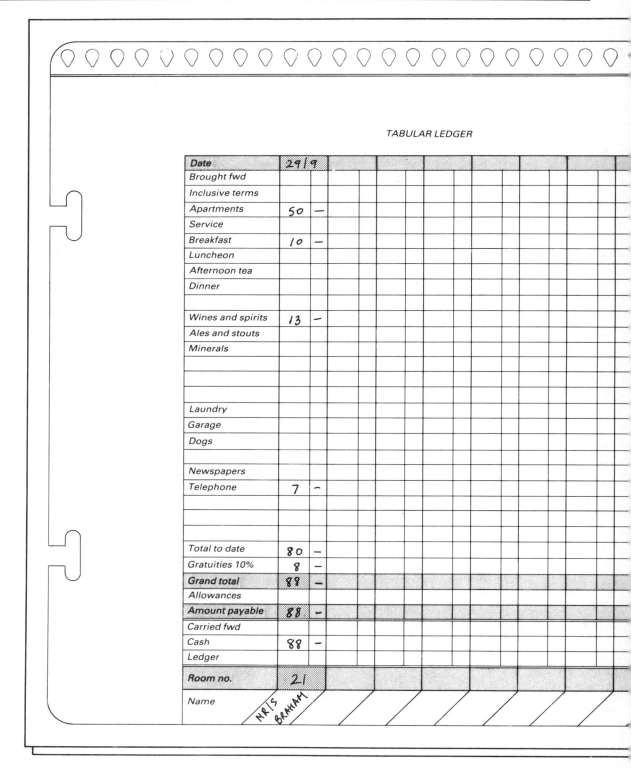

Date	29/9									
Brought fwd										
Inclusive terms										
Apartments	50 —									
Service										
Breakfast	10 —									
Luncheon										
Afternoon tea										
Dinner										
Wines and spirits	13 —									
Ales and stouts										
Minerals										
Laundry										
Garage										
Dogs										
Newspapers										
Telephone	7 —									
Total to date	80 —									
Gratuities 10%	8 —									
Grand total	88 —									
Allowances										
Amount payable	88 —									
Carried fwd										
Cash	88 —									
Ledger										
Room no.	21									
Name	NR/S BRAHAM									

Figure 77   *A tabular ledger of the 'vertical' variety*

TABULAR LEDGER

	American bar				
	Cocktail lounge				
	Chance/total				

	Total
	50 —
	10 —
	13 —
	7 —
	80 —
	8 —
	88 —
	88 —
	88 —
	CHECKED BY
	29/9

Date	29/9																

Hotel and Catering College of Technology   Cheques by arrangement only

Bournemouth   Rate:

MR/S B.R.V. BRAHAM   Number of guests: 2   Room no. 21

	29/9																
Date																	
Brought forward																	
Inclusive terms																	
Apartments	50 —																
Service																	
Breakfast	10 —																
Luncheon																	
Afternoon tea																	
Dinner																	
Wines and spirits	13 —																
Ales and stouts																	
Minerals																	
Laundry																	
Garage																	
Dogs																	
Newspapers																	
Telephone	7 —																
Total to date	80 —																
Gratuities 10%	8 —																
Grand total	88 —																
Allowances																	
Amount payable	88 —																

PLEASE LEAVE KEYS AT THE OFFICE

Figure 78   *A guest bill produced from the 'vertical' tabular ledger shown in Figure 77*

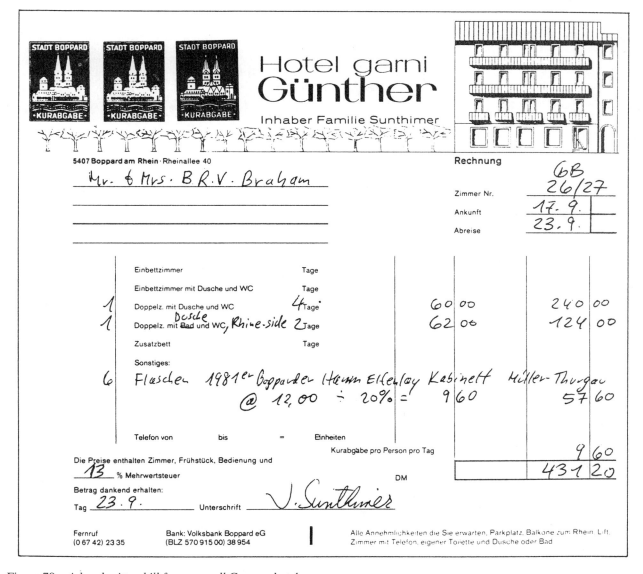

Figure 79   *A handwritten bill from a small German hotel*

hotel billing machines have often only come to make machines with hotel applications once they have exhausted other markets. Most of the hotel billing machines in operation are direct successors of machines employed originally in supermarket check-outs but with the addition of a different analysis and a printer that produces a much more detailed bill than the till roll receipt common in retail shops.

There is often a feeling of nervousness experienced by new staff when confronted with a billing machine but really they are very simple to use because of their evolution from supermarket machines. Billing machines do, of course, satisfy our need for an efficient guest billing system by producing both guest bills and an analysis of the business being carried out throughout the hotel.

While electromechanical machines are now regarded as 'vintage' the more modern billing machines rely on microprocessors for their operation and indeed many may quite rightly be regarded as

Figure 80   *The old billing machine and its keyboard that was in operation at the Majestic Hotel*

computers. The range of work that may be handled by an electronic billing machine is enormous when compared with the restrictions of its predecessors and many of the previous problems are overcome with ease.

The first major advantage of using a billing machine of the electronic type is the quantity of information that it is able to store adequately. Most machines will quite happily hold sufficient information for 1000 rooms which will adequately cover the vast majority of potential establishments likely to make use of them. Equally a very large number of analysis functions may be available so that management information can be compiled.

To clarify this point all the machines are doing is producing the same information as a tabular ledger that would have had 1000 rooms downwards and maybe thirty departmental analysis columns across. The possibility then of reaching a grand total accurately would be fairly slim but an electronic billing machine will do this as it is in effect an 'electronic tabular ledger'.

A machine will calculate a grand total accurately because it takes away from the receptionist the lengthy mental arithmetic and mathematics that are necessary with the tabular ledger. Errors of the arithmetical variety are therefore totally eliminated and the accounts may be produced very speedily, as well as an eventual balance.

As far as customers are concerned they are now able to check-out at any time with their bill up-to-date and ready for them as the machine will keep all bills constantly totalled and ready for presentation. Unlike the tabular ledger, which requires a bill to be written up for the customer at the time of departure, in itself a fairly lengthy process, the machine will allow a speedy check-out from the hotel by having all the information instantly ready.

The guests will also appreciate the clarity of the bill that they are receiving as the machine will in most cases produce a bill that is far easier to read than the handwritten versions found with other systems. However, machines may sometimes go wrong, with overprinting taking place, but this is the exception rather than the rule. In Figure 81 the charges are easy to comprehend and clear.

Regarding the bills themselves, the machine eliminates the need to write out a bill separately from the accounts record as both are automatically produced at the same time. In other words, as amounts are being placed onto the guest bills the same amount is being recorded simultaneously into the memory of the machine to add to the information relevant to the particular department.

From Figure 81 it will be seen that each transaction is given a code number by the machine. Code numbers 570, 606, 696 and 703 start certain lines and these indicate each time the receptionist has added some extra information or posting onto the guest's bill. The coding of all the transactions allows very strict control to be exercised over the operation of the machine as well as helping to identify transactions on the machine's audit roll. The audit roll is a continuous strip of paper on which all transactions appear in chronological order within the machine and the codings correspond with those on the bill. Only senior staff have access to the audit roll, which is locked away inside the machine, as it helps to control, and even locate, errors if they occur while also helping to combat fraud.

Machines are normally equipped with what is called an 'X-key' which allows the management, for example, to extract the total amount of business done under any particular heading instantly at any time during the day. The X-key is also used for balancing the figures at the end of the working period which may be at the end of each shift or overnight. It may be imagined how long it would take to extract similar information or balances for an equivalent amount of business using a tabular ledger; the machine therefore allows very swift control of financial information.

One of the important features that a billing; machine will provide is the opportunity for the vouchers coming through to reception to be verified. Needless to say a whole host of vouchers will be coming through to reception and quite often ending up on a spike or a pile in the office of the member of staff compiling the accounts. It would be quite easy either to forget to enter a voucher onto a guest's bill or not to know whether it had been entered or not if the member of staff is in a hurry or under pressure. Consequently there is often a facility on machines which allows vouchers to be over-printed when they are being posted, to act as a proof that they have been entered onto the guest's bill. This is a very useful facility that protects the member of staff, who cannot be accused of

Room No.	No.	Name
230	2	MR/S B BRAHAM

Arrival	Departure

Rate	Remarks/Deposit
2 x £25,00 AO	

CARLTON HOTEL
East Overcliff
Bournemouth
Telephone:
Bournemouth 22011
Telex:
41244 Carltonian

Company Address

31/05#5128

Ref.	Charges	Credit	Balance
++++++++++++++++	£££.00		
DBAL			.00
TERMS	50.00		
E.BFST	6.00		
BAL A1	# 023-8		56.00
31/05#5129			
DBAL			56.00
H.LNCH	8.50		
H.BAR	2.50		
BAL A1	# 023-8		67.00
31/05#5130			
DBAL			67.00
H.DINN	25.00		
H.BAR	5.00		
BAL A1	# 023-8		97.00
31/05#5131			
DBAL			97.00
PHONE	1.00		
LAUNDY	6.50		
BAL A1	# 023-8		104.50
31/05#5132			
DBAL			104.50
TERMS	50.00		
BAL A1	# 023-8		154.50
31/05#5133			
DBAL			154.50
2@	.75		
E.M.T.	1.50		
E.BFST	6.00		
C.BFST	4.25		
BAL A1	# 023-8		166.25
31/05#5134			
DBAL			166.25

Your room rate is →

EXPLANATION OF CODES

E.BFST	English Breakfast
C.BFST	Continental Breakfast
H.LUNCH	Horizon Lunch
C.LUNCH	Causerie Lunch
H.DINN	Horizon Dinner
C.DINN	Causerie Dinner
AFT.T	Afternoon Tea
BEVS.	Beverages
E.M.T.	Early Morning Tea
RMSERV	Room Service
TRAYCG	Tray Charge
BANQFD	Banqueting Food
R.BAR+	Room Bar Stock
R.BAR−	Room Bar Returned
CELLAR	Cellar Sales
H.BAR	Horizon Bar
C.BAR	Causerie Bar
BANQDR	Banqueting Drink
NPDRNK	Night Porter Drink
LAUNDY	Laundry
PHONE	Telephone
TELEX	Telex
FLORST	Florist
ENTS.	Entertainment/Bands
TOBAC.	Tobacco
GRATS	Gratuities
PORTER	Porter Paid Out
MISC.	Miscellaneous
SGL DP	Single Demi Pension
T/D DP	Twin/Double Demi Pension
DS/ODP	Double for Single Occupancy Demi Pension
KIDSDP	Children Demi Pension
CRP AB	Corporate Rate Apartment & Breakfast
EN P.1	EN Pension
EN P.2	EN Pension
CONF.1	Conference Rate
CONF.2	Conference Rate
TRNFER	Room Transfer
S.RM	Sitting Room
SNGL	Single Accommodation Only
DBLE	Double Accommodation Only
DS/O	Double Single Occupancy
CC.S	Causerie Club Single
CC.D	Causerie Club Double

VAT Reg. No. 185 3027 65

VAT CONTENT OF THIS ACCOUNT £

SIGNATURE

Figure 81 *A machined bill demonstrating the clarity and analysis that may be achieved*

not posting items, and satisfies the management that all charges have been properly recorded.

Probably the most important function of the use of a billing machine is that it allows receptionists more time to deal with customers as much of the tedious mathematical work is taken away from them and the drudgery of adding up long lists of figures is removed. There is no doubt that staff who have operated a machine will be very loath to return to a tabular ledger system of guests' accounts. Therefore the resultant job satisfaction of staff must be looked upon as a major advantage of using a machine.

However, there are certain hurdles that must be overcome if a billing machine is to be used in any hotel. There is no doubt that a machine is a relatively costly piece of technology for some small hotels to contemplate but leasing or hiring might well be the way of overcoming the initial high capital outlay which might deter some hoteliers. A hidden cost is often the stationery which is normally purpose designed for particular machines and which may be costly. If carbonless paper is used this too may increase the cost, which may be substantial, although one should always bear in mind that even with a manual tabular ledger, bills will still have to be produced, so there is already some existing cost.

This book has deliberately refrained from giving a specific method of operating a machine in detail because, as there are a variety of makes, manufacturers and types, to give one system's details could be misleading. The same problem faces hoteliers where new staff are concerned as almost certainly some detailed training or at least a familiarization exercise will have to be undertaken to introduce people to the new system. Often with a billing machine the training is quite lengthy and consequently, especially if new receptionists have not worked one before, will be much more involved than trying to familiarize them with a tabular ledger-type system.

The biggest problem with all technology is that none is ever going to be 100 per cent reliable; invariably a machine will break down at the worst possible moment probably in the middle of a busy check-out. While immediate action will have to be taken to produce guest bills ready access is needed quickly to a maintenance engineer for repairs to be undertaken. The maintenance arrangements should be examined carefully before purchasing a new machine to ensure that not only is every type of breakdown covered but also that an engineer will always be available quickly. It is no good in a hotel with its twenty-four-hour operation waiting two days for an engineer or to be lent a replacement machine that is completely different while your original machine is taken away for repairs. Machines will go wrong so maintenance that is effective should be a priority at the time of purchase.

While the Majestic did for some time exist on a billing machine for producing guest accounts it eventually incorporated billing into the larger computer facility that already handled reservations and therefore much of what we are going to discuss about computers at the International will also apply to the Majestic.

The International Hotel's computer guest billing system

In Chapter 6 we saw how a computer may be used to store the vast amount of information necessary to deal with customers due to arrive at the hotel having booked accommodation. It should be apparent that a computer is also ideally suited to any figure-work in a hotel and consequently the handling of guest's accounts is one of the best applications.

As far as reception is concerned many of the advantages and disadvantages of a billing machine apply also to a computer but really a hotel of any size, these days, would be unwise to ignore the economies expressed, both financially and in time, that a computer may bring to the handling of guests' bills. There is no doubt that guest billing is probably *the* ideal application for a computer in a hotel.

It is immaterial to the computer whether it is dealing with individual or group accounts which are always kept up-to-date either for the addition of new items or for printing and presentation to the guest. Much of the tedious posting of individual vouchers may be taken away from the front office staff as charges may be added to a guest's account direct from the place where the charge was incurred.

Earlier in the chapter we examined the number of departments and the information that they could all be sending through to the front office for addition to the guests' bill and we assumed that paperwork was the way in which this information should be transmitted. While we stated that paperwork could not completely be dispensed with there is a great saving in time if terminals, of one sort or another, are situated throughout the hotel in various departments and information is fed to the guest's bill held electronically in the computer, by the staff in those departments. The information concerned may be entered either manually, as may be the case of the coffee shop supervisor informing the computer of a meal, or automatically by another element of the computer system that is monitoring phone calls. It may therefore be seen that a guest's bill is kept completely up-to-date and there will be no need to wait for paperwork vouchers to come through before the guest may check out unless a charge is disputed and a signature needed for verification.

It is quite possible for small point-of-sale terminals to be interfaced with a larger mainframe computer in a hotel the size of the International. For example, if a guest has a drink at the bar having produced a key card as identity the bar staff will ask the guest to sign the voucher. This information may then be inserted into the bar's terminal, which may also be a till, and the charge will then be instantly transmitted online to the main system processor where it is recorded onto the guest's 'electronic' bill. As a double-check of identity the terminal will then register the name of the guest who should be incurring the charge so that the bar staff are then satisfied that the transaction was valid (Figure 82).

At the International it will be the cashier's office which is concerned with the preparation of bills for guests but much of the work will also be carried out within the computer's central processor where all the 'electronic' bills are located until information needs to be accessed (Figure 83). Any credits, adjustments or transfers may be transacted rapidly while room charges, for example, may be charged automatically to guests' accounts purely by telling the processor which rooms are occupied.

At any time by reference to the VDU in the cashiers office the current balance of a customer's bill may be ascertained whether this consists of just a single 'page' of entries or a large multiple series of 'pages'. Management may also rapidly keep track of the individual status of each guest's bill so that action may be taken quickly if necessary. There will no longer be any problem about calculating percentages for service charge or VAT. With the latter the total will be

Figure 82   *A member of the bar staff entering guest details into the bar terminal at the International Hotel*

calculated automatically to take into account those items which are zero-rated.

By use of the computer the guests' bills will be far more accurate than would otherwise have been possible with other billing systems and provided sufficient printers are used the check-out of guests will be far quicker than by using traditional systems. It is simple to tell the computer how payment was made and if necessary to transfer the amount to the ledger carrying the business credit accounts. If charges that have been disputed need to be credited then this may be done with ease. Every transaction requires the cashier to give his or her own code so that the member

Figure 83   *One of the cashier's terminals at the International Hotel*

of staff concerned may always be identified (Figure 83).

In the same way as the billing machine the computer will automatically keep running totals of the business being undertaken by each department so that the management may receive instantaneous information concerning the operation of the hotel. There is therefore an automatic departmental accounting record.

Where the computer is especially useful is in the situations where calculations are not quite as straightforward as they might normally be. It is common, for example, to quote customers a total 'package' price for their stay involving many separate charges to be apportioned to various departments. With a tabular ledger or some billing machines it is a tedious process to split up all these charges but with a computer these may be programmed automatically. Tours or groups are often a problem and in this case 'extras' bills may automatically be produced for charges not included in the package price which again would be very time-consuming with other systems. Some guests will be set credit limits and the computer will stop charges being incurred over these limits at the points-of-sale so that the customer will then be obliged to pay cash thereby short-circuiting a possible managerial problem. With deposits made in advance the computer will hold this information until the guests arrive and automatically adjust their account accordingly so that he is not inadvertently charged 'twice', which can happen in some systems. The computer may even produce individual bills for two guests sharing the same room if required. The computer can be adaptable provided it has been properly programmed.

It may be seen in a hotel the size of the International that the computer is indispensable. To use any other system would involve either the employment of far more staff or much more time for existing staff to be able to carry out the business accurately. While the International's computer system is a large mini computer network many of the features mentioned may be applied to smaller systems in smaller hotels as is the case at the Majestic.

What does a night auditor do?

In all hotels there will be a need for a separate external check on the work that the receptionists and cashiers have carried out during the working day to ensure that errors with the guests' bills and accounts are kept to an acceptable level. While in a small establishment it may well be the accommodation manager who undertakes this work, in a hotel the size of the International there will sometimes be a night auditor employed where a computer system does not undertake a lot of the work automatically.

As the job title suggests the night auditor will come on duty late in the evening, probably at 11 p.m. and will work through until reception comes on duty again the following morning at 7 a.m. He or she may well be part of the night reception shift at the International and may even have to undertake several tasks as a night manager. However, these should be kept to a minimum, as the main work relies on the fact that the reception will be quiet during the night, enabling the night auditor to concentrate on auditing the day's work.

All the paperwork that has been generated within the front office during the day, and especially the guests' bills, will be checked in minute detail, or by the use of spot-checks, to ensure that accounts are correct. Any charges that remain outstanding prior to the next morning's check-out will be posted, with the rest of the night taken up preparing managerial reports on the revenue from the food and beverage outlets, the rooms and balancing the accounts. The management will therefore receive a summary of the previous day's business as well as the daily trading accounts in the knowledge that a good control procedure has been followed. Indeed the night auditor may be able to spot mistakes immediately prior to the check-out of the guest concerned, thereby forestalling what could have been a major complaint from that customer.

Invariably night auditors will check the numbered vouchers with the entries on the accounting system's audit roll in detail so that the work of the daily staff is monitored. He or she may well act on behalf of management producing lists of customers who, for example, may be close to exceeding their credit limits so that managerial action may be taken quickly to eliminate potential bad debts. However, the last function may well be undertaken by a properly programmed computer but by no means every system has this facility.

Guest accounting is yet another reason for the computer installation at the International to be completely reliable. For the system to go down at all would considerably inconvenience guests and affect the whole bill-collating process. It is therefore very necessary in a hotel of this size to have a secondary processor to take over if the first goes down and even to invest in stand-by generators or battery-packs to ensure operation even in a power cut. Once a large computer system is operational it is almost impossible to do without it so every precaution must be taken to avoid loss of use.

8 Check-out

Having completed their stay in the hotel the final morning arrives, when customers have to pay for all those services that they have made use of during their stay. They will have their room to pay for as well as the meals which they signed for in the restaurant. The drinks in the bar and miscellaneous items that cropped up while they were in the hotel will hopefully be recorded accurately on their bill which will be presented to them when they call at the cashier's desk.

Unlike any other kind of sale, should customers be surprised at the amount they are asked to pay there is no way that they can return the 'goods' they have purchased. They are committed to finding the correct payment. Rather than pay up immediately, guests may want to check their accounts – they may not believe that they have run up such a total!

It is at moments like this that the *cashiers* have to exercise their social skills as there is no doubt that people are sometimes loath to pay their account. In order to demonstrate to guests that they really did incur those charges the cashier will need to have to hand all the documentary evidence that is needed. Whatever the method of billing, whether it be tabular ledger, billing machine or computer, the vouchers with the guest's signature will have to be easily accessible so that it may be established whether in fact the guest is correct if a charge is disputed. The vouchers themselves should be kept in batches corresponding to the room numbers to which they refer at the desk in the cashier's office. Delay in dealing with a dispute will only aggravate what could already appear to be a serious problem. Sometimes the cashiers may be on the receiving end of some hostility through no fault of their own especially if the eventual settlement involves the checking of such things as credit ratings.

If the staff undertaking the compilation of the guests' bills have done their work correctly then half the problems facing the cashier will have been overcome. However, the problem still remains of the method of payment selected. Guests will expect to be able to settle their bill by any one of a large number of different methods ranging from sterling cash to travellers cheques and will assume that the cashier is competent to handle the transaction accurately. Guests will expect the correct change as well as an accurate calculation of the relevant exchange rate should foreign currency of one sort or another be involved. There is no better way of upsetting a customer on departure than for the cashier to make an error that is to the detriment of the guest's wallet.

What are the duties of a cashier?

The cashier's work is universal, whatever the type of hotel, with only the scale of the cashier's office differing between one establishment and another. The basic work of the front office cashier in a hotel the size of the Ship is to receive payment for customer's bills, which is undertaken by a single receptionist. In hotels the size of the Majestic there may well be a separate receptionist specializing as a cashier on each shift while at the International there will undoubtedly be a separate office in the foyer whose cashiers specialize solely in cashiering duties. No matter what the size of the hotel, the basic rules of being a cashier will always apply as the same methods of payment are being used by all customers.

The cashiers in hotels will generally be responsible for accepting payment for guests' bills as well as dealing with the exchange of foreign currency. It is also an important task to undertake the safe custody of guests' valuables if so required. The cashier will make up the floats for staff throughout the hotel as well as accepting these departments paying-in at the end of the working day. In some hotels the cashier will total the cash ready for paying-in to the bank as well as preparing orders for change so that the hotel does not run out.

In those hotels that do not have a separate hotel accountant it is likely that the head cashier will be responsible for the entire system of handling money throughout the hotel. Not only will guests' payments be the head cashier's responsibility, but also the payment of bills to tradesmen and anyone who has supplied goods to the hotel, thereafter compiling the relevant records. In some cases the cashier may even be responsible for making up the wages of staff with all the inherent problems that this involves. The administration of the hotel's petty cash may also be the cashier's responsibility.

Therefore, it can be seen that the cashier in some hotels has a particularly responsible job especially as so much finance is involved. Whatever the size of hotel, it is essential that whoever is employed as a front office cashier will have a proven track-record of honesty. It is therefore vital to take out the most detailed of references on persons entrusted with so much money. In many cases, as a final safety net, the hotel will take out a 'bond' on each cashier so that any loss of money attributed to the negligence of a particular member of staff may be reclaimed from the insurance company.

How does the law affect the payment of guests' bills?

Surprisingly customers are legally obliged to pay their bills in legal tender in full, which when translated literally means that only cash to the exact amount of the bill is acceptable. Needless to say that if the law were complied with fully very few customers would be able to settle their accounts as cash payments are an increasingly small proportion of the total business carried out in any hotel. Interestingly enough the hotel is not obliged to give change in settlement of a bill paid by cash and the onus is therefore on the customer to tender the exact amount but if both this and the insistence upon cash were actually enforced then hotels would quickly go out of business and would lose their reputation for hospitality.

Legally the position is that hotels need only accept payments by methods other than cash at their own discretion which means that the manager or cashier may well use the law to their advantage in situations where customers are being difficult or where credit payment is thought to be too risky. Needless to say most payments are normally accepted in the vast majority of hotels but it may be necessary to fall back on the law in those difficult situations where payment by some guests is thought likely to be problematical.

The law mainly becomes involved in situations when it is thought likely that a guest will be unable to pay his or her bill or in the event of definite non-payment. Under section 16 of the Theft Act it is an offence to leave a hotel without paying and the hotel may prosecute in order to obtain payment. The problems regarding the definition of 'good faith' arise in this situation as the case may well be that, for example, a credit card is presented in payment and for some reason payment is refused and the transaction is not honoured through no fault of the customer who has acted in 'good faith'. If this is the case then prosecution may not be possible. If the non-payment were deliberate then, of course, prosecution would be perfectly possible.

If it is found that guests are for some reason not able to settle their bill or if it is obvious that they have no intention of doing so then 'innkeeper's lien' may be exercised. Innkeeper's lien is the legal term for the right that the hotel proprietor has to keep the guest's property in settlement. While it is permissible to retain the baggage of the guest certain items such as guests' cars and their clothing may not legally be withheld and it should be remembered that any physical attempt made to stop the guests leaving may be interpreted as an assault in the eyes of the law.

Under the Innkeeper's Act of 1878 the goods that are held by the hotel proprietor may be auctioned after six weeks should payment have not been received. An advertisement must be placed in the press at least one month in advance of the auction and should the sale produce more than the outstanding amount of the bill then the residue remaining must be returned to the guest.

Cashiers must keep their floats secure

A float will be issued to each cashier in the hotel consisting of sufficient small change to enable them to deal with the large number of transactions with which they will be faced during their shift. While we are dealing primarily with the front desk cashiers there will also be similar floats issued to all the cashiers at the various points of sale throughout the hotel.

The float contains the small denominations of money necessary for the settlement of bills and in a hotel the size of the Ship may only consist of less than £100.00, whereas it may be composed of several hundred pounds in a hotel like the International. The size of the float will vary considerably from one hotel to another and may well fluctuate with trends in business but its size will certainly depend upon the tariff or prices charged, the total quantity of settlements expected, the predominant payment methods and the amount of overseas currency being handled. In the last case it should be realized that if one is receiving currency from overseas to any extent then this will be useless for giving change to other customers and therefore allowances must be made to compensate with a larger float.

The total quantity of floats in the hotel should be kept to as small an amount as possible as valuable cash is being tied up that might well be put to better use thereby assisting the 'cash flow' of the business. Another very good reason for keeping floats as small as possible, without the risk of running out of change, is the possibility of robbery which increases the larger the floats are. Fraud and petty theft is often a problem where floats are concerned and the cashiers should be provided with, and also make use of, every possible precaution to protect their money. It is often the case that cashiers are made personally responsible for shortages in their float and therefore precautions should be taken to avoid theft. The best policy is to issue each cashier with a lockable cash box that is their sole responsibility and for which they sign each time they start a shift. The head cashier will have made up the floats to the required size and will have itemized them out on 'float slips' which cashiers will agree and sign for when starting work. At the end of the shift cashiers will deposit their takings and sign in the float as they might also do if handing over to a subsequent cashier. This will certainly happen at 'handover' time between shifts in reception. In order to discourage mis-use of the floats issued to cashiers the auditors and management will undertake spotchecks to make sure that the money is not being used elsewhere and also that there are no 'IOUs' in the float. While working with the float the cashier should ensure that it is kept under close supervision and also that lockable till drawers are used to lessen the risk of theft.

One of the larger floats will be that for the hotel's 'petty cash' which exists so that items may be purchased for cash outside the hotel on behalf of guests. It is essential that every withdrawal of money from the petty cash is balanced with a corresponding petty cash voucher properly authorized or by a VPO (visitors paid out) or disbursement voucher. An analysis of the usage of the petty cash will be completed each day to ensure that the relevant guests are billed as well as to see what the petty cash is being used for. Items such as flowers, theatre tickets, medicines and taxi fares will be common items that will be paid for on behalf of the customer using the petty cash.

While serious robbery is unlikely in a hotel it is always a possibility and the cashiers should be given instructions not to put themselves at any personal risk if threatened and to hand over the money if this is demanded. This is the best policy to avoid risk to both staff and customers.

How may customers settle their bills?

Even though legal tender or cash is the only method that customers may utilize by right to settle their bills there are very many other types of payment that hotels willingly receive. Not all of them will be common to every hotel, but there are the more usual payments with which cashiers must be familiar and it is generally up to the policy of the hotel's management as to which are taken in settlement of a bill.

Cash payments

First, we must examine the various *cash* methods of payment and look at the various problems with which cashiers may be faced. Sterling cash must be accepted if tendered and poses the biggest security problem for the cashiers; it is obviously the most risky of methods of payment as it is easily 'lost' by a thief. The main problem with sterling cash is therefore keeping it secure and ensuring that it does not fall into the wrong hands. Wherever sterling cash is accepted in the hotel it must therefore be kept in a secure tray or box and collected regularly so that large amounts do not accumulate, thereby becoming a tempting target for potential thieves. When dealing with cash the cashier must always keep the amount given in payment separate from the float until the change has been counted back into the hand of the customer. Many tills are equipped with a clip for this very purpose and if this is used there will be no opportunity for customers to maintain, for example, that they handed over a large denomination note when in fact they gave a smaller one. Even though sterling cash is the simplest form of transaction for the cashier it should never be underestimated and every settlement must be treated with care.

Sometimes there is confusion over the currencies from our immediate neighbours in Scotland, Ireland and the Channel Islands. In the case of Scottish and Channel Islands banknotes they are readily acceptable and may be taken in directly in exchange for a bill as they have exactly the same value as their sterling counterparts. A cashier should not, though, apply the same rules to the currency of Southern Ireland (Eire). This has a different value and may only be paid into banks in the same way as other types of *foreign currency*.

Foreign currency is increasingly popular as a method of payment in those hotels where there are a large number of overseas customers staying. It is important, though, that the cashiers in these hotels are familiar with those currencies that are acceptable in the UK both from the point of view of their value and their design. In order to avoid the inadvertent acceptance of forgeries all cashiers should be familiar with the unusual, to our point of view, designs of banknotes from countries overseas. It is also by no means the case that every overseas currency is negotiable in the UK and therefore the cashier should be issued with a list of those countries whose currency is acceptable. This list should be obtained from the hotel's bank to which the money will be taken in the daily banking. It is common for banknotes from Eastern European countries to be unacceptable as well as currencies from countries where exchange rates are known to fluctuate dramatically. There are also certain countries whose currency is not acceptable due to political problems with the UK and these should not be taken by mistake as they may well not be accepted by the bank.

In accepting foreign currency the hotel is in fact undertaking a service to the guest which is more often given by a bank; as with the latter organization, the hotel will charge for this service. A consequent commission rate is therefore always charged on top of the rate for the particular currency to allow for any changes in the rate, as well as covering the charges the bank will apply when the foreign currency is eventually paid in to them. The commission is sometimes also regarded as extra revenue for the hotel and in some establishments is regarded as the 'perks' of the cashiers. If it is managerial policy to allow the cashiers to keep the commission as a form of incentive or tip then a strict watch must be kept by the management to ensure that extortionate rates are not charged.

The commission is charged on top of the usual exchange rate for the particular currency which may be obtained from the bank each day. Indeed it is a good policy to ask the bank to send (or fax) a daily exchange rate sheet to the hotel with the member of staff who has completed the banking so that the rates are kept up to date. To rely on the rate printed in the daily paper is not sufficient, as with print schedules they may be a day out of date. If in any doubt the bank should be contacted direct. Current rates may also be found out by referring to the financial 'pages' of the Teletext service on TV, as these are kept up-to-date throughout the day by reference to the foreign exchanges. A common mistake is to confuse currencies with the same title; extra care should therefore be taken to identify the correct nationality of the dollars, francs, marks or krone being taken. Even the difference in rate between American and Canadian dollars is very marked and the wrong rate charged could result in a substantial loss on an individual bill.

The point should be made that only banknotes

```
Cashier's instructions for payment by:

FOREIGN CURRENCY

1   Is the currency acceptable in the UK?
2   What is the exchange rate?
3   Watch out for dollars, francs, marks and krone.
4   Has correct commission been charged?
5   Have you completed a foreign exchange receipt?
6   Give sterling change only.

NB If in any doubt regarding a currency's acceptability
or its correct exchange rate check with the bank.
```

Figure 84

should be accepted in payment as the bank will be unlikely to accept overseas coins. Even if one has the correct change in an overseas currency only sterling must be given in change to satsify the foreign exchange regulations. The cashier, for good accounting purposes, should always issue a receipt for each currency transaction so that errors may be determined and readily identified as well as enabling fraud, or at least its potential, to be reduced. When the foreign exchange is banked a separate paying-in slip should always be used, and again, to satisfy the foreign exchange regulations, all foreign exchange *must* be paid into a bank.

The most common type of payment in many hotels is by the use of a bank *cheque* drawn on a personal current account. A cheque settlement contains many pitfalls for the unwary cashier and should the exact procedures set down by the bank not be followed there are many reasons why the bank itself may not accept the cheque for payment.

The cashier may be faced either with a request to cash a cheque or to receive the cheque in settlement of the guest's bill. Whatever the situation there should be managerial policies to cover every eventuality. Generally the cashing of cheques is discouraged for non-residents and will not be contemplated if the cheque is not backed up by a valid cheque guarantee card. Indeed, the issuing of cheque guarantee cards has greatly simplified the procedure for accepting cheques but the regulations must be followed exactly (Figure 85).

It will almost certainly be managerial policy to accept only cheques that are backed up by a valid

cheque card but many cards only guarantee up to £50 in any single transaction. Many hotel bills involve far larger sums than £50 and therefore there is a temptation to ask the customer to write out more than one cheque for a large transaction and to ask for them to be dated on separate days. While this may appear a logical answer to the £50 problem it is not acceptable to the bank and if it is spotted the bank may well refuse payment.

From the regulations it will be seen that it is necessary for the cheque to be signed in front of the cashier. If this is not the case the guest should be asked to sign again on the reverse of the cheque and the signatures compared again. This is to stop those thieves who have laboriously copied a signature before presenting the cheque in the hope that they will not be asked to repeat the signature when confronted. The signature should be checked with that on the card and here the cashier should be extremely vigilant. If the card has been damaged at all or the background under the card's signature is in any way tampered with the payment should be refused. A pet technique involving both bank cheque cards as well as credit cards is to respray the signature area with matt white paint and then use a more natural signature on the stolen card. The background should not be clear white and should definitely not show the effects of being tampered with (Figure 86). Increasingly cards boast holograms and some have the owner's photograph. Make sure that these have not been tampered with and also correspond to the person who is using them.

It is a stipulation of a transaction that the same bank sorting code is on the cheque card as on the cheque, while the most important of all the requirements is that cashiers write the cheque card number themselves on the back of the cheque. This is proof that the cheque has been examined by the cashier and also acts as a memory aid to make the cashier examine the other points that are necessary. The bank might refuse payment if the guest has put the number on the reverse of the cheque themself as they might if no number appears at all. Some cashiers are equipped with imprinter machines which will allow the card to have its details printed directly onto the reverse of the cheque. Another good technique is to have an ink stamp that asks for the relevant items and which is printed onto the reverse of the cheque. This is a very good memory aid for the cashier.

National Eastminster Bank Limited guarantees the payment of one cheque only **not exceeding £50** in any single transaction if it:

(a)   is signed in the presence of the payee, the signature corresponding with that on this card;

(b)   is drawn on one of its cheque forms bearing the code number shown on this card and dated before the expiry date of this card;

(c)   has the card number written on the back by the payee.

Figure 85   *The regulations that apply to a cheque guarantee card*

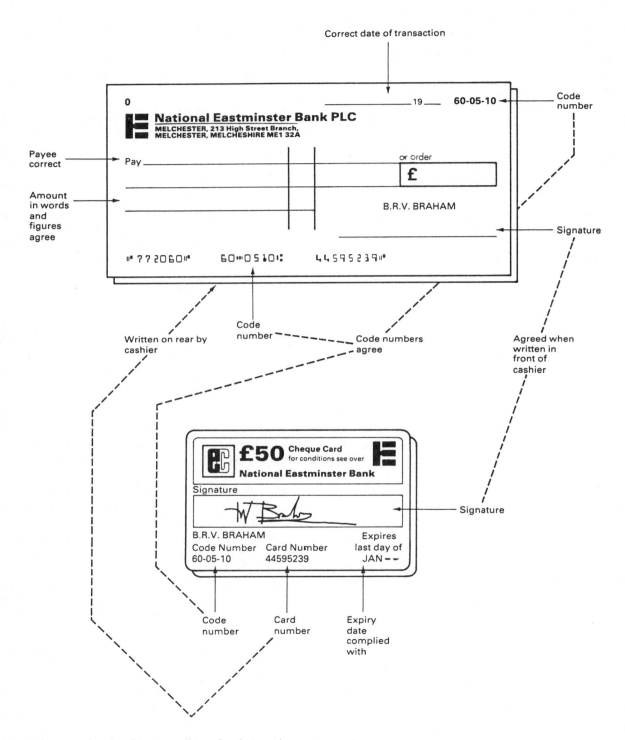

Figure 86   *Items for a cashier to examine closely in a cheque transaction*

On the cheque itself the cashier should examine the date to make sure it is the actual date of the transaction. Postdated cheques made out for dates in the future should not be accepted as the account could even be closed or the customer deceased by the time that payment is possible. Equally cheques should not be accepted that are more than six months old as they will be regarded by the bank as 'out of date'. Regarding dates, the cheque guarantee card itself will display an expiry date and no transactions should be carried out if this has expired.

In the detail on the cheque it should be ensured that the hotel is correctly described as the payee and also that the amounts in words and figures agree. If this is not the case the cheque again will not be acceptable to the bank. The cheque must be written in a permanent ink, although the colour is immaterial, and any alterations must be signed by the drawer.

If there is any doubt over a particular transaction it is possible, during banking hours, to ask the hotel's bank to check with the guest's bank that the latter has sufficient funds to cover the bill. There are also a number of agencies that will reveal from the records the creditworthiness of individuals.

In many hotels if payment is intended by cheque, which may well be asked at the time of registration, the bill may have to be settled three or four days before the guest leaves in order to guarantee that the cheque is cleared. In certain circumstances a 'special clearance' may be arranged through the hotel's bank so that a cheque may be cleared within twenty-four hours; even so, there is little opportunity to validate a transaction if the guest wishes to check-out immediately.

While it is often useful to ask guests to place their address on the reverse of the cheque, so that they may be contacted if inadvertently some error has been missed, on its own an address is not going to help with deliberate fraud. After all it is hardly likely that a person committing a fraud will give a correct address, but it is surprising how many cashiers ask only for this information and do not request the details of a cheque guarantee card. This is, of course, asking for trouble and the instructions shown in Figure 87 should be taken as a good guide line.

Debit cards, such as Switch, are becoming an increasingly popular method of handling transactions. Basically the plastic cards, that may be identified by the relevant logos, enable payment for the customer's

Cashier's instructions for payment by:

CHEQUE

1   Only cheques accompanied by a valid *cheque guarantee card* are acceptable.

2   On the cheque itself:
   (a)   Is the *date* correct?
   (b)   Are the *payee's* details correct?
   (c)   Does the *amount* in words and figures agree?
   (d)   Was the cheque *signed* in front of you?

3   On the *cheque guarantee card*;
   (a)   Has the card *expired*?
   (b)   Does the *signature* agree with that on the cheque?
   (c)   Does the *code number* correspond with that on the cheque?

4   Write the cheque guarantee card *number* on the reverse of the cheque *yourself*.

NB If in any doubt regarding a cheque transaction check with management and if necessary the bank.

Figure 87

bill to be transferred directly from their bank current account to the establishment's account. Most hotels and restaurants undertake the transaction electronically but it is still possible to use a manual system of vouchers in locations that do not have access to validation terminals. It should be realized that organizations such as Switch are confident enough in their systems to 'guarantee' transactions, which is a major selling point to businesses that are watching their cash flow closely, but that a commission rate is charged on each and every transaction so handled which reflects the cost of offering the guarantee.

The system that is used for validating debit card payments, as well as those made by credit card, is known as the *Electronic Fund Transfer From the Point of Sale* or EFTPOS system. The cashier uses a small terminal through which the relevant card is 'wiped'. The terminal reads the number of the card from the magnetic strip and communicates with a host computer by telephone line to see whether the card is on any lists of lost or stolen cards. If not, the cashier punches into the terminal the amount of the bill to be settled, and authorization must be given by the computer for the transaction to proceed. The guest is asked to sign a receipt slip which also gives permission for the amount concerned to be transferred from their account. The cashier compares the signatures and gives the customer one copy of the receipt. The whole operation can be very swift and the only problems that might occur involve damaged cards. If the damage is only minor, it is always possible to punch the card number into the terminal manually but this takes a little longer.

It will not be too long before the magnetic strip on both debit and credit cards is replaced by a small microchip containing more details about the customer and creating what is called a 'smart card'. Whilst these are common on the continent they allow PIN numbers (Personal Identification Numbers) to be used in addition to the normal card number and carry much more in the way of financial information about the customer. Smart cards will become commonplace

before too long and the methodology of their handling will be very similar to that described above for EFTPOS.

Another type of cheque that a cashier must know about is the *travellers cheque* which is a common way in which overseas customers or tourists pay their bills while in another country. Travellers cheques suffer from the problem that they are issued in fixed denominations by many different banks as well as travel agencies and therefore there is no common design. They may also be issued in any of the common currencies so the same exchange problems occur as were encountered with foreign currency. As far as their value is concerned identical precautions should be taken to those for foreign currency.

What is common, though, is that when the travellers

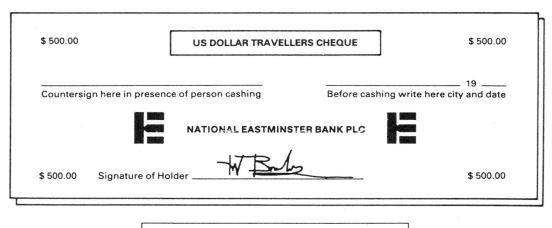

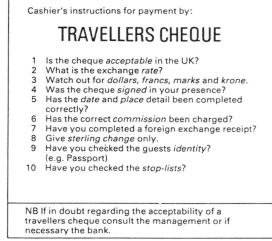

Figure 88   *Outline of a typical travellers cheque*

cheques are bought in the bank or travel agency they must be signed once before being issued. The process of validation in the hotel will therefore require the cashier to watch a second signature being placed on the travellers cheque by the customer and thereafter ensuring that the two are similar. If the cheque comes ready-signed to the cashier she should ask for it to be signed again on the reverse. All the customer has to do otherwise is to insert the place and date of encashment and the travellers cheque is then treated as foreign currency and may equally be readily paid into the bank. Whether being exchanged for cash or for settlement of a bill, change will almost certainly be necessary and should be issued in sterling notes and coinage.

If there is any doubt about the identity of the customer, identification should be asked for and a passport is usually the best solution. Reference should also be made to the stop-lists issued by the banks and travel agencies so that any lost or stolen travellers cheques are not accepted inadvertently as they will be of no value if the hotel has been informed of their loss.

Eurocheques are a convenient method for travellers to pay their bills in approximately 40 countries throughout the world. They are identified by the distinctive blue and red EC symbol and, where acceptable, they have the advantage that they may be made out to the exact amount of the bill in the local currency of the particular country involved. There is therefore no need for the establishment to charge a commission. They are guaranteed by a corresponding Eurocheque card complete with the EC symbol, which must display the same signature that is on the cheque and must be valid. Where their acceptance by cashiers is concerned the methodology is very similar to that of a current account cheque. (See figure 89.)

Credit payments

An increasingly popular method of payment being used in many hotels and restaurants is the *credit card* which has really gained popularity in this country since the introduction by the large banks of Access and Barclaycard credit cards.

Although it is immaterial to the cashier, there are three main types of credit card. First, there are the 'all-purpose shopping credit cards' such as Barclaycard, Access, Mastercharge, Visa and Bank Americard for which the owner usually pays a subscription as well as paying interest on any outstanding amounts of money from transactions not settled after one month. Second, there are the 'travel and entertainment' cards such as American Express, Diners and Carte Blanche for which the owner pays an annual subscription and pays off the outstanding bill at the completion of each month. Third, and last, there are the 'company credit cards', such as those issued by the major hotel companies, which enable bills to be settled in the particular company's outlets and nowhere else. It is up to the company as to whether credit is allowed beyond a month and as to whether a subscription has to be paid. The difference between these cards is only evident in the accounting after the guest has completed payment and at the time of settlement they are all treated in the same way

It must be made clear, though, that not every management of every hotel or company believes in accepting credit cards of every type for settlement of their establishment's bills. While it may be argued that the risk of not receiving payment is cut for a hotel by the use of a credit card, as it is up to the credit card company and not the hotel to actually obtain payment for the hotel bill, the cash flow of the establishment is drastically affected by the enforced wait that the hotel has for its money when compared with a cash transaction. It is evident that to accept credit cards will attract owners of those cards to a hotel, thereby substantially increasing custom, but balanced against this is the substantial commission that a hotel has to pay to a credit card company that may also eat into what might be small profit margins. While credit cards help to increase the spending of guests in a hotel and are firm favourites of businesspeople, who like to avoid using their personal finances and who like to keep track of their expenses, there is a large security problem to the hotel due to the number of stolen or 'lost' cards. If a hotel accepts payment on a card they have been told is no longer usable then the hotel is responsible and there is no redress to the credit card company.

It may therefore be seen that the idea of a credit card, first established by Diners Club in the early 1950s, is by no means popular with all hotel managements; consequently those cards that entail the highest commission rates may well be unacceptable in some hotels. The point should also be emphasized that not every hotel accepts every credit card; indeed they

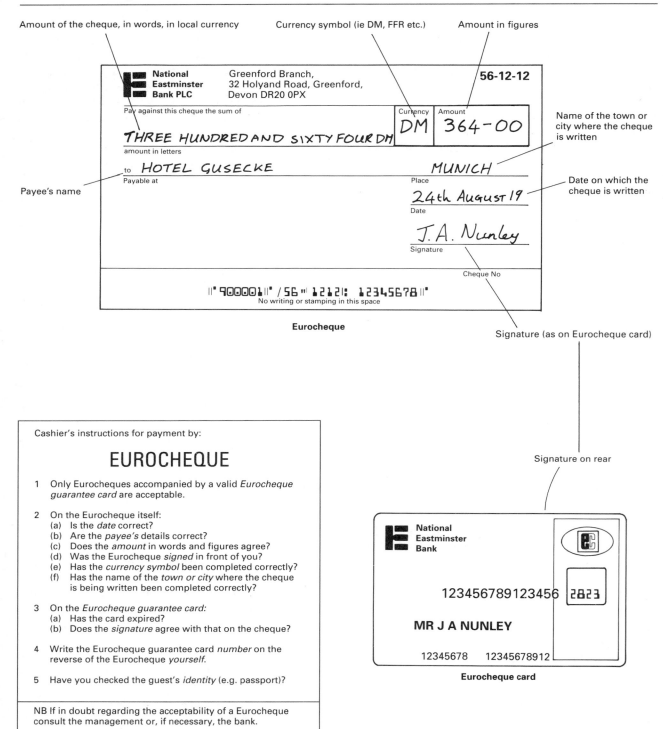

Figure 89   *Dealing with a Eurocheque transaction*

may only take on the 'franchise' for maybe three or four credit cards at the most due to the cash flow and accounting problems sometimes associated with credit cards.

In accepting payment on a credit card the first thing cashiers should do is to establish that the card itself is one of those that the hotel accepts. If by accident they accept a card for which the hotel does not have a franchise then there is no comeback, but it is surprising how often a cashier in a hurry does this. Each hotel will also be given what is called a 'floor limit', or, in other words an amount of money of a total bill over which the cashier *must* obtain authorization before accepting payment. Depending entirely on the business concerned this may vary widely between two hotels situated next door to each other accepting the same card. Whatever the situation, if the bill is over the floor limit then the cashier must obtain authorization from the particular credit card company's twenty-four-hour authorization centre. This sometimes involves a Freefone call which costs the hotel nothing.

By now the card itself will have been obtained from the customer and it should be ascertained as to whether it is within the expiry date printed on it. The card should also be checked against the stoplists received from the credit card company to ensure that it has not been stolen or that it is not required to be returned. Usually a reward is offered for the return of some cards by the credit card companies as an incentive to cashiers to look at cards closely. In most cases if a card is on a stop-list it is common policy for cashiers to have to phone the authorization number again and they will then be told whether to confiscate the card or to call the police in the case of a card that has been stolen.

Having checked that the card is valid and that the amount of the bill is satisfactory for settlement the cashier will either complete a sales voucher for the correct credit card company or use the EFTPOS terminal. If using the paperwork system many cashiers unfortunately do not use the correct voucher so all the credit card companies swap vouchers that they receive in error; but the time taken to balance the accounting means that it is far better to sort out the problem initially by using the correct stationery. This is quite difficult as most of the multi-ply vouchers look identical; all the same, extreme care should be taken. The card will then be placed on an imprinter machine given by the credit card company and the details on the card will appear on the voucher. With the card kept out of sight, so that the signature cannot be copied, the guest is asked to sign the voucher and the two signatures are then compared. If everything is similar the guest is then given back their card along with one ply of the voucher as a receipt and a copy their bill. The transaction is now complete. It may therefore be seen that there are plenty of checks which have to be carried out, but if a cashier is under pressure it is still very easy for a stolen card to slip through.

At the completion of the day's business all the credit card vouchers will be separated out into their respective companies. Some may be paid directly into a bank while others will be sent off to head offices for payment, less commission, in a few days' or weeks' time. Depending on the time taken for settlement the cash flow of the hotel is, therefore, affected by the slowness with which final payment may be achieved. It should also be noted that as far as the hotel is concerned the contract over payment is between the credit card company and the hotel and not with the guest, so this should be remembered if a dispute is likely to be the result of an argument over a bill settled by credit card (Figure 90).

In hotels where there is a substantial business clientele a large number of *credit ledger accounts* will be granted thereby giving individuals or companies the opportunity to pay their outstanding bills at the end of

Cashier's instructions for payment by:

CREDIT CARD

1 Is the card one of those *acceptable* to the hotel?
2 If the amount of the bill is outside the card's *floor limit* phone for authorization.
3 Has the card *expired*?
4 Is the card on the credit card company's *stop-list*?
5 Is the card in the same *name* as the guest?
6 Have you prepared the *correct sales voucher*?
7 Has the imprint come out *clearly* on all the plys of the voucher?
8 Does the guest's *signature* agree with that on the card?
9 Did you *obscure* the card from the guest's view?
10 Return the card and the *copy* of the voucher to the guest along with his copy of the bill.

NB If in any doubt regarding a credit card transaction consult the management or telephone the credit card company direct.

Figure 90

their accounting periods rather than on departure. In order to administer what may be a complex and cumbersome account system there may well be a separate ledger clerk who sends out demands for payment and records both the quantity and amounts of ledger business transacted. Indeed in many commercial hotels a substantial amount of money is always owing to the ledger and therefore there is a need to operate this efficiently if cash flow is to be maintained.

The management of the hotel are the only people who will be allowed to grant credit ledger facilities to an individual guest or a company as it must be established that there is some good reason for allowing this person or organization a credit facility to the detriment of the hotel's cash flow. As it may well be three months after a guest has stayed at the hotel that the settlement is actually made of the account it would be foolish to allow too many ledger accounts that would tie up too much cash that could otherwise be being used in the business. In extreme cases the hotel might have to borrow money from the bank to cover those amounts tied up in the ledger. To reach this situation, without good reason, is bad financial management.

Credit ledger accounts will therefore be kept to a minimum although it should be realized that they are a great attraction to business customers who use the hotel a lot as they then only have to settle a monthly account rather than each individual bill incurred. In the case of a large company using the hotel for its representatives a combined total of all the bills incurred by those persons will be sent to the company, making their accounting processes much simpler. There is no doubt that this will be a valuable sales weapon for the sales manager in the hotel to utilize to tempt commercial business to the hotel provided the financial situation justifies this.

Before granting a credit ledger facility the management will have closely checked the credit-worthiness of the individual or company concerned. This may be carried out with the assistance of the hotel's bank, a credit checking company or, if the hotel is in a group, through the finance department at the head office. It will be realized that in allowing payment for a bill at a date long after a guest has stayed will give more opportunity for non-payment to occur than if payment had been made at the time of

---

Cashier's instructions for payment by:

CREDIT LEDGER ACCOUNT

1　Is the firm or individual on the hotel's *credit ledger account list*?
2　Have you checked the *identity* of the guest against nominated users?
3　Is the bill within the *ceiling* amount set by the account holder?
4　Is there a necessity for an *extras bill*?
5　Has the customer *agreed* and *signed* his account?
6　Has the guest left the details of where the bill should be *sent for payment*?
7　Once settled pass the bill to the *ledger clerk*.

NB If in any doubt regarding a credit ledger account transaction consult the management or contact the account holder direct.

Figure 91

departure; consequently every safeguard must be taken to ensure that only customers that are 'good risks' are given credit facilities to guard against bad debts. It should be carefully agreed also with the customer that bills will be settled within a stated accounting period, otherwise the facility will not be granted, as some of the largest and best known companies that are household names are sometimes the worst at settling accounts on time. It is rumoured that legislation will be introduced to solve this. As their accounts tend to be the largest there is a considerable effect on the hotel's financial situation if payment times are not strictly negotiated initially.

As far as cashiers are concerned they will have a list in front of them of those companies and individuals that are granted credit ledger facilities. They will be aware that no other persons are allowed credit and they should *never* offer these facilities themselves if the person is not included on the list. They will also have at hand the names of those persons who are authorized by their company to use credit facilities and will check their identity at the time of settling the bill to ensure that only the correct persons are using the facility. There will undoubtedly be 'ceilings' put on what may be charged to a company account and this will differ from one arrangement to another so cashiers will ensure that any amounts or items not stated in the original agreement are charged on a separate 'extras' bill that will be settled in cash by the customer. On departure guests therefore simply have to check and agree their bill, by signing it, and then to pay for any extras, on the separate bill, that are their own responsibility.

Tour groups and travel agents' customers are frequently accommodated in the majority of hotels and they both provide another challenge for the cashier as they tend to settle their arrangements with the hotel by use of what is commonly called a *travel agent's voucher* (Figure 92).

Before sending an individual customer to a hotel the travel agent will have negotiated a price with the management for their customer's stay.

This price will then be what the travel agent charges the guest but they will actually make their money later when the hotelier sends a demand for payment less what is usually a 10 per cent commission. In other words, customers pay the travel agent the full amount for their stay while the agent only pays the hotel 90 per cent of the total, keeping the balance as their charge.

The exact terms of the agreement will be finely negotiated by the management who will be aware that to attract more business to the hotel they may have to offer higher commission rates to travel agents at certain times. Whatever is agreed the agent will confirm the individual arrangements to the hotel using a travel agent's voucher. This is really a piece of paperwork, which unfortunately has no common design, varies hugely between one agent and another, and which has several copies. One, as already stated, is sent to the hotel as a confirmation of the details of the arrangement and an identical copy is sent to the guest.

As far as cashiers are concerned a customer coming from a travel agency is very simple to check-out as they simply have to confirm that the two copies of the voucher are identical, for identity purposes, and then examine the details that are agreed in the voucher between the hotel and the agency. This purely means establishing what the agency is going to pay for and what charges are the guest's own responsibility. What then happens, rather like a credit ledger account, is that the guest signs the bill that goes back to the agency, and then settles any extras on a separate extras account. The ledger clerk will administer the system for regaining payment as well as the calculations to allow for the deduction of commission from the total bill if this has not already been done.

Where a large tour is concerned a 'bulk' voucher may well be used and similar arrangements made to make guests pay for their extras separately. While commission is unlikely, as the price charged to a tour will be discounted anyway, depending on the amount of business brought by the operator and the season, the tour guide or courier may well be required to agree the totals of customers and rooms used before departure so that an accurate account may be sent to the tour company by the ledger clerk at a later date.

One of the problems with travel agent's vouchers is if they are accepted from overseas when currency values are likely to fluctuate. Should the amount not actually meet the requirements of the bill then there is always an awkward problem in working out whether to bill the agency or the guest for the extra. The best policy is to ask overseas travel agents to quote their amounts in sterling.

We have therefore examined the most common ways in which payments may be accepted by the cashier, but before moving on one important point should be made. Because of the pressure on the cashiers at the time of check-out it is often necessary to prepare details concerning many of the payments involved in advance to avoid a queue of aggravated customers building up at the desk while long credit checks are carried out. There should therefore be considerable liaison between the receptionists and the cashiers as a lot of time may be saved if customers are asked on arrival, perhaps on their registration forms, how they intend to settle their bill. If a cheque is indicated it may be necessary to ask the customer to settle well in advance of check-out to allow for clearance; or, if a credit card is the intended method, its number may be taken on arrival to allow for authorization to be checked during a quiet period in preparation for check-out. Liaison between the departments of the front office will considerably ease the pressure at time of check-out.

The golden rule of the cashiers, though, should be *never be rushed* as a simple taking of a short-cut in settling a bill could lead to a considerable loss of money to the hotel which might otherwise have been avoided.

A lasting impression is as important as a first impression

Having paid the bill, the customer is usually given a copy (Figure 94) which is neatly receipted, either by a machine or by the issuing of a receipt from a separate

R.E. BATH TRAVEL SERVICE

The *top* (customer's) copy

Ref:

Registered Office: 4 Albert Road, Bournemouth BH1 1BZ
Registered No. 288173 England

BRANCH

Offices in
BOURNEMOUTH, BOSCOMBE, WINTON
CHRISTCHURCH, POOLE, FERNDOWN
DORCHESTER, FARNBOROUGH
ALDERSHOT, ANDOVER, SALISBURY
RYDE (IOW), NEWPORT (IOW)
YEOVIL and SHERBORNE

HOTEL MAJESTIC .... CENTRE MELCHESTER ....

Accommodation reserved 1 x DOUBLE ROOM WITH BATH ......

....

Commencing with DINNER ....

on 21 JANUARY ....and terminating

with BREAKFAST .... on 28 JANUARY ....
Including room, continental breakfast, luncheon, dinner, service and taxes

ADDITIONAL FACILITIES
ROOM MUST BE QUIET AT BACK OF HOTEL. ....
R.E. BATH TRAVEL SERVICE LTD

Name(s) MR and MRS B. BRAHAM ......

....

R.E.B

Registered Office:
Registered No. 288

Offices in
BOURNEMOUTH, BOSCOMBE, WINTON
CHRISTCHURCH, POOLE, FERNDOWN
DORCHESTER, FARNBOROUGH
ALDERSHOT, ANDOVER, SALISBURY
RYDE (IOW), NEWPORT (IOW)
YEOVIL and SHERBORNE

Commencing with DINNER ....

on 21 JANUARY ....and terminating

with BREAKFAST .... on 28 JANUARY ...
Including room, continental breakfast, luncheon, dinner, service and taxes

ADDITIONAL FACILITIES
ROOM MUST BE QUIET AT BACK OF HOTEL. ....
R.E. BATH TRAVEL SERVICE LTD

Name(s) MR and MRS B. BRAHAM ....

....

The Manager,

Dear Sir,

   With reference to your letter confirming the above reservations, we have pleasure in enclosing duplicate copy of the hotel coupon. Full payment of your account will be made as soon as it is received at this office, and we are grateful to you for your co-operation.

The *bottom* (hotel) copy

Figure 92   *A specimen travel agent's voucher (Not all travel agents are as well organized as this)*

Cashier's instructions for payment by:

TRAVEL AGENT'S VOUCHER

1 Has the *copy voucher* been received from reception?
2 Which *charges* is the travel agent responsible for?
3 Is there a necessity for an *extras bill*?
4 Has the customer *agreed* and *signed* his account?
5 Have we the exact *name* and *address* of the *travel agent*?
6 Once settled pass the bill to the *ledger clerk*.

NB If in any doubt regarding a travel agent's voucher transaction consult the management or contact the travel agent direct.

Figure 93

receipt book, the receipts being checked later in the day to make sure that they agree with the total amount of the bills that have been paid, as a form of control. The cashier will then inform reception that the room is vacated. They in turn tell housekeeping.

One would imagine that the guest is now free to leave but it may well require a luggage pass to be issued by the cashier to enable the porters to take the customers' luggage out of the main entrance. This is a simple precaution to stop the uniformed staff unwittingly carrying out the bags of customers who have not paid their bills. All the luggage pass does is establish that the customer is leaving legitimately.

Social skills are once again put into action when the customer leaves as the cashiers or receptionists may pleasantly wish the guest a safe journey and may even put their sales techniques into action. After all, if the guests are known well enough this may be the time to ask them if they would like to book again for next year or maybe to make a reservation in another of the group's hotels in the town to which they are travelling. Not only will this sort of care and interest in guests impress the customer it will also benefit sales. That is not to say that the receptionists should force themselves on the guest; the last thing that is required is for the lasting impression of the hotel to be a bad one. All interaction with guests should be left to the receptionist's discretion as not every customer may be-treated the same way and the bland use of stock phrases such as 'Have a good day now!' or 'Missing you already!' may not work in all situations.

Before the guests leave they must deposit their key, if the traditional systems are in operation. The loss of a room key may not only be costly but, of course, casts a doubt over the security of the particular room involved. Quite often keys are dropped into a slot in the cashier's desk where they are secure and may not be picked up by a potential thief and this is undoubtedly the best policy.

The overriding aim at the time of departure is therefore to create a good lasting impression of the hotel so that the customer might be encouraged to return.

What other duties might a cashier undertake?

Apart from the settlement of guests' bills the cashier quite often has the responsibility in a hotel of administering the system employed for protecting guests' valuables.

The obligations on a hotelier regarding liability for the loss of guests' possessions or valuables are quite clearly stated in the Hotel Proprietors Act of 1956 and are well summarized in the statutory notice which must be prominently displayed (Figure 95). If it were not displayed then a hotelier might in certain circumstances be liable for the full amount of any possessions lost by a guest.

A hotelier is obliged therefore to take reasonable care of the property of guests who may reasonably expect valuable items to be looked after by the hotelier on their behalf. Consequently a system of safety deposit boxes or a separate safe may well be utilized for the safe custody of guests' valuables. The cashiers are usually responsible for administering this.

In the eyes of the law, in the event of loss, if the guest wants to obtain full compensation for the loss of any article valued at more than £50 then this is possible only should the item have been offered to the hotelier for safe keeping. In practice many articles that a guest carries are worth in excess of £50 and therefore it tends to be the most expensive items such as money, cameras and jewellery that are offered to the cashier. The cashier will keep a special safe deposit receipt book and will record in this the details of the item offered for safe keeping which will normally be placed into a sealed envelope which has the number of the receipt clearly displayed on the outside. The item may only be recovered from the cashier at a later time when the receipt is produced by the customer and will not be released in any other circumstances. The receipt is

MAJESTIC HOTEL
1 HIGH STREET,
MELCHESTER,
MELCHESTERSHIRE, ME1 2ZF
Tel: 9876 54321

VAT registration no. 123 4567 89

Room no.   No. of guests

803

Rate £ ....

Departure 23.8

Name .....GRANT

.....................PA.B

A/c to ....

....

Explanation of code

	A apartments
	R room hire
	B breakfast
	L luncheon
	D dinner

FOOD	banquet food
	teas and coffees
	restaurant drinks
	banquet drinks
BAR	bar drinks
	telephone and telegrams
	laundry
	trips
MISC	miscellaneous sundries
%	service charge
CASH	cash received
ALLW	allowances and corrections
LDGR	transfers to ledger

Please leave your key

Signature ......

Serial no.: **63671**

Date cons. no.	Code	Amount

```
22/08#0110
****************.00

DRAL                      .00
DRINKS        1.20
RAL A1      #0303-9       1.20
22/08#0128
DRAL                     1.20
DRINKS        1.20
RAL A1      #0303-9       2.40
```

No. **80737**   Date......23.8

M   GRANT   **Received £**

the sum of 2.40

....

For 803   2 | 40

VAT no. 123 4567 89   **HOTEL MAJESTIC**

Figure 94   *A guest bill and its subsequent receipt. This is an 'extras' bill for a tour customer*

**Hotel Proprietors Act 1956 – Loss Or Damage
To Guest's Property**

Under the Hotel Proprietors Act 1956 a hotel proprietor may in certain circumstances be liable to make good any loss or damage to a guest's property even though it was not due to any fault of the proprietor or the staff of the hotel.

The liability however
(a) extends only to the property of guests who have engaged sleeping accommodation at the hotel;
(b) is limited to £50 for any one article and a total of £100 in the case of any one guest, except in the case of property which has been deposited, or offered for deposit, for safe custody;
(c) does not cover motor cars or other vehicles of any kind or any property left in them, or horses, or other live animals.

This notice does not constitute an admission either that the Act applies to this hotel or that liability thereunder attaches to the proprietor of this hotel in any particular case.

Figure 95

then stuck back into the receipt book to show that the item was reclaimed. Should the guest not wish to reveal what is in the envelope then only an estimate of the value will be placed on the receipt and a note to the effect that the contents of the envelope are unknown will be made.

Should an item of value be lost from safe keeping then guests are entitled to complete compensation of its total value; but should they have been unwise enough to leave items of value in their bedroom then they will only be entitled to £50.

The cashiers will also be involved in preparing the banking and may even take this to the bank themselves. As far as the banking is concerned, the totals of finance obtained during the particular day of business must first be agreed with the accounting and billing system in use and cross-checked before the relevant paying-in slip is completed. The cashiers will be involved with the problems of maintaining the correct levels of change available for floats in the hotel and therefore not all money will necessarily be paid in as some may well be retained for the floats.

In order to keep the checking of the paying in simple for the bank cashier the paying-in slip should be completed as shown in Figure 96.

If this sort of system is used the time taken to pay in will be considerably reduced.

The cashier should also take to the bank the hotel's order for change, which may have been phoned through earlier to facilitate its preparation, and will also collect the daily sheet of foreign currency exchange rates.

An important consideration when a member of the hotel's staff is transacting business at the bank is that he or she is a likely target for robbery. Large hotels will employ a security firm for transferring money; but in smaller establishments, as a safeguard, the cashier should not take the same route to the bank at the same time every day. Ideally, the cashier should also be accompanied.

PAYING–IN SLIP ONE

Cheques: Drawer's name and bank code number.
    Largest cheques first.

Sterling notes: Bundled all the same way up into amounts stipulated by bank.
    Largest denominations first.

Coins: Silver, bagged into amounts stipulated by bank.
    Bronze, bagged into amounts stipulated by bank.

PAYING–IN SLIP TWO and subsequent slips
(one for each overseas currency being handled)

Traveller's cheques: Name of issuing agency and itemized into amounts.

Foreign currency notes: Bundled all the same way up.
    Largest denominations first.

Figure 96

9 The work of the accommodation manager

The importance of the accommodation manager

In all of our three hotels the manager who is responsible for the accommodation is ultimately in charge of the area of the establishment that will at the end of the day produce the most revenue and consequent profit. The accommodation manager's job is therefore both responsible and sometimes onerous in that failure to sell the bedrooms profitably will undoubtedly result in the insolvency of the total business.

From the Ship Inn through to the International Hotel there is little doubt that rooms have to be sold to encourage business into the other facilities provided by the hotel. If the financial controllers of these hotels were consulted they would almost certainly regard the operation of the restaurants, bars and other departments as very secondary trade, contributing, as they would, only a small percentage of the total revenue and yet forming a large part of the expense of running the hotel.

It is hardly surprising therefore that the managements of most hotels quite rightly devote themselves to selling rooms, with the aid of a professional accommodation manager, and only spend time on the secondary spin-off trade from selling those rooms.

Much of the time of the accommodation manager is taken in keeping financial track of the business; therefore, he or she will be compiling or requiring staff to give him or her the most accurate business statistics that have been set so that the achievements of the hotel against any particular budgets may be compared. As the major task is to maximize the occupancy and consequent revenue of the hotel the accommodation managers will be deeply involved in monitoring the business to see that targets are being achieved and hopefully exceeded. Indeed their personal future may be determined by their ability to achieve targets as judged by their immediate seniors and by their employers at a head office, so a large amount of their time must be spent making sure for their own career that the hotel is 'on budget'.

Not only are accommodation managers responsible for the financial attainment of their rooms but they are also charged with the job of ensuring customer satisfaction; a hotel is, after all, providing a very personal service to guests. Not only must they therefore liaise extensively with the housekeeping department to ensure that the rooms are maintained and serviced to the required standard but they must be prepared to be public relations people in being able to deal with any complaints that may arise from the accommodation operation of the hotel. Complaints have already been discussed in Chapter 7 from the point of view of the receptionist, but it is ultimately up to the accommodation manager as to whether a complaining guest is given a credit off their bill, a free stay or is asked to leave the hotel as the level of service required is not possible in the establishment!

Do not be fooled, though, into thinking that accommodation managers escape from the task of supervising staff; not only will this very task take up a considerable amount of their time, despite having conscientious heads of section or department working for them, but they will also have to organize and direct them, becoming involved in all the administrative tasks such as rotas, allocating days off and holidays and therefore ensuring that there are always sufficient staff to cope with peaks of business. They will be personally involved in the hiring and recruiting of new staff to the department and will undoubtedly organize their training, whether this is on-the-job or release to college.

Probably the most important time for accommodation

managers each day is around 6 p.m. when the amount of business for the night becomes apparent and decisions have to be made as to whether to release rooms or not. Accommodation managers need to make positive decisions at this time to enable the 'house' to be filled to its maximum and will also therefore be taking decisions as to whether to overbook or not. They will, of course, have to make the decision to stop taking reservations should it become obvious that this is necessary; consequently they will be continuously monitoring their computer VDU display or the reservation rack to keep watch on the situation.

Accommodation managers will be taking decisions, along with the sales managers in large hotels, as to the rates to quote to large groups or business customers and will be personally involved in formulating the discounting policy. In smaller hotels the accommodation manager may also be the sales manager so he or she will directly liaise with potential new customers, especially those conference and tour operators who may place large amounts of business with the hotel.

It should now be apparent that the accommodation manager has a wide and varied responsibility in a hotel and his or her position is charged with achieving the largest part, by far, of the possible revenue for the hotel.

In order to monitor the business the accommodation manager must make use of business statistics

From a cursory glance into reception at the number of guests being accommodated or the number of rooms being let it is not possible to keep an accurate check on exactly how the business is performing from minute to minute. Indeed, many of the decisions that the accommodation manager has to make relate to statistics that need to be calculated rapidly and then have to be compared with last year's achievement as well as a detailed budget. A very important part of the accommodation manager's work will be analysing statistics that may well have been prepared by other front office staff and then taking the appropriate managerial decisions.

The first series of statistics involves looking at the performance of the staff at letting the rooms of the hotel; this is called an analysis of occupancy. The occupancy statistics that are calculated purely let the accommodation manager know how effective the sales of rooms have been but it depends exactly on how the eventual figures are worked out as to how meaningful the result will be. In order to understand the implications of calculating occupancy by varying methods let us examine the results of a week's accommodation sales at the Majestic Hotel (Figure 97).

From the figures it will be seen that totals have been produced for the business both daily and weekly and it is common to produce cumulative statistics so that in addition the monthly and annual results may be compiled. While the numbers of rooms sold, the results of bedspaces let and the total income has been isolated the figures have also been expressed in percentage occupancy terms. This is the common way for the performance of the accommodation departments to be analysed.

The whole point of calculating the various types of occupancy is to make sure that the hotel maintains a profitable performance and does not sink below the break-even point that has been set. The break-even point will depend upon the multitude of fixed and variable costs involved in letting the rooms and operating the hotel in total but there will be a minimum overall percentage occupancy that the hotel must achieve to remain solvent. As every hotel has infinitely variable operational expenses, the break-even occupancy level will be peculiar to every separate hotel but it is the basic base line below which an accommodation manager must not sink if the hotel is to continue in business; it always has to be remembered that the majority of revenue comes from letting the rooms.

The first basic way of calculating occupancy is to work out the *room occupancy* which tells the accommodation manager how efficient the staff have been in letting the rooms. Room occupancy may be calculated as follows:

$$\text{Percentage room occupancy} = \frac{\text{actual rooms sold}}{\text{total rooms in hotel}} \times 100$$

This statistic is the most basic of the occupancy statistics. It is useful but will not reflect that the hotel is being undersold if only one customer is placed in a double room. All the statistic shows is how many rooms have been sold but not to how many people, which is far more meaningful.

MAJESTIC HOTEL

Analysis of the accommodation department's performance for the week commencing 12 September

	Total rooms sold	(%) Room occupancy	Total bedspaces sold	(%) Sleeper occupancy	Total income	(%) Income occupancy
Mon. 12	150	100	250	100	£8,800	88
Tues. 13	150	100	250	100	£9,600	96
Wed. 14	150	100	250	100	£10,000	100
Thur. 15	150	100	250	100	£9,200	92
Fri. 16	75	50	135	54	£5,400	54
Sat. 17	30	20	55	22	£2,200	22
Sun. 18	90	60	110	44	£4,400	44
Weekly total	795		1300		£49,600	
	75.7% Weekly room occupancy		74.2% Weekly sleeper occupancy		70.8% Weekly income occupancy	

Total rooms in hotel 150 per night or 1050 per week.
Total bedspaces   250 per night or 1750 per week.
Total possible income £10,000 per night or £70,000 per week.

Figure 97

In order to cope with the inadequacies of the room occupancy statistic a more accurate way of gauging occupancy is to calculate the *sleeper occupancy*. This records the. number of bedspaces (a double bed for statistical purposes is two bedspaces) that have been let in the hotel and may be calculated as follows:

$$\text{Percentage sleeper occupancy} = \frac{\text{actual number of bedspaces sold}}{\text{total bedspaces in hotel}} \times 100$$

Even though the sleeper occupancy statistic is more important, the astute accommodation manager could easily fill all the rooms and all the bedspaces by selling at give-away prices which might satisfy the statistics but still mean that the hotel is unprofitable. Consequently *income occupancy* is often calculated to show how much of the potential income that the rooms can make has actually been achieved. Income occupancy may be calculated as follows:

$$\text{Percentage income occupancy} = \frac{\text{actual income}}{\text{total possible income}} \times 100$$

Income occupancy is far more meaningful and provides the best possible statistic from the point of view of the finances of the hotel. It is therefore the single most important of all the occupancy statistics.

Having seen how these figures are calculated let us look back at the figures produced for the Majestic (Figure 98). On the daily figures it is apparent that the rooms are full in the hotel from Monday to Thursday but that the weekends show a marked decrease in trade which illustrates why the weekly room occupancy is as low as 75.7 per cent. The weekly sleeper occupancy.is lower at 74.2 per cent, showing that not all bedspaces have been filled to capacity; the real problem was on Sunday night when 90 rooms were sold to only 110 sleepers, giving a very low sleeper occupancy of 44 per cent. As far as income was concerned, Wednesday saw the whole hotel sold to capacity (although on Monday the rooms and bedspaces were full), and yet, due to discounting, the income occupancy figure was down to a low 88 per cent. The problems of the weekend are

reflected in the income occupancy figures especially as they affect the weekly occupancy figure at a low 70.8 per cent. While many assumptions may be read into these figures the accommodation manager would need to improve the income occupancy results especially in view of the problem that arose on Monday night.

Another way of representing these figures may be in the form of a graph which is always a useful reference aid in a back area of the reception office. It is much easier to spot the trends in occupancy by superimposing the various occupancy statistics onto the graph and thereby let the staff witness the effects of their labours. If it is the managerial policy to pay a bonus or give some incentive to staff who fill the hotel to a certain percentage occupancy what better centre of attraction than a graph which shows those staff how they are doing towards their goal? Hopefully a graph will produce the added stimulus to encourage staff to attain their target.

In some hotels it is the managerial policy to look in detail at the number of rooms that could take two guests but in fact are only let to one. This will no doubt affect the sleeper occupancy figure but it may not affect the income occupancy if the customer has in fact paid the full rate for two people, which might anyway be the case if a 'per room' tariff is being used. If the tariff in operation is 'per person' then the management will wish, where possible, to discourage the single occupancy of double rooms and will therefore ask for a *double occupancy* statistic to be produced daily by use of the following equation:

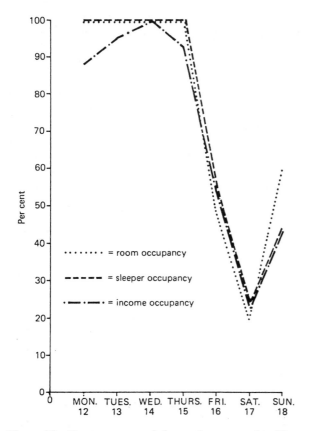

Figure 98   *Occupancy graph for week commencing 12 September for the Majestic Hotel*

$$\text{Percentage double occupancy} = \frac{\begin{array}{c}\text{number of double}\\\text{or twin rooms let}\\\text{to two persons}\end{array}}{\begin{array}{c}\text{total number of}\\\text{twin and double}\\\text{rooms}\end{array}} \times 100$$

The management should, though, always remember that the production of statistics of this sort may have the reverse affect to that originally intended. Staff should obviously be encouraged to fill double rooms, but it may not be possible in all cases and an empty room is far less preferable than a double being used by only one person. At least some revenue is being gained as well as spending being encouraged in other departments of the hotel which might not have been the case otherwise.

In the larger hotels the statistics referring to occupancy will be produced overnight by the night auditor or by computer and presented with the financial reports the following morning to the accommodation manager. The results should not surprise the accommodation manager especially if a percentage in excess of 100 appears. It is in fact quite possible to achieve, for example, a 110 per cent sleeper occupancy if extra beds are placed into some rooms or, in the case of airport hotels, where some rooms are let more than once a day. While this policy of multi-letting rooms can be onerous for the housekeeping department, it has been possible at times to let an airport hotel bedroom for three eight-hour time slots within twenty-four hours and the sleeper and income occupancy figures have therefore benefited correspondingly.

Before leaving occupancy statistics and moving on to some of the other business statistics the point should be made that in some hotels the room, sleeper and income occupancy rates are worked out instead as 'available' room, 'available' bedspace and 'available' income occupancy figures on the understanding that some rooms will always be taken 'off' for redecoration or repairs. This may be true and some hotels would argue that this is a legitimate way of working out the occupancy statistics; but the figures as originally produced will also reflect the number of rooms 'off'. The accommodation manager should not therefore 'adjust' the occupancy figures but should keep a close watch on how many rooms are taken off, and therefore losing income, which will be reflected in the original method of compiling the occupancy figures.

Up to now the statistics we have examined have been expressed in percentages but many hoteliers prefer to use statistics that refer to amounts of money. While it is common practice in restaurants to produce statistics such as the 'average spend per head' this is not quite so common in the accommodation departments but some managers may find a similar figure easier to refer to.

The accommodation manager's equivalent of the 'average spend per head' is the *average room rate* and the *average sleeper rate* which will show, when expressed in financial terms, the effectiveness of staff selling at the published tariff or 'rack rate'. In other words, the more discounting that is carried out on prices the lower the average room and sleeper rate,

which will always be examined with an aim to them being increased. The average room rate may be calculated as follows:

$$\text{Average room rate} = \frac{\text{total room income}}{\text{total number of rooms sold}} = £$$

The same sort of comparison may be made with sleepers, with the average sleeper rate being calculated as follows:

$$\text{Average sleeper rate} = \frac{\text{total room income}}{\text{total number of sleepers}} = £$$

For our figures for the Majestic the average room and sleeper rates would be as shown in Figure 99.

Again the problem of discounting appears on Monday with both averages being low compared with the rest of the week; there are also some other fluctuations which the accommodation manager will have to examine closely along with the breakdown of types of rooms to establish the exact cause. The effect will invariably be that pressure will be maintained by the senior management and head office for the weekly averages to be increased above those achieved especially if they compare unfavourably with both the budget figures and the results from the previous year.

Another statistic that the front office staff may be asked to prepare on behalf of the entire hotel operation is the calculation of the *residents average spend*. This calculation does not take into account only the accommodation charges that a resident guest has incurred but also the entire amount of the bill. This

	Average room rate	Average sleeper rate
Mon. 12	£58.66	£35.20
Tues. 13	£64.00	£38.40
Wed. 14	£66.66	£40.00
Thur. 15	£61.34	£36.80
Fri. 16	£72.00	£40.00
Sat. 17	£73.34	£40.00
Sun. 18	£48.88	£40.00
	£63.55 ↑ Weekly average room rate	£38.62 ↑ Weekly average sleeper rate

Figure 99

average spend therefore tells the management how much guests are spending on their entire stay at the hotel and, if used correctly, will reveal those guests who should be attracted to the hotel because of their high spending. The way in which the residents average spend is calculated is as follows:

$$\text{Resident average spend} = \frac{\text{total of resident bills}}{\text{total number of residents}} = \pounds$$

Having compiled several statistics that reveal the usage of the hotel's accommodation and also the amounts of money that are being exchanged, the astute accommodation manager will also calculate a series of statistics designed to reveal more about the guests themselves. Most of the results will be vital in formulating the hotel's marketing policy as they will reveal trends that may not be apparent from a cursory look at the guest records.

In order that accommodation managers may learn about their customers and the type of business for which they are catering there are several statistics that may readily be produced. The first of these that will have far-reaching implications on the operaton of most of the hotel's departments is the *average length of stay* of guests. This is calculated as follows:

$$\text{Average length of stay} = \frac{\text{total number of bed nights sold}}{\text{total number of guests}}$$

The results of this research will allow, for example, the housekeeping department to make plans for the amount of linen needed for rooms, as the length of stay will obviously affect the number of linen changes required. It may well reveal that short stay customers are being accommodated and therefore that more emphasis should be placed on marketing to long-stay holidaymakers. Maybe families may have to be encouraged rather than businessmen, depending entirely on the results that are reached. It will be realized that this average length of stay statistic cannot be calculated for a single day but has to be over a period of at least a month and probably longer. In many hotels this statistic is produced only annually.

There are two calculations which allow the accommodation manager to assimilate the places that guests and their business come from. The first of these is the *origin of guests* statistic which will break the customers down into nationalities and then counties or even towns to show the accommodation manager where business is coming from. The information for this calculation is readily available from the registration details and the results will show where marketing has been successful as well as highlighting areas that need special attention. A pie chart, histogram or even a map may be good ways of illustrating this information.

Similarly it may be useful to compile an analysis of the *source of reservations* or, in other words, from where reservations come. This analysis will reveal how many customers book through their businesses, how many use a travel agent, the number of individual as well as chance reservations and those who have come on tours or for conferences. Again this will help formulate marketing policy as well as illustrating areas of the trade that have been missed.

There is no doubt that the accommodation manager will need access to statistics like those we have already mentioned in order to keep a close watch on the usage as well as the income from the rooms in the hotel. An analysis of the customers themselves will also help considerably in formulating marketing strategy.

The night auditor or the reception staff themselves will produce the various statistics for the accommodation manager and many of them will appear on the daily trading report that is circulated to the management – usually the day after the actual business has been undertaken. The accommodation manager will be able to see from this report whether the accommodation departments are performing to budget as there will usually be comparative figures not only for the budget itself but also of the previous years' results. Managerial decisions will be made from these figures in order to keep the operation on target and it will become evident from the figures if the business is straying away from its planned course.

It is of course not only essential to look back at what has been achieved but also to plan ahead so that business decisions may be taken in advance. The accommodation manager will therefore be keen to receive forecasts some time ahead of the business likely to be undertaken in the accommodation departments. The expected trade in the hotel established from those reservations already placed as well as reference to last year's figures will allow a fairly accurate forecast to be produced. This will be distributed to the various heads of department so that preparations may be made.

The daily trading report used at the Majestic is illustrated in Figure 100, showing the columns for comparisons not only with the budget but also with last year's results. The sophisticated night report for the International is shown in Figure 101, with not only an analysis of business on 10 October but also a forecast of room availability for the immediate future.

Much of the accommodation manager's time will be

Majestic Hotel

Daily trading report for...19... Prepared by:...

Rooms	Today No.	Today %	Budget %	Last year %	Sleepers	Today	Budget	Last year
Occupied					Room only			
Compliment					R & B			
Staff					½ board			
'Off'					Full board			
Vacant					Children			
TOTAL	150	100%			Complimentary			
					Resident			
Ratio					Weekend break			
Av. rm. rate					Revenue			
Av. slp. rate					Rooms			
					Breakfast			
Total guests					Tdh lunch			
					A.la.c. lunch			
Source of business					Tdh dinner			
Business house					A.la.c. dinner			
Travel agent					Banq. food			
Tour (a)					Room serv. food			
Tour (b)					Comp. food			
Individual					Public bar			
Chance					Tdh bar			
Conference					A.la.c. bar			
Other:					Banq. liquor			
					Comp. liquor			
					Laundry			
					Telephone			
					Casino club			
					Sundries			
					Total:			
Income occupancy:					Residents average spend:			

Figure 100   *Daily trading report form*

INTERNATIONAL HOTEL NIGHT REPORT FRIDAY 10 OCTOBER

Group tours and conference	PAX	Revenue inc. VAT	No. of rms	Average inc. VAT
Tour 8068	25	317.00	14	22.64
Tour 61	13	186.00	7	26.57
Tour 65	27	360.00	15	24.00
Tour 51	29	351.00	15	23.40
Tour 8045	13	155.00	7	22.14
Tour 66	40	480.00	20	24.00
Tour 43	19	274.00	12	22.83
Tour 8069	20	230.00	10	23.00
Discount B	18	216.00	9	24.00
Discount A	19	222.90	9	24.76
Conf. 9108	4	60.00	2	30.00
Conf. 1109	10	150.00	5	30.00
Conf. 742 185	16	287.93	9	31.99
Int. package	15	195.40	9	21.71
Bye tours	9	140.00	5	28.00
BA tours	1	27.50	1	27.50
Aut avia	12	219.00	6	36.50
Atlantis pack	12	238.84	7	34.12
Fan jet	3	63.25	2	31.63
Fan travel	2	36.50	1	36.50
Travellers	2	30.00	1	30.00
Affro pack	2	35.00	1	35.00
Bell UK	2	25.20	1	25.20
Total inc.	313	(i) 4,300.52	168	25.60

Revenue analysis

Inclusive tours	£4300.52(i)
Air crews	£1315.40
Business house	£1126.60
Conference, D/D	£ 923.25
Individual disc	£4656.29
Full rate	£4313.00
Summary	£16635.06(ii)

Total revenue	£16,635.06(ii)
Day lets and extras	£ 186.00
Sub total	£16,821.06
Adjustments to prior business	£ .....
Total including VAT	£16,821.06
Total VAT	£ 2,165.92
Total excluding VAT	£14,655.14(iii)

Rooms sold: 430	Percentage: 71.66%
Vacant : 166	Percentage: 27.66%
Off : 4	Percentage: 0.66%
Total : 600	100%

Room availability forecast

Date 10	11	12	13	14
Occupied	430			
Departures	163	35	69	6
Projected		51	210	100
Available	267	86	279	106
Reservation	46	27	43	42
Groups	80	164	109	71
Total	126	191	152	113
Available	600	600	600	600
Sold	393	277	431	219
To sell	207	323	169	381
% occupancy	65.5%	46.16%	71.83%	36.5%

Analysis of actuals to budget excl. VAT

Day 5	Actuals	Budget	Variance
Av. room rate	34.08	39.30	-5.22
% room occ.	71.66	95.38	-23.72
Net revenue	14,655(iii)	22,479	-7824
Week 1 day 5	**Actuals**	**Budget**	**Variance**
Av. room rate	33.53	39.30	-5.77
% room occ.	91.01	95.38	-4.37
Net revenue	66,506	112,395	-45,889
Period date	**Actuals**	**Budget**	**Variance**
Av. room rate	33.53	39.30	-5.77
% room occ.	91.01	95.38	-4.37
Net revenue	66,506	112,395	-45,889

Figure 101 *Night report Friday 10 October for the International Hotel*

taken up analysing and justifying the figures that appear on the various reports that are produced, and from the night report for the International Hotel on the 10 October there is a considerable amount of interest. The business has been analysed in detail on the right-hand side, but at the bottom the telling figure is that for the particular date showing the hotel to be £7824 down on budget which has led to a shortfall of £45,889 for the period. The accommodation manager would try to discover any way possible at this time to improve these figures to balance out the deficit on rooms by the end of the period. Unfortunately the room availability forecast is gloomy, with only the night of 13 October looking set to exceed the occupancy statistics of 10

October. Perhaps, though, there is a surge of business beyond our short forecast that will explain the very high budget figure set at 95.38 per cent room occupancy during this particular period.

While the night report itself may initially seem intimidating it is purely a record of the business being undertaken in the room that has had a limited amount of statistical analysis added to it. Most hotels will produce a similar breakdown of the business; it is an essential method by which the management may monitor the success or otherwise of the business.

The accommodation manager must monitor the business by means of control

In the larger hotels such as the International there will be a separate control department; in the smaller hotels 'control' will be left to the individual specialist managers. Whatever the organization, the accommodation manager will need to exercise control over the operation of the rooms.

The aim of accommodation control is first to see that the guests are billed correctly and to this end a large number of internal checks will take place in order to make sure that guests' bills are accurate. The easiest check of all, which the accommodation manager and the head receptionist will supervise, is the checking of the receipts against the paid bills as well as the money actually received in the till. Any discrepancy here will almost always indicate sloppy attention to detail in the handling of money and will indicate the efficiency or otherwise of the cashiers. Another important check is on the usage of rooms to ensure that guests have been billed correctly.

It is important that the front office liaise considerably with housekeeping as in all but the smallest hotels it will be impossible for the receptionists to physically check the usage of each bedroom. What will normally happen is that at least twice a day the floor supervisors on the housekeeping staff will check the exact usage of each bedroom and record this on a housekeeper's report which is sent to reception. The report will detail exactly how many bedspaces have been slept in in each bedroom. This detail will be checked against the occupancy figures in reception. What will show up is those rooms where more people are sleeping than are paying, or even those rooms that are occupied without the knowledge

of the reception. There may, in the latter case, be some very logical reason such as staff being allowed to stay in the hotel by a manager who has not informed reception; but conversely it could mean that, for example, a night porter is letting rooms without telling anyone and pocketing the money. This form of control of bedrooms will also show those customers who have left without paying, or those rooms which are thought to have been occupied which have in fact not been taken up by those customers who reserved them. Whatever the outcome it will be important to act on the results of the housekeeper's report so that an exact picture of room status is compiled at least twice a day.

At the International the rooms division manager will have not only a hotel controller but also a member of staff to undertake the control function and, as the manager in charge of accommodation, policy decisions will have to be made in the light of the results achieved. The controller will usually be a person with accountancy skills who is not only responsible for the total work of the control department but who also prepares and analyses the various statistics for management. They may well, if the hotel is in a large company, be responsible initially to the financial director at head office, but they obviously do everything they can do to assist the unit management with whom they work closely. Should the figures produced highlight any particular problems the controller will probably be asked to investigate these errors in conjunction with the accommodation manager so that any problems are identified and rectified rapidly before they get out of control.

Apart from accuracy of accounts and the usage of the bedrooms another duty of the control staff and the accommodation manager is to prevent any fraud by staff or guests. The purpose of the control will therefore be to discourage any acts such as letting rooms on one's own behalf or giving free stays to friends or any abuses that may occur in the hotel. The habit of overcharging on foreign currency exchange rates and similar practices will be eradicated by good control. Another purpose of control is the efficient usage of resources and this may well be applied to the consumables such as cleaning materials in the housekeeping department under the responsibility of the accommodation manager or to such items as stationery in the front office. Control will make the accommodation operation much more cost effective.

Yet another function of control is to ensure that payment is received from customers, especially with credit sales. A hotel is most unusual in that it gives a considerable amount of 'credit' to customers by allowing them to complete their stay at a hotel before presenting them with a bill. Where else may you purchase an item only after you have used it? There are also a considerable number of opportunities open to guests to pay by methods that do not allow the hotel its money immediately and the ledger clerk will be the person who keeps a check on outstanding payments. In order to encourage payments a sequence of 'demand' letters may have to be instigated using the formats shown in Figure 102.

Hopefully this sequence of demands will not have to be put into action, but if it is thought necessary the accommodation manager will give authorization: non-payment of any bills obviously affects the revenue of the hotel considerably.

Another aspect of non-payment that the accommodation manager has to decide upon is that of guests who have not claimed accommodation that they have booked. Legally it is quite permissible to do this as well as sending a bill for any food that they might reasonably have been expected to consume during their stay. In practice it is usually tour or business customers who are sent bills, especially if they have a record of being regular offenders; but the accommodation manager will always balance the effect of loss of goodwill. This might be considerable, but on the other hand so might be the loss involved to the hotel. Customers may only be charged if it has proved impossible to re-let their unclaimed accommodation to another customer.

How does the accommodation manager manage reservations?

It is up to the accommodation manager to monitor bookings carefully and especially to formulate policies on releasing rooms that have been unclaimed and also in deciding on levels of overbooking. The accommodation manager will usually be very evident in the front desk area around 6 p.m. when the deadline is reached in those hotels who stipulate as a term to their reservations that unclaimed rooms may be re-let to other customers after 6 p.m. It will usually be left to accommodation managers to decide which rooms to

release and they will usually go for those which are unconfirmed, bearing in mind the legal rights of those customers who have confirmed in writing or verbally.

Overbooking is another technique that astute accommodation managers will employ in an attempt to compensate for the 'no-shows' and cancellations which look likely to leave them with a hotel that is not full. The major point to make with overbooking is to ensure that it is watched carefully each day rather than there being a policy; for example, to overbook by 10 per cent every day.

Overbooking means accepting more reservations than there are rooms available in order to compensate for no shows and cancellations; at best it is always a risky policy to pursue especially if an accommodation manager is new to the particular hotel. While reference to past situations might be helpful, overbooking may be carried out on a minute-by-minute basis only, keeping a close watch on the local environment which might affect bookings. For example, at the International weather conditions, such as fog, will affect the level of usage of the airport and consequently the hotel; even weather overseas that is adverse for flying will stop planes, and therefore hotel customers, arriving. Industrial action at the airport will affect the level of business in the hotel so the accommodation manager must be very aware of the outside influence on the business.

If overbooking is not calculated daily then the situation will be reached where customers with confirmed reservations will be arriving only to be told there is no room for them. Here accommodation managers have to exercise their social skills, as the guest is legally entitled to alternative accommodation of the same standard at another hotel at no extra expense. The guest will therefore have to be transported to that hotel; should it be more expensive then it is not the customer's responsibility to stand the difference. Needless to say, this sort of situation aggravates customers; it is better to make sure that if overbooking is utilized it is carried out within strict limits. *Never* fall into the trap of overbooking by 10 per cent every day, as this can cause enormous problems.

Another way in which the accommodation manager manages reservations is by the encouragement of large groups of customers to the hotel. By large groups we mean that discussions will take place with tour

1   Sent out immediately after bill incurred:

> MAJESTIC HOTEL
>
> Dear Sir,
>
> We have pleasure in rendering the attached account which we trust you will find to be in order.
>
> In accordance with our terms of business, we would respectfully remind you that we look forward to receiving your remittance within the next 14 days.
>
> We are pleased to have been of service to you and hope to have further opportunity on future occasions.
>
> Yours faithfully,
>
> Accommodation Manager

2   Statement sent 14 days after (1)

3   Sent out 14 days after statement (2)

> MAJESTIC HOTEL
>
> Dear Sir,
>
> Outstanding account totalling £.................
>
> We note from our records that we still have not received your remittance in settlement of the above outstanding accounts now due for payment.
>
> We would remind you that our terms of business are nett cash within 14 days.
>
> We await your early remittance, thus avoiding the need for stronger action.
>
> Yours faithfully,
>
> Accommodation Manager

4   Statement sent 14 days after (3)

5   Sent out 14 days after (4)

> MAJESTIC HOTEL
>
> Dear Sir,
>
> Overdue account dated.....................
> Totalling £..............................
>
> We are concerned to note that we still have not received your remittance in settlement of the above overdue debt, despite sending you previous reminders.
>
> Our terms of payment are Nett Cash within 14 days and, as we cannot allow any further extension of credit, we must insist on full settlement within the next 10 days, otherwise the debt will be forwarded to our Debt Collection Agents.
>
> Yours faithfully,
>
> Accommodation Manager

6   After 10 days details given to debt collection agency.

Figure 102

operators, conference organizers, airlines, local business houses and also travel agencies concerning the policies for allowing their business into the hotel. Having started this chapter by examining statistics it will be appreciated that large groups may well increase the hotel's room occupancy but may well affect the income occupancy specially if large discounts are offered. The accommodation manager will therefore have to balance off any loss in revenue for rooms against the overall benefit to the business of filling the rooms and a large amount of time will be taken on similar decisions.

Groups will normally be selected to fill in the troughs in business but the unfortunate fact is that, like most customers, tours want to come at peak times. It may well turn out not to be worthwhile accepting tour customers at certain times because of the traditional business, paying the full 'rack' rates, that might be turned away; therefore this has all to be considered. In a hotel like the Majestic it may well be felt that tour customers are not the type of business that should be encouraged so there will be little opportunity for a tour operator to succeed there, whereas at the International there may well be plenty of scope for the larger groups especially conferences. The accommodation manager therefore has to be extremely careful in formulating policy as a wrong decision will severely affect the figures in the reports at a later date.

The accommodation manager's job is all about people

As hotel work involves giving a service to customers there is no doubt that the accommodation manager has to play a substantial part in making sure that guests are accommodated with the utmost possible hospitality. The accommodation manager will more often than not be particularly involved in the checking-in and service given to VIP guests and will personally have checked their accommodation prior to their arrival. He or she will certainly have distributed information about the VIP to the various department heads on a VIP form such as that illustrated in Figure 103.

As well as dealing with the VIP guests in a hotel accommodation managers will normally come into contact with other guests at stress times such as when they have a complaint; it requires a member of staff of their seniority to solve the problem. It is, after all, only

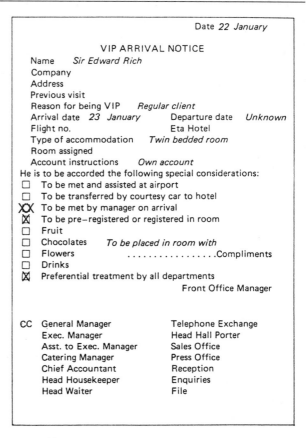

Figure 103

a member of management who may authorize a discount or a refund should a complaint be serious enough to warrant this. The impression should not be given that they hide away in their offices as they will almost certainly be involved as duty managers each day, thereby entailing their presence in many areas of the hotel. This requirement to run the hotel as duty manager also explains the necessity for them to have had training in non-accommodation departments so that they know how to administer, for example, the restaurant when necessary.

Where staff are concerned they will, of course, be involved in their recruiting and training so that they must be aware of all the techniques of personnel management in order to be a motivator of the front office staff. Quite literally they should have the experience and confidence to undertake any of the jobs that are carried out in the front office and by being able to do this will command the respect of their juniors.

It may therefore be seen that the accommodation manager has a large task in a hotel of any size, being totally responsible for the major profit making area of the establishment. The hotelier who has reached this position should be justifiably proud of the attainment in what is a most challenging and rewarding position.

Appendices

1 Legislation relevant to the provision of accommodation

The operation of accommodation in Great Britain is subject to much legislation and there follows a brief list of that which is relevant accompanied, where possible, by a number of the cases of precedent. This list and the accompanying explanations should be regarded purely as an indication of the scope of individual Acts and Orders, and specialist textbooks or a solicitor should be consulted in practical dispute situations.

The following Acts and Orders are an integral part of Common Law and have historically been created to protect the rights of both the person operating a business – within the hospitality industry this is often the *hotel proprietor* or *innkeeper* – as well as the rights of the customer – the *traveller, lodger* or *guest*.

The hospitality industry itself is made up of establishments technically known as *Inns* which are in fact those hotels defined within the Hotel Proprietors Act of 1956 and which would include our theoretical examples of the International and Majestic Hotels and the Ship Inn. Hotels outside the Hotel Proprietors Act definition are commonly known as *private hotels*.

Hotel Proprietors Act (1956)

The Hotel Proprietors Act defines a hotel as 'an establishment held out by the proprietor as offering food, drink, and if so required, sleeping accommodation, without special contract, to any traveller presenting himself who appears able and willing to pay a reasonable sum for the services and facilities provided and who is in a fit state to be received.'

The hotel proprietor (the owner, company or manager), who may also historically be referred to as an innkeeper, is therefore under an obligation to accept travellers, who may make use of the hotel's facilities for whatever period of time, at any establishment that fits the Act's definition. A traveller, incidentally, in law is anyone who wishes to make use of the hotel's services and may also, once they have booked in to stay, be referred to as a lodger, customer or guest.

The Hotel proprietor is obliged by the Act to cater for all travellers, whether they have booked in advance or not, although it is unclear in law when a traveller, once accepted, becomes a 'lodger' and then subject additionally to legislation including the Law of Contract. The proprietor may, though, refuse to accept a traveller requiring accommodation should the hotel's bedrooms be full whilst the late arrival of a traveller, unless this has been agreed in a contract, is no reason to refuse accommodation.

In making a judgement on the acceptance of travellers the hotel proprietor is not allowed to discriminate in any way on the grounds of the traveller's colour, creed or sex. They, in turn, must be in a fit state to be accepted or served which means that they must neither be under the influence of drugs nor drink and that their behaviour is not unreasonable. It is deemed important too that the traveller is appropriately dressed to be accepted but a definition of the standard is difficult to come by and is obviously appropriate to an individual establishment. The hotel proprietor has discretion too as to whether or not to accept a traveller who is accompanied by a dog. Should, incidentally, a dog be accommodated it may not of right accompany its owner into the hotel's public rooms (although exception may obviously be made for guide dogs) and the relevant Food Hygiene Regulations (1970) should be adhered to so that 'no person shall expose food to the risk of contamination'. A traveller may not be accepted into a hotel if accompanied by a dangerous or dirty dog.

Travellers are entitled to expect a reasonable price to

be charged for the hotel's services whilst the hotel proprietor is protected by the Hotel Proprietors Act against travellers who are not trustworthy by permitting a reasonable sum to be paid, in advance of the hotel's services being used, in other words, a deposit. The non-payment of a traveller's bill is also catered for with appropriate solutions being available within the Act which are explained a little later.

The hotel proprietor is obliged by the Act to provide travellers with refreshment, although there is no definition of what that refreshment should be. Refusal to do so, provided the request is not proven to be unreasonable, is punishable by a fine.

Where accommodation is concerned the hotel proprietor is obliged to provide accommodation that is of a reasonable and proper standard and in effect fit for the purpose. The accommodation, whatever the standard, must be clean and hygienically equipped. The traveller has no right to demand a particular room, although an astute proprietor will obviously try to satisfy such requests. Should a proprietor promise to provide a particular room, and then fail to do so, the contractual arrangements will have then been broken and the traveller may be entitled to damages.

Under the Act the proprietor is not only obliged to accept travellers but also their luggage provided it is not of an exceptional nature. The proprietor does have a right (or lien) to subsequently seize and hold the traveller's luggage in lieu of an unpaid bill. Additionally the hotel proprietor has no obligation to provide garaging for a traveller's car above the provisions normally made available for vehicles.

Those travellers who have booked and are paying for accommodation will find that the Act specifically addresses the potential problems with their belongings. Where a traveller's property is concerned, provided a statutory notice is prominently displayed (as illustrated in Figure 95), the hotel proprietor is personally liable for any damage or loss to that property up to a limited amount whether negligence of hotel employees is involved or not. If the fault, though, lies with the traveller there is no liability on the hotel proprietor. The definition of 'property' is wide but specifically excludes animals, horses and vehicles and belongings left within vehicles. Liability of the hotel proprietor ceases once the traveller becomes a 'lodger' unless negligence is involved. Property handed in to the hotel proprietor for safe custody is not subject to

any limited liability and, if lost or damaged, would require the hotel proprietor to refund their full value. The proprietor may obviously insure against such claims.

As already mentioned the hotel proprietor has a lien where traveller's property is concerned. This means the proprietor is entitled to hold on to that property until an outstanding bill is paid. The lien applies to all travellers and not just those who have booked accommodation and gives a hotel proprietor the right to auction the property after the correct procedure has been carried out. (See Innkeepers Act (1878)).

Private hotels are those which decide not to open their doors to every traveller. For example, they may advertise through external signs such as 'No coaches'. In these hotels the proprietor may not only pick and choose their customers, but there is also no liability for customers' property, unless negligence is established, and there is no lien over that property in the case of unpaid bills.

Cases:

Armistead v. Wilde (1851)	Loss or property
Behrens v. Grenville Hotel (Bude) Ltd	Loss of property
Bennett v. Mellor (1793)	Loss or property
Browne v. Brandt (1902)	Refusal as hotel full
Carpenter v. Haymarket Hotel Ltd. (1931)	Loss of property
Constantine v. Imperial Hotels (1944)	Refusal to accept a traveller
Cunningham v. Philip (1896)	Definition of Inn
Dixon v. Birch (1873)	Definition of Innkeeper
Lamond v. Richmond (1897)	Definition of Lodger
Marsh v. Commissioner of Police (1944)	Lien
Orchard v. Bush (1898)	Definition of Hotel/ Restaurant, Traveller and Inn
Pidgeon v. Legge (1857)	Traveller's dress
R. v. Higgins (1947)	Refusal of refreshment
R. v. Rhymer (1877)	Traveller's dogs
R. v. Ivens (1835)	Late arrival
R. v. Sprague (1899)	Traveller's dress
Robins v. Gray (1895)	Traveller's luggage

Rothfield v. North British Hotels (1920)	Removal of guest
Shacklock v. Ethorpe Ltd. (1939)	Traveller's property
Williams v. Linnitt (1951)	Definition of Traveller Loss of property
Winkworth v. Raven (1931)	Liability for property (car)

Race Relations Act (1976)

The Act maintains that a hotel proprietor may not discriminate against a traveller, lodger or guest, when deciding whether or not to accept them or to supply them with services, on the grounds of colour, ethnic origin, nationality or race. The same Act applies to every type of business. Small establishments, with facilities for six or less lodgers in addition to the operator's family, are excluded from the Act in the specific case of residential accommodation only.

Where employment is concerned any person concerned with the employment of others is not permitted to discriminate against a potential employee on the grounds of colour, ethnic origin, nationality or race. The only exceptions are where discrimination is either on the grounds of integration or authenticity – the latter being, for example, where one might deliberately seek to employ Indians in the Indian restaurant.

Cases:

Constantine v. Imperial Hotels (1944)	Refusal to accept a traveller
Showboat Entertainment Centre v. Owens (1984)	Refusal to discriminate
Manla v. Dowell Lee & Others (1983)	Discrimination
Seize v. Gillette Industries (1980)	Alleged discrimination
Zarcynska v. Levy (1979)	Refusal to discriminate

Sex Discrimination Act (1975)

The Act maintains that a hotel proprietor may not discriminate against a male or female traveller, lodger or guest on the grounds of sex when deciding whether or not to accept them or to supply them with services.

Where employment is concerned a hotel proprietor may not discriminate against a potential male or female employee on the grounds of sex or marital status when deciding whether or not to employ them. The Act also amends the Equal Pay Act of 1970 to try to ensure that where men and women are employed in similar situations they are employed and remunerated under the same conditions and terms.

Cases:

Gill & Another v. El Vino Co. (1983)	Discrimination in pub
McLean v. Paris Travel (1976)	Marital status
Sorbie v. Trust Houses Forte (1977)	Equal pay

Licensing Act (1964)

Should a hotel possess a justices' liquor licence the hotel proprietor may ask anyone who is either under the influence of alcohol or disorderly to leave the premises.

Public Health (Control of Disease) Act (1984)

If a traveller or guest suffers from a notifiable disease or food poisoning whilst in the hotel the doctor involved is obliged under this Act to inform the proper officer who may be from the local authority's environmental health department or the area health authority. Should it prove necessary other guests must be warned and the affected bedroom disinfected.

Innkeepers Act (1878)

This Act permits a hotel proprietor (innkeeper) to auction a traveller's property over which there is a lien. This happens when a guest's property has been retained against settlement of an unpaid bill. In the case of a bill remaining unpaid details of the property and the traveller whose property it is must be advertised in both a local and London newspaper a month before the auction and at least six weeks after the lien was first imposed. Any extra money raised by the auction must be returned to the traveller once the outstanding bill and auction costs have been deducted.

Cases:
Chesham Automobile Supply Ltd.
   v. Beresford (Birchington) Ltd.
   (1913)   Lien

Development of Tourism Act (1969)

This Act requires hotel proprietors, innkeepers, restaurateurs, public-house managers and guest-house as well as self-catering operators (in fact, all operators of establishments offering accommodation and catering with the specific exception of holiday camps and youth hostels) to make their prices more public than had sometimes previously been the case. The requirements are outlined in the tourism (Sleeping Accommodation Price Display) Order (1977).

Tourism (Sleeping Accommodation Price Display) Order (1977)

Where an establishment has no fewer than eight beds or four bedrooms a notice outlining the detailed pricing of accommodation must be displayed in a prominent position. The notice must specifically show the details of maximum and minimum prices for bedrooms (or beds where appropriate), inclusive of any service charge, for single and double occupancy as well as the clear implications of VAT (i.e. whether the price is inclusive or exclusive of tax). If the price excludes VAT then the full price to be subsequently incurred by the guest must be displayed as must the implications of any meals included in the price.

This Order also obliges the hotel proprietor to charge travellers a reasonable price although the definition of what is and is not a reasonable price has never been exactly defined. The quality of the establishment will obviously have a bearing.

Consumer Protection Act (1987)

Where the pricing of accommodation is concerned the Consumer Protection Act is closely allied to the Tourism (Sleeping Accommodation Price Display)

Order of 1977. The former Act states that 'a person shall be guilty of an offence if, in course of any business of his, he gives (by any means whatsoever) to any consumers an indication which is misleading as to the price at which any goods, services, accommodation or facilities are available (whether generally or from particular persons).'

Occupiers Liability Act (1957 & 1984)

The hotel proprietor (the occupier) is made liable by these Acts for the personal safety of everyone legally entering the premises whether they be traveller, lodger or employee. It is therefore the proprietor's responsibility to ensure that there are no hazards and that the premises are reasonably safe.

Cases:
Campbell v. Shelbourne Hotel
   Ltd. (1939)   Guest accident
MacLenan v. Segar (1917)   Emergency procedures

Health and Safety at Work Act (1974)

This Act makes the hotel proprietor legally responsible for the personal safety of 'all persons who may be affected by his activities' which obviously includes both travellers, lodgers and employees.

Fire Precautions Act (1971)

This act was updated by the Health and Safety at Work Act (1984) which then applied the legislation to 'all places of work' which had not been the case previously. The 1971 requirements applying minimum fire safety standards still apply as does the necessity to possess a valid Fire Certificate that indicates the satisfaction of the Local Fire Authority with the establishment concerned.

Case:
Berry v. Smith (1983)

Shops Act (1950) and Shops (Early Closing Days) Act (1965)

Whilst these Acts are intended to govern the working hours and conditions of employees in retail establishments in the widest sense, catering establishments are referred to specifically and are the subject of compromise regulations. The employment of staff under the age of eighteen is specifically addressed.

Unfair Terms of Contract Act (1977)

This Act makes it unlawful to insert unreasonable exemption clauses into contract documents in situations such as reservation confirmations, brochures or notices. It means that hotel proprietors are unable through such means to protect themselves from breach of contract liability.

Case:
Olley v. Marlborough Court
   Ltd. (1949)   Terms of contract

Trade Descriptions Act (1968)

The Act makes it a criminal offence 'to make any statement in the course of any trade or business which falsely describes any facilities or services offered. This includes any false descriptions as to quality, quantity, availability, price or location of goods, services and accommodation.'
The Act is mainly applied to 'invitations to treat' or advertisements which may misrepresent the service or facilities on offer. Advertisements do not form part of the law of contract.

Cases:
British Airways Board v. Tyler
   (1976)   Overbooking
Partridge v. Crittenden (1968) Status of
                                   advertisement
R. v. Sunair Holidays (1973)   Lack of advertised
                                   facilities

Sunair Holidays v. Dodd
   (1970)   Lack of room facilities
Wings v. Ellis (1984)   False brochure
                                   statement

Law of Contract

The legally binding agreement that is made between the hotel, proprietor and the traveller for the provision of accommodation and/or refreshment is a contract subject to the wider Law of Contract and is therefore regarded as a civil matter.

The implications regarding accommodation in particular are outlined in Chapter 3.

Cases:
Jackson v. Horizon Holidays
(1975)   Misrepresentation
Jarvis v. Swans Tours (1972)   Misrepresentation

Theft Act

See Chapter 8.

Diplomatic Privileges Act (1964)

See Chapter 5.

Aliens Orders (1953/57)

See Chapter 5.

Legislation bibliography

Hotel and Catering Law in Britain, David A. Field, Sweet & Maxwell (London) 1989
Principles of Hotel and Catering Law Alan Pannett, Cassell (London) 1989

2 Value Added Tax

In the billing examples found in Chapter 7 it has been assumed that Value Added Tax, the tax payable on goods and services administered by HM Customs and Excise, is included within all the prices shown. It is important to make the point, though, that this is not always the case in every establishment and, even if it were, the business must legally provide returns at three-monthly intervals demonstrating how much VAT has been both charged for by the business (outputs) as well as that paid to suppliers (inputs).

VAT on sales (outputs) is allowed for in the accounts by making use of one of three rates: *standard, reduced value* or *zero*.

Accommodation

Accommodation is a hotel, inn, boarding house or similar establishment is standard-rated. This covers sleeping accommodation and ancillary accommodation such as bathrooms and living rooms in residential suites as well as rooms supplied for the purpose of a supply of catering. An establishment is deemed to be liable for VAT if it provides furnished sleeping accommodation which is generally used, or held out as being suitable for use, by visitors, travellers or others for whom the accommodation is not 'permanent', whether or not there are some 'permanent' guests. From the definition it will be seen that the VAT regulations here, and that follow, cover accommodation in the International Hotel, the Majestic Hotel and the Ship Inn as well as all motels, guest houses, bed and breakfast establishments, residential clubs and hostels such as those run by the YHA. Furnished service flats are also included if they normally cater for, or are held to be suitable for, people staying away from home, such as business people or tourists. Also included are other establishments which provide both overnight accommodation and food or drink to be consumed in a restaurant, bar, dining room or elsewhere on the premises. In most cases establishments will be providing one or more meals, either at an inclusive charge or for additional payment. However, board, or facilities for the preparation of food, are not necessary for an establishment to be regarded as a hotel, etc.

In such establishments VAT is due at the standard rate on most types of accommodation which are provided in it or in its grounds although the supply of non-bedded accommodation in a hotel or similar establishment other than 'rooms used for catering' is generally exempt. This includes the letting of halls, conference rooms, shops, kiosks and of sites for amusement and gaming machines, display cases, etc. It is permitted, though, to choose to standard-rate such supplies under the 'option to tax' (Notice 742b). The supply of 'rooms used for catering' includes both short-term lets, such as those for wedding receptions and private parties, and some longer term lets, such as the granting of a catering concession (a concession to operate kitchen, restaurant, bar, cafe or kiosk facilities for the preparation and/or serving of food or drink in the course of catering).

The standard rate of VAT is applied additionally to the hotel or similar establishments' catering and any other facilities provided as well as any extras which are charged for separately, such as telephone calls. 'Facilities' includes car parking, cleaning, room service, laundry, porterage and the provision of a television or radio.

If a service charge is levied, it is standard-rated but

if a customer freely gives a tip over the above the total charge, no VAT is due on the tip.

Reduced value rules for stays of over four weeks

For the first four weeks of any stay VAT is due on the full amount payable in the normal way. If an individual (or any individuals who share the costs of the accommodation) personally stays for a *continuous* period of more than four weeks, VAT is due on a reduced value from the 29th day of the stay. This also applies if, for example, a shop is let within the hotel for longer than four weeks.

Persons likely to benefit from the provisions include homeless persons living in bed and breakfast accommodation booked by the local council, elderly residents of seaside hotels and students occupying taxable accommodation in term time. Persons working away from home for lengthy periods may also qualify if there are minimal breaks in stay to return home.

Therefore from the 29th day VAT is no longer due on the part of the charge which is for accommodation. That part of the charge is not, however, for an exempt supply. But VAT must still be charged in full on other elements such as meals, drinks, service charges and facilities. At least 20 per cent of the combined charge must always be treated as being for accommodation and facilities but if the true value of the facilities is more than 20 per cent of the combined charge the higher percentage must be used.

There follow a number of Customs and Excise calculations based on the old standard-rate of VAT of 15 per cent. It will be realized that this percentage rate has already changed and may well change again in the future with little warning. The examples should therefore be treated purely as mathematical illustrations of principles.

Examples of calculations for the reduced tax value for accommodation exceeding four weeks

The weekly terms for accommodation, facilities and meals in a boarding house are £115.00, i.e. £100, 00 plus £15.00 VAT at a rate of 15 per cent; of which £46 represents the tax-inclusive charge for meals. Tax is chargeable on the full amount for the first four weeks and on the reduced value thereafter. After the first four weeks of occupation the reduced tax value may be calculated in one of the following ways. (For the purpose of these examples the proportion for meals has been taken to be 40 per cent but this will not always be so.)

1 If the charges are expressed in tax-exclusive terms the weekly rate of VAT is calculated as follows:

a) Total tax-exclusive weekly charge: £100.00

b) Tax-exclusive charge for meals: £ 40.00   VAT due £6.00

c) Tax-exclusive balance (a–b): £ 60.00

d) Tax-exclusive value of facilities: £ 12.00   VAT due £1.80
not less than 20 per cent of the balance)

e) Total tax: £7.80

The weekly terms are therefore £100.00 (b+c) plus £7.80 VAT.

2 If the charges are expressed in tax-inclusive terms; but the total charge is reduced after the first four weeks to take account of the reduced element of tax the weekly rate of VAT is the same as in example 1 but the calculation is a follows:

a) Total tax-inclusive weekly charge for first 4 weeks £115.00

b) Tax-inclusive charge for meals: £ 46.00   Incl VAT of £6.00

c) Tax-exclusive charge for meals: £ 40.00

d) Tax-inclusive charge for facilities and accommodation (a–b): £ 69.00

e) Tax included in d) (3/23 of £69.00): £ 9.00

f) Balance (exclusive of tax): £ 60.00

g) Tax-exclusive value of facilities: £ 12.00   VAT due £1.80
(not less than 20 per cent of the balance)

h) Total tax: £7.80

The weekly terms are therefore £100.00 plus £7.80 VAT.

3   If the charges are expressed in tax-inclusive terms but the total charge is not reduced to take account of the reduced element of tax, the weekly rate of tax must be calculated as follows:

a)   Total tax-inclusive
     weekly charge: £115.00

b)   Tax-inclusive charge
     for meals: £ 46.00   Incl VAT of   £6.00

c)   Tax-exclusive charge
     for meals: £ 40.00

d)   Tax-inclusive charge
     for facilities and
     accommodation
     (a–b):   £ 69.00

e)   Tax included in d
     (3/103 of £69.00)[1]:   VAT due   £2.00

f)   Tax-exclusive charge
     for facilities and
     accommodation: £ 67.00   _____

g)   Total VAT: £8.00

The weekly terms are therefore £107.00 (c+f) plus £8.00 VAT.

[1]In this instance, when the rate of VAT is 15 per cent, the tax fraction to be applied to the facilities and accommodation is:

$$\frac{(15 \times \text{facilities }\%)}{100 + (15 \times \text{facilities element }\%)}$$

Thus where the facilities element is 20 per cent, the tax fraction to be applied to d) is:

$$\frac{15 \times 20\%}{100 + (15 \times 20\%)} = \frac{3}{103}$$

Reproduced from VAT Leaflet 709/3/90 Courtesy of HM Customs and Excise.

Although VAT is only chargeable on the reduced amount, the full tax-exclusive amount (£100 in the first two examples, £107.00 is the third example) is to be included in the establishments' VAT return. This is because the accommodation element of the total charge continues to be the consideration for a standard-rated supply even though the value for the purposes of calculating the tax becomes nil after the first four weeks.

Breaks in stays – reduced value rules
Normally it is not possible to use the reduced value rules unless the guest stays for a continuous period of more than four weeks. If, for example, a guest stays for three weeks in every month the tax must always be charged in full. similarly, if a guest stays for five weeks, is away for a week, and then returns for another five weeks each stay must be treated separately and the reduced value rules can only be used for the fifth week of each stay. There are two exceptions to this. A guest's period of absence need not be treated as ending if:

a)   the guest is a long term resident and has simply gone away for an occasional weekend or a holiday. This might happen where the guest is working away from home or where an elderly resident visits relatives. Students' vacations can be treated as acceptable breaks provided the student returns to the same accommodation the following term; or

b)   the guest pays a retaining fee to reserve the accommodation

In these cases the guest's stay may be treated as continuous and VAT need only be charged in full for the first four weeks of the overall stay. A guest need not always occupy the same room for their stay to be treated as continuous.

If a guest pays a retaining fee for a period of absence during the first four weeks of their stay, VAT is due on it at the standard rate. If a retaining fee is paid for a period of absence after the first four weeks then the reduced value rules apply. If the fee is no more than the amount which is treated as the payment for accommodation under the reduced value rules no tax is due. Otherwise the fee must be treated as payment for both accommodation and facilities as previously outlined.

Deposits, cancellation charges, forfeited deposits and book fees
Deposits serve primarily as advance payments and the VAT must be accounted for on the amounts received in the return covering the period in which they are received. If a customer cancels a booking and has to forfeit a deposit, VAT already accounted for can be reclaimed in the next return. If a cancellation charge is made to a person who cancels a booking, no VAT is due on the amount charged.

If the hotel arranges or provides a guarantee or

insurance against customers having to pay cancellation charges, VAT is due on the charge which is made. Any commission received from a person permitted, under section 2 of the Insurance Companies Act (1982) to carry on an insurance business, is exempt.

Booking fees should be treated in the same way as deposits.

Holiday accommodation and camping facilities

The letting of holiday accommodation in houses, flats chalets, villas, beach huts, tents, etc., or in caravans and houseboats is taxable at the standard rate.

Sunset Quay is obviously covered within these definitions as is the camp site alongside the Ship Inn because 'holiday accommodation' in general includes any accommodation *advertised or held out as such*. For example, holiday accommodation is being provided if:

a) the terms and conditions on which the accommodation is let indicates that the letting is for holiday purposes rather than as a permanent dwelling;

b) the accommodation is advertised specifically as holiday accommodation, or under a general heading of 'Holiday accommodation', or in publications specializing in such accommodation;

c) the local tourist office, local council, etc., has been informed that the accommodation is available for holiday lettings;

d) it is sold or let for occupation during the holiday season only.

Residential accommodation which happens to be situated at a holiday resort is not necessarily holiday accommodation.

Off-season letting of holiday accommodation
Holiday accommodation advertised or offered at a lower rate or rates during the off-season can be treated as residential accommodation, provided the let is for more than four weeks. In such cases the whole of the let, including the first four weeks, counts as an exempt supply. This arrangement applies only in resorts where the holiday trade is clearly seasonal. The season in such resorts would normally be expected to be at least

from Easter to the end of September. London, for example, is not regarded as having a seasonal holiday trade.

Holiday accommodation: time-share and multi-ownership schemes
If holiday accommodation is supplied in a house, flat, chalet or other building under a time-share or multi-ownership scheme, it is standard-rated. VAT must be accounted for both on the initial charge that is made for the right to occupy the accommodation for a specified week or weeks each year and on any additionally maintenance or other periodic charges. VAT is due whether the weeks are sold by lease in perpetuity, lease for a fixed term of years, licence or in some other way, such as through membership of a time-share club or a shareholding in a company set up for the purpose.

Caravans
If holiday accommodation is supplied in any caravan (whatever its size) already sited on a pitch, the supply is standard-rated. Holiday accommodation includes any accommodation advertised or held out as such. If accommodation other than holiday accommodation is let in a caravan already sited on a pitch the supply is exempt.

If caravans are hired for a holiday or any other use and they are suitable for use as trailers drawn by motor vehicles having an unladen weight of less than 2030 kilogrammes or are caravan units designed to be mounted and carried on, and demounted from, motor vehicles, their supply is standard-rated.

Where the provision of holiday or seasonal caravan pitches, including pitches for touring caravans is concerned, the supply is standard-rated.

(More information may be found in the VAT leaflet *Caravans and houseboats.*)

Camping
If holiday accommodation is provided in either a ready-erected tent or on provided pitches for tents, the supply is standard-rated.

Value for tax purposes
VAT is due on the full amount payable for holiday accommodation or standard-rated pitch rentals or camping facilities (including any incidental services provided) no matter how long the customers stay.

Cancellation charges, forfeited deposits and booking fees

The VAT treatment of cancellation charges, forfeited deposits and booking fees is identical to that already explained for hotels.

Catering

The supply of most food and drink of a kind used for human consumption is zero-rated. But some supplies are excluded from the zero rate and are therefore standard-rated.

A hotelier or restaurateur must account for VAT at the standard rate on any food or drink:

a) supplied in the course of catering
b) included in the list of items which are always standard-rated. This list includes ice-cream, confectionery, chocolate biscuits, alcoholic drinks, most soft drinks, crisps and salted or roasted nuts.

The word 'catering' is not comprehensively defined in the law but it includes everything which would be regarded as catering in the ordinary everyday sense of the word. It covers, for example, the supply of food and drink at functions such as wedding receptions, parties or dinner dances and at sporting events, exhibitions, conferences or the theatre. It also includes any meals, snacks, etc., which are delivered to a customer at their home or place of work. If food provided by the customer is cooked or prepared, for example if a meal is prepared for a dinner party at the customer's home, this is standard-rated.

In addition the law provides that the following are to be regarded as catering: food and drink to be consumed on the premises where it is sold; hot take-away food and drink.

Food and drink to be consumed on the premises where it is supplied

If a restaurant, cafe, canteen, snack bar or similar business is being run then the operator must account for VAT at the standard rate on any food or drink sold for consumption on the premises where it is sold. This applies not only to complete meals but also to snacks, sandwiches, hot dogs, hamburgers, teas, coffees, etc.

'The premises' includes more than just the location from which the meals are sold, etc. It includes: the rest of any office, factory or hotel in which the catering outlet is situated; the grounds surrounding an office block, factory, hotel, cafe or public house; the whole of any enclosed space such as a football ground, race-course or other sports ground, a garden in which a fete takes place, a show ground, amusement park or safari park. As a general guide, any site or space is 'premises' if it has a clear boundary or limit.

The caterer must standard-rate food and drink for consumption on any part of the premises even if it is taken away from the point of sale to some other part of the premises. for example, food or drink taken into the forecourt or garden of a public house or restaurant (such as might happen at the Ship Inn), or eaten sitting at tables outside a cafe is standard-rated.

Information reproduced courtesy of HM Customs and Excise from VAT leaflets 709/3/90 and 709/2/85.

Index